Confessions

Confessions

ADMISSIONS OF SEXUAL GUILT

EDITED BY SAGE VIVANT *and* M. CHRISTIAN
FOREWORD BY M. J. ROSE

THUNDER'S MOUTH PRESS | NEW YORK

CONFESSIONS
Admissions of Sexual Guilt

Published by
Thunder's Mouth Press
An Imprint of Avalon Publishing Group Inc.
245 West 17th St., 11th Floor
New York, NY 10011

AVALON
publishing group incorporated

First printing November 2005

Library of Congress Cataloging-in-Publication Data is available .

ISBN: 1-56025-758-X
ISBN 13: 978-1-56025-758-5

9 8 7 6 5 4 3 2 1

Book design by Pauline Neuwirth, Neuwirth & Associates, Inc.

Printed in the United States of America
Distributed by Publishers Group West

For anyone who knows
the erotic power
of spilling one's guts

Contents

Foreword

WHEN WE LIE TO TELL THE TRUTH

M. J. Rose

IT WAS A blistering hot day in July, and I'd walked to the top of a hill to visit a seventeenth-century convent and its chapel. By the time I'd reached the oversized wooden doors, I was hot and tired. Inside was a silent oasis of cool air and dark shadows. According to the guidebook, this small church was where the convent nuns came to celebrate mass. Now, years later, it was a tourist destination in a remote area of the Italian countryside where few tourists visited.

I'm not religious but I am an art lover, and the chapel was a gem that boasted a lustrous altar painting of the Virgin Mary and a glorious stained-glass window that washed the interior in lavender light. To the right of the entryway, a carved wooden confessional stood like a sentry. It might have been sacrilegious, but I pulled open the door and went inside the tiny enclosure. The air smelled musty, and I wondered how long it had been since anyone had knelt where I was kneeling. Putting my hand up to the decorative grille, I felt the intercrossed metal design with my fingertips and whispered the words that, although not part of my religion, were familiar to me as they are to most of us: "Forgive me father for I have sinned." How many nuns had knelt there and confessed their sins to the priest on the other side of screen?

THE STORY CAME to me without effort. It was not sweetly religious but sinfully erotic–about a young nun and a priest who had met in this confessional. Invisible to each other that first Sunday, she had whispered her secrets and he had listened. Week after week, she exposed more and more of herself to him, and as her soul became naked, he became aroused. Soon he was in her thrall and begged her to meet him just so he could see the face of the woman who had shown herself to him so completely.

As I began to imagine their face-to-face meeting, it was then, for the first time, that I became aware that confession is one of our oldest forms of storytelling. It is our need for intimacy that pushes us to reveal more and more of ourselves. It is our desire to be completely accepted that drives us to disclose our most private thoughts and deeds. It is our fear of isolation that gives us the courage to open up and take the chance that we will be understood–or worse–that we won't be redeemed.

One way we can and do share our deepest sins and our most dangerous secrets is to spin them into tales that we can tell our listeners. In other words, we use fiction to reveal some of the more complicated facts. We explore darkness through fantasy in order to connect with someone in the orgiastic light of revelation and acceptance.

Let me tell you this thing I have done. It is wrong (or bad, or evil, or illicit, or blasphemous). It may be a burden for you to hear it, but just as possibly it will be a revelation. If you listen and you respond, we might experience a sudden intimacy. It could create an emotional bond between us. It might bring us closer, allow us to be spiritually naked together.

As fiction writers, we take risks every time we put pen to paper, because even though we are not saying that *this* very thing happened to us, we are confessing that it might have happened in some way. How else could we understand it so profoundly? How else could we communicate it with such pathos and credibility? And so we take chances. We make up fantastical, sensual stories; we confess our imagination's machinations. If what we expose, if what we write, touches our readers, then the reward is not only deeply satisfying for both of us, but it also reassures us that we are not alone.

Each of the authors in this anthology, and all of us who write erotic fiction, put ourselves on the line with what we write, even though none of our stories is true in the literal sense. As confessions, they are all lies. But they are lies that tell the truth.

Introduction

WE HAVE A confession to make. The act of disclosure, of telling all, of spilling the beans, absolutely fascinates us. Oh, not so much when we do it, mind you, but when somebody else decides it's time to uncork some secret, we're all ears. We want to know why they chose this particular moment, who they've deemed worthy of hearing their confession, and ultimately who will be affected by the disclosure.

'Fess up—you want to know, too.

Just look at when and how confessions are delivered and you instantly get a sense of their importance. The old man on his deathbed whispers with painstaking clarity just how he embezzled thousands of dollars from his employer. The woman in love with another man lives out her life never confiding her betrayal to her husband. The phrase "we need to talk" precedes an inordinate number of confessions, all of which begin with a long intake of breath and that dizzying feeling one gets before a roller coaster soars downward. When a confession looms in the air, tension is thick and misunderstandings are common.

Sounds a lot like sex, doesn't it?

So, when the confession is actually *about* sex, what ensues is nothing less than earth-shattering. No confession is without risk, and few are without consequences, which means that when the stakes are sexual, somebody is bound to get hurt. Or happy. Or laid.

One of the strongest human urges is the need to confess. The act is credited with relieving the conscience–but to what end? Nothing is the same for the person who decides, for whatever reason, that a sexual secret is no longer worth safeguarding. But is that because the confessor is changed somehow–or is it because the person hearing the confession reacts to the confession and changes the direction of the relationship?

Confessions–or the lack thereof–determine what we do with our guilt and how we'll behave in the future. For some, confessions grant permission. For others, they are the precursor to absolution. What a person hopes to gain from a confession versus what actually happens may mean the difference between suffering and happiness–or the difference between continued bad behavior and redemption.

Some confessions pour out in one hideous blob of information. Others leak out slowly, sometimes over a period of years, insidiously affecting an ever-broadening arc of lives. And perhaps the most dangerous are those that are never given a voice–the ones that fester and metastasize.

Our goal was not to be too maudlin about the whole thing. We didn't want people to feel any guiltier about sex than they already do. What we really wanted was a direct and honest look at what—and why—humans choose to divulge when it comes to sex. And does sex then get better, or just more complicated?

We wanted to put together a book of stories that explores the broadest possible range of effects that result from letting the cat out of the sexual bag. We wanted writers to take a look at the sometimes devastating, sometimes exhilarating aftermath of letting go of whatever it was that brought guilt to a situation. We imagined those stories would run the gamut from hilarious to life-altering, and damn if we weren't right.

We wondered what might make a person tell all and how that might affect all sexual decisions going forward. Did confessions feed or starve the libido? Was there a place for confession in sex play? And most important, is it ever better to just shut up?

The writers in this volume apparently have one hell of a grasp on guilt. They've placed their characters in the kinds of sexual situations virtually all of us know on some level, and then let them determine their destinies by what they do or do not confess. Some characters made quite a mess of things, and some characters saved their own asses quite nicely. Amid well-intentioned confessions and doomed disclosures, we watch characters who resemble each of us do what they believe is necessary to continue to get, enjoy, avoid, justify, or understand sex.

We'll tell you this: After working on this collection of sexual confessions, we don't know if we're any more enlightened about human sexual behavior, but we know we've been entertained. And that's all we're going to say.

Sage Vivant
M. Christian,
San Francisco
January 2005

Confessions

Playing the Part

EDO VAN BELKOM

THEY'D HAD SEX again and it had been good, but there was definitely something missing–namely, heat.

"Sorry," she apologized.

"What? Why?" he said. "You don't have to be sorry."

She smiled at him and ran a finger through the thick mat of hair on his chest. "Yes, I do. I've been so busy with rehearsals . . . and now that the show's up and running, I feel like I don't have any time for you."

Marion had gotten a part in a local dinner theater production of *Meet You Upstairs, My Love* and had been rehearsing the play every evening for the past six weeks before it opened. Now that it was running and looked as if it was going to be a success, Marion seemed to have less and less time for everything else in her life–including her husband.

But Ross didn't mind his wife's foray into acting. Not only had she wanted to do something like this all her life, but she happened to be good at it. The play was a bedroom farce about a middle-aged wife who's caught with a young lover in her bedroom by her husband, a man who also just happens to be coming home early from work with a young woman of his own. The older woman and younger man are interrupted just as they are about to have sex, and the rest of the play is all about the wife and husband accusing the other of infidelity while trying to get their own lovers out of the house.

Marion was utterly convincing as the oversexed mature woman who needs more loving than she's getting. And, if he dared say it, she was also pretty sexy in the role, showing a side of herself that he hadn't even known existed.

Ross ran his hands over her thigh and around her buttocks. "I don't mind you being in the play."

She smiled at him. "You're just saying that."

He shook his head. "No, I'm not. To be honest, I actually enjoy watching you up on stage."

"You do?" There was an odd hint of relief in her voice, as if a weight had been lifted from her shoulders.

"Yes, in fact, it's more than that . . ." His voice trailed off.

"What is it?"

There it was, the question that he desperately wanted to answer truthfully, only he was scared to death of what she might think of him if he did.

"Tell me," she prodded.

"I, uh . . . , I don't know how this is going to sound, but–"

"Oh, c'mon, Ross."

This was it. No turning back now. He took a deep breath and sighed. "I love watching you up on stage. You look hot and sexy, and maybe even a little bit slutty."

"You like that?" The look on her face was one of genuine surprise and–again–relief.

"Why wouldn't I? You've got great legs . . ." Marion spent the entire play in a silky pink slip that ended at her mid-thigh. She wore pantyhose, too, but no shoes. There was something about the outfit that made her look as if she'd have sex at the drop of a hat.

"You always did like them," she said, lifting her left leg until it was ninety degrees to the bed, her feet pointed at the ceiling with her toes in a tight curl.

"But that's not all of it."

"There's more?"

He nodded, and paused a moment. Why he was going this last extra step, he had no idea. Things would have been fine if he'd just stopped there, telling her how good she looked on stage and having another session of lovemaking just a little bit hotter than the first. That would have been nice, but he was strangely compelled to take this last giant step; it was now or never.

"What is it?" She said the words so playfully, with such innocence, that he was sure he was about to make a big mistake, one of the biggest of his life, but there could no turning back now.

"I know you're just acting, but . . ."

"But what?"

"I like watching you in the play and imagining that you've been having sex with another man."

Her face went blank, and the bedroom was eerily silent for what seemed like forever. Finally, Marion began to giggle, slowly at first, but eventually the giggle grew into a full-blown laugh.

"You find that funny?" He could feel the anger growing within him. He'd envisioned a dozen different reactions to his confession, but none of them had included laughter. And even though he couldn't tell if she were laughing with him or at him, she was still laughing . . . and it hurt.

Marion must have sensed his pain, because she did her best to calm herself. "Oh, no, darling," she said, moving in close to kiss his shoulders, neck, and cheek. "I'm not laughing at you. I'm laughing because *I'm relieved.*"

"Relieved?"

"Yes. My god! Slinking around on stage in that little slip . . . climbing on top of young Bertram on the bed, and pretending to seduce him just as my husband comes home . . . then stealing kisses for another hour as I'm trying to shoo him out the door . . . Do you have any idea how horny I am at the end of the show? My crotch is soaked and a couple of times in that opening week I had to *take care of myself* after the final curtain, just so I could think straight."

Ross could hardly believe this rather shocking turn of events. He'd been worried that she'd think he was a freak of some kind, but instead she was getting just as turned on by the whole situation as he was.

Even though they'd just finished having sex, Ross's cock was hard again–and throbbing.

"Really?"

"Oh, yeah," she said, beaming.

"Tell me about it."

"No, I've got a better idea."

"What is it?"

"Just wait lover," she said, crawling off the bed and heading to her closet. "I'll be right back."

She went to the closet, grabbed something, and left the bedroom. Ross could hear her moving about in the bathroom but couldn't be sure just what she was doing in there. Whatever it was, the anticipation of it all had him rock hard and ready for whatever she had in mind.

And then she walked back into the bedroom wearing a slip similar to the one she wore on stage. It was cut low in front, showing a hint of cleavage, and the material was thin enough to let her nipples poke through when they got hard . . . like they were right now. She was wearing pantyhose too; they were a cheap pair that she could walk around in shoeless and throw away when they wore out, but they still made her legs look great on stage, and in the bedroom.

"Well?" she asked, putting a knee up onto the bed. "What do you think?"

She wasn't wearing a bra, and every time she moved, her heavy breasts swayed deliciously from side to side.

"Gorgeous," he said. "Hot!"

"I was hoping you'd like it."

"I do," said Ross, stroking himself with his right hand. "But what I really want to know is what it's like."

"What what's like?"

"Being with Bertram."

She smiled and put her other knee on the bed. "Well . . ." she began slowly. "When we began rehearsals, I was uncomfortable about being dressed like this in front of a bunch of strangers. That first night I was wearing my bra and two pairs of panties under the slip just so I wouldn't feel so *naked* on stage."

Ross reached out and pulled her close to him. She lay on top of him for a moment, then spread her legs and pushed herself up by her arms until she was straddling him. He could feel the Lycra of her pantyhose pressing against his cock . . . and liked it.

"But you don't feel that way now."

"Oh, no." She shook her head. "Not since opening night. I don't know what it was, but there was something about being on stage in front of a full house that made me want to be as sexy as I could be. I don't wear a bra on stage anymore . . . or panties for that matter." She lifted the front of the slip to offer him proof, then began to grind her pussy against his cock until he could feel the wet warmth coming from between her legs. "I wanted every man in the theater to lust for me, and every woman to want to be me."

He put his hands on her legs and began running them up and down her thighs. The material of her hose felt different under his fingertips—sexy and sensuous, and maybe even a little bit slutty. "*I* lusted after you," he said, moving in time to her gyrations.

"I was hoping you would," she said. "It turned me on to know you were out there with everyone else . . . watching me."

"My cock was hard every night."

She pushed one of the thin straps of her slip off her shoulder, exposing a breast and the long stiff nipple that jutted from the wide, dark brown areola. She fingered the nipple as she spoke. "Yours wasn't the only one."

"What do you mean?"

"Bertram," she said with a coy smile. "He gets hard, too."

"Does he?"

"Yes." She stopped gyrating and began moving forward and back, rubbing her Lycra-sheathed pussy against his shaft. "And, oh my god, it's so big!"

Her breath was labored now, coming in short, sharp gasps that made her chest and body shudder.

Ross couldn't be sure if his wife was telling him the truth about her fellow actor or simply getting lost in the moment, playing yet another part. But whatever the reason she was doing it, it was turning Ross on to hear her talking about another man's cock. After all, seeing her up on stage fooling around with another man had been a turn-on, but this . . . this was orgasmic.

"How do you know it's big?"

"I've felt it. . . . When I'm on top of him I can feel it rubbing against me–against my pussy–through his silk boxers." She tilted her head back and put a hand to her naked breast. "You have no idea how many times I've wanted to pull down those shorts and fuck that gorgeous big prick of his–"

"With everybody watching you."

"Yes, with everybody watching me."

Ross was harder than he'd ever been in his life. This had all begun as an innocent little confession on his part. But Marion had had a little secret of her own to confess, and now that the two were out in the open, things were hotter than either of them could ever have imagined. And while their confessions had been the starting point, this encounter was quickly taking on a life of its own.

"What else would you like to do to him?" Ross asked.

"Suck his cock."

"And make him come?"

"Oh, yes."

She got off him and grabbed hold of his cock. She took it forcefully, grasping the base firmly in her right hand, then lowering her lips over the head in one smooth motion until she'd taken the entire length of the shaft inside her mouth and down her throat.

"And while you're sucking his cock, what do you want him to do to you?"

She pulled her mouth away from his cock, leaving a long glistening thread between the two. "I want him to lick my pussy…"

"And what else?"

"… and suck on my clit."

She turned on the bed and straddled him until her pussy was inches from his face. Her lips were full and swollen, and her slit was so slick, the crotch of her pantyhose absolutely glistened.

He licked her once, trailing his tongue along the length of her pussy through the thin sheath of hosiery covering her sex.

"Like that?" Ross said.

"Yes," she gasped.

He licked her again, and as she moaned her appreciation, fingers suddenly appeared between her legs. She hooked a finger into the crotch of her pantyhose and pulled so that her nail broke through the material and it began to tear. A moment later, Marion's naked pussy was proudly displayed before him.

Ross lifted his head, took her swollen clit into his mouth and sucked on it.

He had heard squeals of delight come from Marion before, but none quite like this one. It was a scream of pleasure that was led by a high-pitched shrill, but driven from behind by a bass sound that suggested she was feeling it from somewhere deep inside.

"You want everyone to hear, don't you?" Ross said.

"Yes," she panted, sucking on his cock between breaths and grinding her pussy hard against his mouth.

"Even the people in the back row."

"Yes!" she screamed. "But mostly I want *you* to hear."

"Why?" he said, giving her clit a kiss and then sliding his tongue up and down the lips of her cunt.

"Because I want you to know that another man is making me come..."

Just the thought of it brought Ross to the edge of climax.

"And I want you to be jealous . . . so the next time you fuck me, you do it hard, like I've been a bad, bad girl."

"You *have* been a bad girl," Ross managed to say just before his cock spasmed, shooting a massive load all over Marion's face and hands. "But it's never felt so good."

Marion's entire body shuddered then, and for the first time since they'd been together, Marion let loose a stream of cum.

"Encore!" said Ross breathlessly. "Encore!"

ROSS CLOSED THE front door behind him slowly so as to not make a sound. It wasn't that he didn't want to disturb anyone—he'd be doing that in just a few minutes—but rather, he wanted to hear what was going on in the house.

And there was something going on, upstairs in the bedroom.

"Give it to me!" Marion screamed.

It was a livelier cry of pleasure than she'd managed in weeks, and it bode well for their lovemaking later on.

"Fuck me harder with that gorgeous cock of yours!"

Very well indeed.

Without a sound Ross crept up the stairs, slowing as he reached the top. Marion had been good about leaving the bedroom door open the past few weeks, and today was no different. Ross peered around the corner of the upstairs hallway and had a clear view into the bedroom . . . where his wife was being fucked from behind by a muscular young man in his early to mid-twenties. He was an athlete most likely, or possibly an actor; it was hard to tell these days with the shape many of today's young thespians were in.

While he watched Marion getting reamed, his wife looked over at him and smiled. Knowing he was there watching her being fucked would bring on an almost instantaneous orgasm. But as enjoyable as that might be to observe, it wouldn't be half as much fun as what happened next.

As careful as he'd been on the way up, Ross silently went back down the steps and retraced his route back to the front door.

There he waited.

And waited.

Until . . .

"Oh God, that was fantastic!" sighed Marion.

That was the cue.

Ross opened the front door and slammed it closed.

"Honey!" he said. "I'm home."

Salvation Tango

LUCY TAYLOR

THE BEARDED MAN who stood next to Quinn Farris at the edge of the dance floor nudged him and said, "See that girl?"

"Which one?" But Quinn knew. He'd been staring at her ever since she came onto the floor.

"Black hair. Red leotard. Skirt slit all the way to her crotch."

"Oh. Marcella."

The guy, whose name was Ricardo something, turned his head to get a better look at Quinn. "You know her?"

"Some. I've danced with her a few times."

"So then you'd be the person to ask–the stuff people say about her, is it true?"

Quinn hesitated, then proceeded with caution. "You mean that she studied tango in Montevideo?"

"Monti–I don't know anything about that. But I heard she works for one of those uptown services. You know, a thousand dollars an hour. They only deal with diplomats and tycoons and dignitaries."

"Just a rumor," said Quinn, who had heard something similar at a *milonga*, an Argentine social dance, a few weeks earlier.

"I heard something else, too."

Don't bite, Quinn told himself. *Just walk away.*

But he stood rooted as the dark-haired girl glided past in fishnet stockings and scarlet stilettos so vertigo-inducingly high that Quinn didn't see how she could stand up in them, let alone perform backward *ochos* with her left hand barely brushing her partner's back for support.

"Lady friend of mine was in the bathroom with her at a dance and she dropped her purse. Spilled everything out. There was a membership card my friend said looked like it was for this place called L'Eglise."

"Lay what?"

"It means church in French. Anyway, it's not a church ... It's a sex club."

Quinn was getting irritated. "And your girlfriend just happens to know this for a fact?"

"Not my girlfriend. Just a woman who's into tango. She says her sister-in-law's best friend is a vice cop. That's how she knows about L'Eglise."

"Oh, well, it's gotta be true then," said Quinn, his voice hot with derision. He turned his back on the man, walked over to the first woman he saw who was free, and asked her to dance. But even out on the floor, when technically he was supposed to be watching to avoid collisions with other couples, he scanned the room for a glimpse of Marcella–her endless legs, heavy breasts, the cascade of hair down her back like a bolt of black silk.

His partner, unaware that for all the attention he was paying her, he might have been dancing with a mannequin from the window of Saks Fifth Avenue across the street, said, a trifle breathlessly, "You dance really well. You must have been doing tango a long time."

Only since my wife left, thought Quinn. Which seemed like both forever and only yesterday.

In truth, tango had saved him.

After Elle left, when the wound was so raw and the grief so bitter that just getting up for work every morning required all his fortitude, there were many nights when Quinn wandered out onto the balcony of his eighteenth-story condo, Scotch in hand, and stared out at the dark a little too intently, a little too long.

To jump would be cowardly, and he was not a coward–at least he hoped not–but his pain and anger were such that he wanted to murder someone. And if it couldn't be Elle, who had dumped him after nine years of marriage for a Greek fitness instructor, for God's sake, or his father, who had shamed him as a failure and then added insult to injury by dying before Quinn had made his first million, then hell, to paraphrase the song, *if you can't kill the one you hate, kill the one you're with*–in this case, himself.

He knew he was capable of it. Despite his outward success, his self-hatred ran virulent and deep–Elle's leaving had only been the seismic crack in the psychic shell that allowed the poisons to seep to the surface. Her swift and utter abandonment had raised his darkest fears, that in truth he was inadequate, a fraud. Her parting words confirmed it.

I always thought there had to be more to you, Quinn. That underneath the boring, good little boy surface, there was a man I could respect. That someday you'd figure out that making love is supposed to be exciting, not a fucking task to get through–touch this, kiss that, thrust three times, and get it the hell over with–when you can get it up at all!

He would gaze out at the outlines of high-rises festooned with lights on the east side of Central Park, then at the park itself, which cut through the ocean of lights like a dark river, and finally straight down onto Central Park Avenue West, where at certain hours of the night no pedestrians stirred, and only the ubiquitous taxis and occasional police cars served as a reminder that he lived in one of the busiest, most exciting cities in the world.

And although in reality New York was never silent, at these times Quinn would curse the absence of din, and, going back inside his luxurious condo with the vaulted ceilings and flat-screen TV costing more than many small cars, he would turn up the stereo and think about women he'd been to bed with before he met Elle–not a lot of them, but what until now he'd thought was a respectable number–wondering if they, too, had been secretly bored with him and if the porno Web sites he sometimes perused were right–that there were secret skills and abilities known only to a few, arcane erotic secrets practiced by only the most experienced and wanton of women.

He felt like he was nineteen again, in need of seasoning. But where does a thirty-eight-year-old man turn when he believes his masculinity is dreadfully deficient?

A hooker? With some trepidation and a couple of stiff drinks, he'd tried that and felt doubly humiliated–once when he failed to function and again when the girl was so condescendingly understanding about it that Quinn suspected she felt relieved.

But it didn't matter, because he had been relieved, too. After all, what does it say about a man's virility when he has to purchase sex, as if it were an iPod or a luxury SUV?

One night, not long after the fiasco with the hooker, he had seen a poster outside a theater on Forty-fourth Street advertising tango lessons followed by a *milonga* at the Marquette Theater on Saturday night. The poster showed a smoldering Latina beauty bent back in the arms of a matinee-idol-handsome man, one leg thrust almost straight back, the other laced around her partner's upper thigh. And although Quinn didn't call the number printed on the poster that night, or for many others, the image was burned into his mind.

Finally, thinking he had nothing to lose, he showed up for the introductory lesson and wound up staying for the dance that followed. Something happened. It wasn't so much that the dancing itself captured Quinn, although tango was beautiful and certainly challenging, but part of what kept him coming back, what kept him signing up for private lessons and classes, was that it seemed to him that tango permitted one to revel in the sizzle of sexuality without actually having to perform sex—a possibility that Quinn both devoutly longed for and passionately feared. As he explained to a colleague at work who questioned him about the expensive dancing shoes he carried with him in a suede bag, "no pun intended, but it has the tang of sex without really being sex."

To which the other man replied, "So what fun is that?"

Quinn only shrugged. In his younger days, he would've said the same thing. But now, being able to act sexy without actually being sexual seemed like a relief, a postponement of the inevitable moment when he would bed a woman and Elle's words would be there in his head, like a razor blade held to his balls.

And then there was Marcella. She'd been at that very first dance, wearing a glittery silver dress that clung to her skin like champagne, black hair coiled into a gleaming figure eight and fixed to her neck with a crimson comb. He'd thought she must be a teacher or one of the professional dancers who'd flown up from Buenos Aires to perform. Her movements seethed with sensuality, her body seemed to vibrate with erotic energy even when she was standing still, nibbling hors d'oeuvres at the buffet table or, as he had observed her a few times, outside cooling off, staring into space in a pensive, distracted way that made him wonder if she had a husband or a lover who was away somewhere, someone she pined for.

Then he watched her dance again and decided no one who moved and posed and arched like that could long for any man alive, that Marcella was one of those people who had never pined for anyone in her life.

After the first few weeks of attending dances and watching Marcella, he realized something else–that not only must he dance with her, but he must bed her, too. Only then would Elle be proven wrong and the evil spell she'd cast around his cock be broken. Making love to Marcella, he was sure, would be the erotic event of a lifetime, would purge him of insecurity and self-blame and the remembered lash of his father's tongue and belt. Sex with her would not be just sex, but wild, carnal fucking that would make him feel potent and virile and male.

He started having fantasies.

After Elle's departure, he had perused an adult bookstore and bought half a dozen videos. Only one had held his interest. The tape itself featured a dozen or so women having unremarkable sex with various uninspired-looking partners. Quinn wasn't interested in the tape, though, but in the woman whose picture appeared on the box. She wasn't in any of the sex scenes, and her face was tilted slightly away from the camera, so you only saw her at an angle, but the body and profile reminded him very much of Marcella.

Enough that it might even *be* Marcella.

Now this rumor about the L'Eglise membership card further fired his imagination. No one who danced like that could just dance. Everything about her performance reeked of the erotic, seductive; her gestures were always on the delectable fringe of taboo.

And that mouth . . .

"I'll bet that chick Marcella can suck a man blind," said Patrick, a bony fellow Quinn shared a cab uptown with after another *milonga.* "I'll bet she does it for money–hey, Quinn, what are you doing?"

The cab had stopped at a light. Quinn threw some money on the seat, got out, and, giving the door a vicious slam, stalked off into the night.

He jogged back to his apartment building, not caring that he was ruining a perfectly good pair of dance shoes, his heart hammering with a combination of anger and shame. Furious at Patrick for his comments about Marcella, ashamed of the fact that they mirrored his own thoughts. There was a story behind this woman–there had to be. Something lurid, dark. Maybe a former sex worker, but not an ordinary whore. No, if she'd worked in the sex trade it had to be at the highest level–a thousand-dollar-a-night call girl supplying the international set or a porno star performing live for European royalty.

If she made love the way she danced, thought Quinn, then she was probably one of the great lovers of all time. Could keep a man going all night, drive him crazy.

He had to have her. The balcony no longer obsessed his nights. Marcella did.

But he had to be canny about it. He couldn't approach her in a clumsy or obvious way. After all, all the men wanted her.

So he'd embarked on a campaign to seduce her, using all the skills of patience, analysis, and detachment that had made him one of the top strategists at a major Manhattan marketing firm. His first step had been to spend thousands of dollars on private lessons from a famed dancer from Buenos Aires who was now living in Soho–enough that in a matter of a few months he became an exceptionally good dancer. Not nearly as good as Marcella–even though Quinn had talent, he wasn't *that* talented–but good enough to make sure she enjoyed dancing with him.

Finally, he summoned the courage to suggest a drink after class. Prepared to be rejected, amazed when she said yes. Then, a few nights later, a dinner date, followed by tickets to a performance of Argentine tango dancers. He dressed for success, as though he were going in for a major job interview, and made sure to mention just enough about his work to let her know, without boring her senseless, that he was a top executive earning a six-figure income.

The emerald green Jaguar he started leasing just so he could chauffeur her around didn't hurt either.

When they were together, Marcella did most of the talking, but Quinn didn't mind. There wasn't a whole lot he cared to share about himself anyway, beyond the success implied by the Rolex, the Jag, and the expensive restaurants they went to. He certainly didn't want to talk about Elle, the elegant, expensive wife who'd found him inadequate, who'd dumped him for a nobody.

Besides, the things Marcella told him were interesting—how she'd learned to dance growing up in Montevideo, attended Catholic school, then lost her father to cancer and emigrated to the United States when she was nineteen. There was a brother somewhere in the picture, but apparently they didn't speak. Nor did it sound like she was on good terms with her mother.

Probably because she did something back home to disgrace them, thought Quinn. There was something dark she hinted at, something left unsaid but talked around, a season of her life spent with an aunt that she referred to as "hitting bottom." Quinn didn't ask for specifics, but his imagination ran riot—a prison term, a penchant for women or married men, an affair with an underage boy. Something she no longer did, but that explained the aura of wantonness, of animal carnality that clung to her.

He never pushed, never intruded, never touched her in an inappropriate way—not even on the dance floor—when the temptation to let a hand slide or a palm wander was sometimes unbearable.

"You're the first man I've gone out with in a long time," she told him over coffee at a twenty-four-hour deli on Eighth Avenue. "I have trouble trusting men. They only want to get me into bed."

"It's hard to blame them," he said. "You're so beautiful, and some of your outfits—well, a monk would be sorely tested."

"On the dance floor, I am someone else, a different person. I can dress however I like." She smiled. "I think sometimes men are afraid of me." She gave Quinn a vixenish smile that went straight to his crotch. Surprising even himself, he reached across the table and took her hand. As the fingers, long and smooth with bright scarlet nails, folded into his palm, his thoughts swirled into an unexpected and distracting fantasy—not of Marcella in any of the wonderfully erotic ways he'd envisioned her, but one of Elle, walking into the coffee shop at just that moment, seeing him in an intimate tête-à-tête with this exotic creature.

And the words he would say to her pounded into his brain like nails. *Maybe you wouldn't think I'm so boring if you saw me with her. Maybe you'd realize I can be a fantastic lover—I just couldn't do it with you. Because really, honey, the truth is, it was* you *who bored* me.

"Why are you smiling?" asked Marcella.

"Just thinking how lucky I am," he said quickly. "To be sitting here with you. So many men would like to be in my place that I can't help wondering . . . why me? I'm nothing special."

Waiting for her to contradict him, hoping she would.

She said finally, "You aren't afraid of me, Quinn, I can tell. So I am not afraid of you."

But at night, alone on that balcony with a Scotch in his hand, he remembered how she felt when they were dancing, the aliveness of her, the way the inside of her foot caressed his calf and how her hot breath found its way into his ear, and he knew that he was scared to death of her—but he didn't care. He was more scared of that balcony and the blackness of the park and the secret, twinkling lure of the drop. In his mind, he translated her dance floor moves into bedroom ones—what passed behind his eyes was every act he'd ever lacked the nerve to try with Elle, arcane positions and practices, every kind of sexual game, from whimsical to dark and decadent.

He thought Marcella was the most intriguing, most seductive woman he had ever known, and he hadn't even made love to her. Only once had she shown a side of herself that seemed off-kilter and incongruous, even a little sinister.

He had taken her to a Broadway play and then downtown for dinner at new French restaurant that had been highly praised in the *New Yorker*. On the way they passed a woman dragging a bawling toddler out of a store, screeching at the little girl in some language that, to Quinn, sounded like tin cans being mangled. Marcella halted, her face dead white. Then her mouth contorted and she began screaming at the woman with such fury that Quinn was both embarrassed and alarmed.

"My mother used to beat me," she said later. "And while she was doing it, she'd yell at me just the way that woman was doing to her little girl. I would feel my heart close up like a fist, I felt like I was drowning in shame, and I would pray to die."

Quinn put his arm around her awkwardly, not knowing what to say. In actuality there was quite a bit he could have said–that his father had been a physically punitive man, too, erratic as a summer storm with mood swings that spanned the full spectrum of emotional instability. He had no tolerance for failure or neediness and heaped shame on his son for the smallest infraction or weakness.

But these were not things Quinn cared to recall, much less share with the woman he was trying to impress with his confidence and sophistication, so he made some vague noises of consolation and changed the subject.

When he did talk to Marcella of personal matters, they were always carefully chosen to enhance his image of success and worldliness. He spoke of his marriage to Elle, a former model, but implied that it was he who'd tired of her, that Elle's small-town Midwestern roots and coldness in bed had ultimately been the undoing of their marriage. His choice of tango as a pastime had nothing to do with the opportunity to meet women, but was merely a pleasant way to relax and unwind after a mentally strenuous day.

He played his role and she played hers, prolonging the suspense into a delicious agony. Quinn put no pressure on her, letting her decide the pace. Finally, the night came when she invited him to her apartment.

She lived in a third-floor walk-up off Union Square, next door to an Italian leather goods store and a Tunisian restaurant. The décor was as exotic as she was, smelling of incense and decorated with colorful rugs and wall hangings from South America. Quinn wrapped his arms around her, pulling her close. For the first time since Elle had left him, he felt good about who he was, proud to be Quinn Farris.

But to his surprise, when he began unbuttoning her blouse, he felt her stiffen and caught her staring out the window with a flat, dead gaze, a thousand miles away, as though she were preoccupied, already dreaming of another. Her flirtatious animation faded away like a mirage. She barely breathed. Quinn felt a stirring of alarm, like a trickle of ice down his spine. Was she realizing she'd made a mistake? That he wasn't the man she'd thought he was, but a poor facsimile, a sham?

Still, he had come this far and he persisted, thinking surely she would come to life beneath his lips and hands, that the sensuality he saw on the dance floor would naturally ignite.

But when he removed her bra, her face flushed with color and her hands went across her chest. Then, apparently embarrassed by her own modesty, she quickly bared herself, almost defiantly, like a woman exposing herself before a room full of strangers to win a dare.

He kissed her breasts. She was still as stone. Only a vein at her temple throbbed madly, like something captured trying to escape.

When he suggested she undo his pants, she fumbled with the catch and he finally had to help her. Once they were naked, he led her to the bed, where she lay unmoving on her back, eyes fixed on the ceiling as though she were willing herself to be somewhere else, anywhere else.

Quinn felt himself growing first desperate, then enraged, then panicky. Was this some kind of cruel trick, and would she recount this tale tomorrow to her friends, laughing at his ineptitude, his stupid certainty that he would bed her?

Of one thing he was already certain–he wasn't going to be able to perform. To the degree that she'd grown stiff and hard as they undressed, he'd felt himself go flaccid. He thought of suggesting that she use her mouth on him, but couldn't ask, too afraid that she'd react with revulsion or scorn.

"Obviously this was a mistake," he said, drawing back. "I'm not sure what happened, but I can see you don't want to do this. I'll go."

"It was a mistake, yes," she said miserably.

"Sorry I wasted your time."

"No, wait, please." She sat up on her elbows, flicking the hair out of her eyes, face wet with tears.

"I really want to do this. I've been thinking about it for a very long time. It's just that–I need to tell you something–"

Jesus. His mind leaped ahead to predict what she would say, one alarming possibility after another–she was a lesbian, a transvestite, she had HIV, she expected him to pay.

"I've never done this before."

It was as though she'd spoken in a foreign language. He'd heard her, but he couldn't comprehend. "You mean you don't bring men to your apartment?"

"I mean I've never *done* it."

"You can't . . . you're not trying to tell me you're a virgin?"

She shut her eyes, tears webbing her lashes. "I'm almost twenty-eight years old. I'm so ashamed. It's much too old to be . . . without experience."

"I don't understand. The way you dance, the way you dress and move . . ." He tried for levity. "Honey, you could be a lot of things, but a virgin isn't one of them."

"My older brother used to touch me, make me do things. When I told my mother, she said I was a dirty liar and threw me out of the house. I went to live with my aunt, but she thought I was a liar, too. Told me it was all my fault, that I'd brought grief to my family. I hate the thought of sex, it brings back all the shame and fear."

Quinn was still baffled. "I don't understand. The way you look, the way you dress–"

"I can't help the way I look," she said. "As far as how I dress, it's not because I want a lot of men–I dress this way because it scares men off. You aren't afraid of me, you're confident, strong . . . you've had so much experience. I thought that you could help me."

She sat up, swiping at her tears with the back of her hand, smearing mascara on her cheeks. She took his hand and met his eyes. "Now that I've told you the truth, I feel better. I don't feel so frightened anymore. Please, Quinn, I want to do this."

All the air seemed to be rushing out of the room. He found that he could barely speak. "I can't. I don't . . . it's late and I'm not feeling well . . . I need to get back home."

He fled her apartment as though it were on fire, caught a taxi going in the wrong direction and snapped at the turbaned driver when the man complained he should have hailed a cab already headed uptown.

"So make a 'U,' goddamit," he yelled and received some grumbled utterance in a language he didn't understand.

Once safely back at his apartment, he walked out on the balcony and leaned against the railing with his head in his hands, berating himself for being such a fool, to have picked as the woman who was going to initiate him into the erotic mysteries a woman who'd never even had sex.

It's her fault, he thought. *She deceived me. She could have told me the truth before it was too late. She didn't have to wait until the last possible goddamn moment.*

A memory came back to him so strongly it made him shudder. Of him and Elle one summer night on this very balcony, her in a little cotton sundress leaning over with her arms against the railing, him behind her, spooning her body, cupping her breasts. The breeze had blown her hair back into his face, and it had smelled minty and clean. They'd been talking about the mundane things that couples talk about.

It had seemed to him a perfect moment, yet when Elle spoke her voice was flat and harsh. "You never talk to me about what's really going on. It's always superficial. We've been together for years, and I feel like I don't know you."

He'd made some kind of joke, trying to jolly her out of what he figured was just a mood. After a bit, it seemed to him that all was well.

It was only a few weeks later that she left him.

At that time, he'd thought that he could never possibly feel more alone. Now he realized he'd been wrong.

My wife left me for another man. I hate her for leaving me. I hate being alone.

He came back into the apartment, picked up the phone. Started to dial. *Jesus, what am I doing?* Put it down.

She laughed at me when she left. She said the other guy was great in bed and I was . . . boring . . . mechanical . . . inept . . . even when I was able to function. I thought with you it would be different. I thought with you I'd be the man I want to be.

He couldn't tell her that. Couldn't tell *anybody* that.

And yet . . .

He picked up the phone, held it in his hand for a long time as he stared out at the darkened park.

After a while he began to dial.

Maybe . . .

Voyeuse

MORGANA BARON

HELLO? IT'S MARTHA Coleman, from the other building. Please don't hang up! I desperately need to explain. You must think I'm weird–perverted even–but I didn't mean what happened to happen. You're both on the line? Good. I don't think I could tell it twice. Yes, what I did was wrong, very wrong, but I want you to understand. I'm not a bad person. It was a slippery slope. I yielded to a small temptation that led step by step to last night's "incident." Maybe it's menopause. Hormones make women do strange things. Can a healthy woman of fifty-two claim "middle-aged crazy?"

I was recently widowed when I moved into this apartment. What did I need a four-bedroom house for? I chose this place for its light. I have floor-to-ceiling and wall-to-wall windows, just like you, but facing north, ideal for my crewelwork.

No, John! I'm not a practicing sadist. My hobby is *embroidery*. May I get on with my confession? Thank you.

Our towers are kitty-corner, but for some reason yours is half a floor lower. It wasn't until I was sorting out my needles and threads and settling down to work for the first time that I noticed that my elevation gave me a clear view into your home.

I pulled my blinds a little, but if I closed them too much they spoiled my light, so I decided to simply ignore the view. That wasn't hard, until I saw movement.

You, John, wearing just your pajama pants, were standing, drinking coffee at your window. You're about ten years my junior, right? Even at forty, you're a fine figure of a man. I dragged my attention from you back to sorting out the precise shade of blue I needed for a Siamese's eyes.

You, Tiffany, joined John. All I saw of you at first were your pajama-clad arms wrapping John's waist, and the top of your head. You were nuzzling his shoulder. In my opinion back then, nine in the morning was far too early for "nuzzling," but people have different ways these days. To my disgust, to my way of thinking back then, it seemed that a relatively innocent show of affection wasn't enough for you two. One of your hands, Tiffany, dropped down and disappeared into the fly of John's pants.

I turned away, quickly. I wasn't so innocent, even then, that I didn't know what can follow when a woman does that sort of thing. Forgive me, but I thought you were a real hussy! If I'd ever done such a thing to my dear departed William, he'd have had a fit.

I went to my kitchen to make coffee, furiously denying that what I'd seen had affected me sexually. When I got back to my window, all I could see were the backs of John's legs on the floor, with your heels digging into his thighs. I told myself I was disgusted. Now I can admit to myself that I was disappointed that you weren't doing what you were doing closer to your window.

"Fucking?" Yes, you were *fucking*, though that's not a word that comes easy to me. Yes, I'll call a spade a spade, if you insist, Tiffany. I'll call it a bloody shovel, if you prefer.

Anyway, when you'd finished, I finally got a good look at you, Tiffany. You're younger than John, right? In your early twenties? No? Thirty-one? You don't look it. You were still wearing the top of John's pajamas, but they weren't buttoned up. I could see your—er—bosom.

"Tits?" If you like, Tiffany. Anyway, they were showing, and they looked younger than thirty-one, to me. You have a beautiful figure, if you don't mind me saying so.

You're welcome. You two are taking my confession very well, I must say.

Yes, I'll get on with it. Where was I? Oh, yes, the both of you were moving about, pausing for kisses and hugs when you passed each other. I would have been touched—romantically—if you hadn't both been showing so much skin. You, John, hadn't tucked yourself in. I couldn't help but make comparisons—you against my poor William.

Yes, John. You're bigger there, much bigger.

He's bigger than most, you say, Tiffany? I wouldn't know. Up 'til then, I'd only seen my William's—thing. Very well, his *cock*. Anyway, I was—it was like I *had* to watch, even though I hated myself for it. I knew it was prurient curiosity, but I just couldn't help myself. You see, my William was unwell for some time before he left this mortal plane. Even before that—well—*that* sort of thing wasn't important to him. What I'm trying to say is, it'd been months, maybe years, since William and I'd . . .

Yes, Tiffany. I was as horny as a nun in a Singapore brothel, as you put it. It's nice of you to be so understanding.

The next day, when I set up my easel, I was kind of hoping

. . . but I saw nothing until around noon and that was just you, Tiffany. You were wearing scarlet—something flimsy.

It's one of John's favorites? I can see how a man might like that sort of thing. At least, I see that now. Back then, I considered you no better than a whore.

John calls you his "little whore," sometimes, in the heat of passion? What a coincidence! It's a term of affection? I can see how it could be, *now*. Back then it was the worst thing I could think of to call a woman. You two have given me quite an education, even if you didn't know you were doing it.

I glimpsed you in several such outfits over the following weeks, Tiffany, usually around four in the afternoon. Being such an innocent and, I admit, a prude, it took me a while to realize that you were readying yourself for John's homecoming. I felt sorry for you and jealous of you at the same time. It seemed like you were prostituting yourself for him. The very idea of a woman transforming herself into a slut to please her husband was alien to me. I thought it degrading at first, and then I saw how loving you two always were together and began to doubt my own values. You two made my life with William seem very dull in comparison.

I found myself wondering all day what skimpy little creation you'd choose for that evening. I obsessed over imagining John's reactions. Would he like the lacy peignoir? Did he prefer the black net see-through bra, or the green satin one that left your pretty breasts virtually naked?

I told myself that it was for some sort of research when I dug out William's old binoculars so I could check just how your nipples showed through that incredibly thin singlet you sometimes paired with an indecently tiny thong.

I didn't see much more than your preparations, Tiffany,

until you got that new couch. The way you have it positioned, just over half of it is visible from my window. I think you two were watching TV that night, cuddling together, John in a toweling robe, and you, Tiffany, in clinging satin pajamas. You two looked so innocent that I almost lost interest until I saw John's hand slide down the front of your pajama pants, Tiffany, and that yours was inside John's robe. I focused my binoculars more sharply. Both of your hands were moving. I couldn't help but imagine why.

It was then that John dragged your pants right off, Tiffany. He knelt on the floor and did something that I had no idea men did.

"Head?" Is that what you call it–"giving head?" I don't have to ask if you liked it. Your face went from blissful to blank and then screwed up like you were in agony. It looked like you shouted something, then slumped, limp.

That was the first time I touched myself while watching you. My body had reacted to what you were doing. I was curious about the strange feeling "down there." Until that moment I'd always kept my hands away from my private parts, except for taking care of hygiene. My mother taught me that. When I witnessed your ecstasy, Tiffany, my private parts–okay, my *pussy*–felt hot and throbbing. I checked myself, briefly, before snatching my fingers away in shame. They were wet.

I put the binoculars down and went to splash my face with cold water. When I got back, you were doing things to John that I'd heard about but had thought only the lowest type of prostitutes did–and charged extra for.

"Blow-job?" Is that what it's called? That's strange. It looked more like sucking, to me.

Why are you two laughing? Did I say something funny?

Yes, I'll continue with my confession. I need to bare my breast completely.

You're laughing at me again! No, no need to apologize. I deserve your scorn.

Did I watch John's face as I'd watched yours, Tiffany? Indeed I did! He didn't have that calm expression that you'd had. He bit his lip and looked sort of strained for a while and then he seemed to convulse. When I directed my binoculars down again, Tiffany, you were licking your lips. That confused me at first, until I realized that you were actually *savoring* the flavor of . . . um . . .

His "jizm?" My vocabulary is expanding rapidly tonight. You say it's delicious? I'll have to take your word for it, I suppose.

Yes, that was about a month ago. You forgive me? That's kind of you both, but my depraved behavior got worse—much worse. I have to tell you it *all*, you understand? My conscience demands it.

I was lured deeper into sin by what I now see was a "Freudian slip." You know how our towers share the underground parking and the pool? It's quite easy, if you make a wrong turn leaving the parking area, to get on the wrong elevator. I did that, either by accident or from my subconscious's prompting. We both live on the twenty-third floor. I rode up and tried my key on 2311. It didn't work, of course. That's when I realized I was in the wrong building, on your floor. Instead of marching back to the elevators, I couldn't stop myself from taking a peek at your door, number 2313.

You'd had a delivery that day. The *Times* was on the floor by your door, wrapped around some magazines. I snooped. There's no other word for it. I bent down, intent on seeing what sort of magazines you subscribed to. As I bent to look closer, my head brushed your door and *it moved!*

I knew that you, John, were at work. I was pretty sure that you, Tiffany, were out. You always do your grocery shopping on Thursdays, and anyway, I'd seen you getting ready to go out earlier.

I trembled with guilty excitement. You two were my *obsession!* The opportunity was too tempting. I tapped, ready to hand you your papers as my excuse. Your door swung open. I called out, softly. No answer. I peeped in. Your apartment felt empty. Heart in mouth, I stepped inside. Once in, with the door closed behind me, I became bold.

I *do* like those little figurines in your curio cabinet, Tiffany.

You're welcome!

Once I was certain I was alone, I made for your bedroom, of course. I love that four-poster bed and must compliment you on your décor, but as you can imagine, it was your closets and drawers that drew me. You have so much lingerie, Tiffany. I'd never seen such a display of robes and gowns and flimsy nighties. Some of your skirts–well–I was shocked! Even the ones that are what I consider a decent length have those high slits. I know you have lovely legs, my dear, but . . .

Anyway, I graduated from closets to drawers. You have things in your bedside cabinets that I still don't understand, but I'm not so stupid I didn't recognize the imitations of men's members.

Very well, "cocks."

Can you really get things that size inside you? I shuddered at the very thought! And your intimate garments–so small! So delicate! So *indecent!*

I remember I was holding a gauzy scrap up to check if I could see my fingers through it when I heard your key at the door. I dropped the garment back and shoved the drawer closed.

My mind raced! Luckily, your apartment is the same plan as mine. I fled your bedroom and darted into your storage closet, just catching a glimpse of your shopping cart as you pushed it in ahead of you.

It isn't very comfortable in there. I couldn't see in the dark. Handles and things jabbed me, and there was barely room to set my feet.

No, I'm not complaining, John. There's no need to tidy your storage closet for *me!*

I endured, hardly daring to breathe. There was a clatter in the kitchen and then the clicking of your heels, Tiffany, and you were humming something, but I couldn't make the tune out. I heard your bathroom door close and a shower start, so I thought I had time to escape, but no sooner had I put my eye to a crack in the door than you exited your bathroom and padded right past me, stark naked!

I froze and stayed frozen, physically. My mind was racing, imagining you in the shower, preparing your body for John.

Doors opened and closed. I couldn't be sure which ones, but I had images of you in one of your daring outfits, fussing in the kitchen, making your face up and so on, all the while walking to and fro, keeping me a prisoner.

You can laugh, you two, but it wasn't at *all* pleasant, I assure you.

After an age, I heard you, John, come home, and what sounded like kisses from the hallway. I agonized while you giggled, Tiffany, and I heard plates and the oven door. Some time later, driven partly by the cramp in my calf, I eased out. Your living room was dark except for the flicker from the TV.

Like some sneaky animal, I crawled, meaning to creep past you while you were intent on your program. I chanced a quick look. Your foot, Tiffany, with a ridiculous muleslipper dangling from your toes, projected over the arm of your couch. Thinking I was safe, I inched forward. Your foot shot up! Your muleslipper flew into the air! Its heel gave me quite a nasty blow just over my left ear before clattering to the floor.

I scuttled back to my closet.

Eventually, long after midnight, I heard your bedroom door close. I crept to it and pressed my ear against the wood. Your bed creaked rhythmically. One of you was panting. There were some squeals followed by animal grunting and a couple of yelps.

I, and my fevered imagination, tiptoed out.

The next morning, a Saturday, I felt I'd been very brave. It was empowering, in a strange way. I'd spied on you and your things, shamelessly, and had gotten away with it.

I had a dirty secret, and it felt good!

When I prepared to settle down to my painting that next day, I felt a craving for excitement. I wanted to be *daring!* Until then I'd always painted wearing an old pair of jeans and a T-shirt, with my smock over it. Throwing caution to the wind, I forwent my usual attire. I put my smock on over *nothing*. It felt very liberating. There I was, alone maybe, but secretly a slut, just as I considered you were, Tiffany. Sitting on my stool, palette and brush in hand, I was incredibly aware that if either of you happened to look out of your window and up, you'd be able to see my bare legs, halfway up my thighs.

You didn't, though. I was almost disappointed.

I didn't see either of you 'til after lunch. When I did, you were both in robes, carrying rolled-up towels. Obviously, you were heading down to the pool.

That's when I got the idea. My veins fizzed like champagne flowed through them. What a lark! What audacity! I'd go down and contrive to actually *meet* you!

As you know, that's what I did. You two swam laps, romped, dived, totally unaware that the nice older lady you shared the pool with knew *exactly* what you both looked like under your swimsuits. You, John, took my breath away when you poised on the diving board in those ridiculous little trunks. They really are indecent, John. You bulge. I was amazed that your private parts didn't . . . And you, Tiffany–how much of you does that blue bikini cover? Four square inches? No wonder you were constantly adjusting your breasts in it. I should warn you both, anyone sitting on the side, as I was, can clearly see through the water. I saw your hand go down the front of John's trunks, Tiffany. I watched what you did to Tiffany underwater, John, when you pretended to be just hoisting her up onto your shoulders.

I was in the way, wasn't I? I could tell that you'd planned to actually *do it* in the pool. It amused me to frustrate you. When you got into the whirlpool and I left, you two were fondling, I knew. That's why I came back and joined you. You, Tiffany, at least had the grace to blush as you sprang guiltily apart.

I didn't understand why you were squirming until I, too, sat close to an incoming jet of water. The sensation is very pleasant, isn't it? Thank you for teaching me that.

When you both got out, I gave Tiffany a moment or two and then followed her. The communal showers gave me a chance to spy on you, naked, again, Tiffany. I'd rather have shared a shower with John, but he was there, in my imagination.

You didn't know that as we chatted about this and that, Tiffany, I had a mental picture of John's big masculine body, all lathered up. I wondered, considering the way you two had been playing, whether he'd been moved to touch himself as he soaped.

"Jerk off?" That's *another* new expression you've taught me.

You didn't, John? Saving yourself for when you got upstairs? I delayed Tiffany with my chatter, John. How frustrating it must have been for you.

Thank you, John. Yes, I'm sure you made up for it later.

I suppose actually meeting you was another turning point in my life. I became totally obsessed. I dreamed about you, usually memories of things I'd watched you do to each other. I opened my eyes each morning wondering if I'd see you, and if so, what you'd be wearing and doing. I was *glued* to my window. I lived on sandwiches so I could eat while I watched. If I suspected either of you went out, I went to the lobby on the off chance of seeing you. I started exercising, simply as an excuse to be in the basement gym when you were there.

I–I stole the towel you'd wiped your sweat off with, John. I still have it. I could launder it and return it, if you'd like.

I may keep it? Thank you.

So–"accidentally" running into each other so often, we became nodding acquaintances, then casual friends. You didn't know that I was quivering with lust when we talked about the price of beef or which phone service was cheapest, did you?

Don't misunderstand, please. Even in my wildest imaginings, I had no designs on your body, John. I didn't want you to do those things you do to Tiffany to me. That would have spoiled everything. I just wanted to *watch*. You two were my vicarious love life. "Vicarious" was exactly how I wanted to keep it.

Each time I spied on you, from then on, I had to fight the temptation to touch myself. It was like an unbearable itch. My being naked under my smock most of the time made it worse, of course. Perversely, I wanted it to be worse. My torment was self-inflicted, but I was *addicted* to it.

"Voyeurs Anonymous," John? Is there such an organization?

Oh, he's teasing me, is he, Tiffany? Yes, I'll get on with it. Please be patient. This isn't easy for me.

It came to a climax yesterday, with the "incident."

You're laughing again, John!

I'd had a couple of glasses of wine, not that that's any excuse. I wasn't expecting to see anything, which is why my lamp was on, but when I saw you, Tiffany, I was transfixed! You were standing pressed hard against your window, gazing out, *stark naked!* Your—er—tits—were squished flat, pale targets with dark bull's-eyes. Your—"pussy" can't be the right word, can it? What's it, plus the surrounding area, called? "Pubes?" Thank you, Tiffany. Your "pubes" were pressed hard onto the glass and *moving!* I thought for a moment that it was some strange way to masturbate, but then I saw John's fingers digging into the flesh of your hips and I understood. He was behind you, *fucking* you!

It was the most erotic thing I'd ever seen, or imagined. I didn't even think about denying my instant itch. Without hesitation, I yanked up my smock and pressed my own pubes against my own window. My legs splayed wide. Wriggling, I managed to part my pussy's lips and spread them on the glass. The chill was a thrill, if you'll pardon the rhyme. Watching you intently, Tiffany, I matched your movements with my own, grinding my little button on the cold surface.

As you accelerated your thrusts, I moved faster and faster. My open flesh smeared the glass with my female excretions. I *squeaked* on my window.

Then you jerked and shuddered, Tiffany, obviously in the throes of climax. I did my best to match you, *straining* for release, and then you looked over and saw me!

I fell back into my room, snatching my light off. It was shame, not sexual completion that convulsed me. Since then, I haven't slept. I've spent all night examining my conscience. My blinds will stay drawn from now on, I swear. I'll not as much as *glance* out my window. If you wish, I'll move away. If we pass in the lobby, I'll retreat. Whatever I can do to make up for what I did, I'll do. I promise you that I have learned a lesson I'll never forget.

You don't want me to move, John? That's kind of you. What's that? I should go to my window and open my blinds right now? I don't understand. You're standing in your window right now, Tiffany, and you two are going to do *what?* You *want* me to watch you, and I'm free to. . . ?

Oh, Tiffany! Oh, John! I'll be right there! Please don't start without me!

Reckless Endangerment

RICK R. REED

THE LETTER ARRIVED in this morning's mail. Thank God it was a Saturday, otherwise I don't know how I would have functioned, standing in front of a classroom of first-graders, helping them get through the fascinating tale of Dick, Jane, and Spot.

But it was Saturday, and I could be alone with my anxiety and fear, the only witness to my trembling and inappropriate sweating a tall glass of vodka, no mixer.

The vodka didn't help.

The letter started off with something simple—a quote. How could the legalese of 720 Ill. Comp. Stat § 5/12-16.2 fill me with such terror? How could it not? Here's the quote:

> A person commits criminal transmission of HIV when he or she, knowing that he or she is infected with HIV, (1) engages in contact with another person involving the

> exposure of the body of one person to a bodily fluid of another in a manner that could result in HIV transmission; (2) transfers, donates, or provides his or her blood, tissue, semen, organs, or other potentially infectious body fluids for administration to another person; or (3) in any way transfers to another any nonsterile IV or intramuscular drug paraphernalia. The actual transmission of HIV is not a required element of this crime. It is an affirmative defense that the person exposed knew that the infected person was infected with HIV, knew that the action could result in infection, and consented with that knowledge.

The quote would have been enough to make my scalp tingle, to acquaint me with how ticklish a line of cold sweat can feel running down one's back, and to cause me to want to burst out into tittering laughter that had nothing to do with mirth. But there was more.

> Dear Paul,
>
> You infected me. You didn't tell me. You need to pay.
>
> All the best,
>
> Trish

The three bald phrases were enough to make me run into the bathroom and throw up. I looked down at the mess of that morning's breakfast, floating on the cold water of the toilet bowl, and reflected how something that comes out of my own body suddenly has the potential to send me to prison.

What kind of punishment, I wondered, was in effect for infecting someone with HIV in the state of Illinois? Worse, what kind of punishment existed in larger realms for giving someone a disease with no cure?

Had I done that?

WHEN I MET Trish, I knew it would be nothing more than a quick encounter, lasting perhaps the rest of that afternoon or maybe into the night, but no longer. I was looking for a girl like Trish (tall, olive-skinned, with black hair and green eyes, witty, or what we here in the Midwest call sarcastic, and a penchant for making fun of those around her), but Trish was not looking for a man like me (short, fair, blue-eyed, with an appreciation for camp and pop culture). Trish was not looking, because she had already found someone like me. The only difference was that her man was in pharmaceutical sales, rather than elementary education, and he was in Seattle on a business trip.

We met in a Starbucks (read: singles bar for the new millennium), a larger, more full-scale Starbucks in the area of Chicago known as Old Town, replete with cushy chairs and window seating, perfect for daydreaming, surfing the Internet on an iBook equipped with WI-FI, and, in general, projecting that look of the cosmopolitan artiste.

I just wanted coffee. Regular with lots of half-and-half. I would have been happy with the same from a 7-Eleven, but Old Town was not that kind of neighborhood.

I probably would have simply left the Starbucks and hightailed it back to my studio apartment on Wells Street, but it was raining that Saturday afternoon (suddenly that day has crazy significance in my memory, and the blur of details—most of them anyway—was sharply clarified by Trish's missive), and the downpour discouraged me from stepping outdoors with my four-dollar beverage.

So I sat down in one of the cushy chairs and carefully removed the lid (contents hot!) from my coffee, letting the aroma waft up to my nostrils. I had nothing better to do. I wished that I had brought something to read; instead, I had to content myself with gazing out the window at the people hurrying by in the rain (like that girl in "Tom's Diner" that Suzanne Vega once sang about).

Trish sat down across from me. Before sitting, she gestured toward the chair opposite (faux blue leather) with her cup of café mocha. "Taken?" She raised a pair of Brooke Shields sexy/bushy eyebrows, and my heart beat a little faster when I saw the pale green of the eyes beneath them.

I smiled and shook my head.

Trish opened a magazine (here, the memory fails to supply details–my guess would be something like the *New Yorker* or *Atlantic Monthly*; in actuality, it was more likely *Vanity Fair* or *W*, but I digress, wouldn't you?) and flipped through a few pages, not really reading. There was a restless air about her.

She was dressed all wrong on the damp September day that felt more like November. She was wearing a T-shirt, plain white, with a short black pleated skirt and open-toed black heels. Her legs were strong and tan, calf muscles defined. She was striking, but not beautiful. Her nose was too big and her lips too full for beauty in the conventional sense.

She nudged me with her toe. "Where's your laptop? Why aren't you reading *Details*? Or something by David Sedaris, maybe?"

I grinned. "Think you've got my number?"

"I don't want your number. Then you'd want mine. Only fair. But that would lead to all sorts of complications."

Good shortcut, Trish. Tell me right off the bat you're involved. Looking back, I wonder now if she'd perfected her seduction technique from experience or from imagination. Looking back, it raises Exhibit A, for the defense.

"Not looking for complications." I returned to looking out the window. In spite of the way her looks arrested me, I was not too titillated by the idea of flirting (or more) with a married or otherwise engaged woman.

"What are you looking for, then?"

I raised my cup. "Coffee."

Trish was quiet for a moment, pretending to concentrate on removing a piece of lint from her black skirt. She looked up. "I'm looking for the zipless fuck."

And that got me. I laughed, maybe too hard; my eyes were tearing up and I was attracting stares. Not many straight men my age (early thirties) would have recognized the reference, coined by Erica Jong in her '70s book *Fear of Flying*. A zipless fuck was a kind of rare sexual encounter where few, if any, words were exchanged before or after sex. The kind of thing that might happen, according to Ms. Jong, in the car of a train, where passion replaces common sense but the lust is so undeniable that proper precautions fly out the train window.

I shook my head as my laughter winnowed down to a few snorts, kind of like the slowing of microwave popcorn. I looked at Trish sitting there smiling at me, her gaze bold.

"Then maybe I shouldn't say much more."

"Then maybe you shouldn't."

I took another sip of my coffee, glanced outside again, and saw that the rain had abated to a gray mist. Trish said nothing, but a slow grin was spreading across her features.

I stood, wishing I *did* have a magazine to hide the obvious proof of my interest in this young woman, who could very well be insane (damn these loose-fitting Gap chinos!). I walked slowly toward the revolving doors. Once there, I turned to look back at Trish.

She was grinning, legs crossed, swinging a foot.

I turned toward the door, my face flushed with the knowledge that she would follow.

I wasn't wrong.

So much for seduction, meaningful glances, and double entendres. So much for the slow buildup of the cosmopolitan mating dance. Trish followed me the two blocks to my apartment (I looked back only to make sure she was still behind me).

I remember the hurried sex, up against my front door (like the wedding reception scene in *The Godfather* with Sonny and the bridesmaid with the oversized vagina), the tearing off of each other's clothes, the kisses so hard they left reddish bruises all around the circumference of my mouth, the gasping, the hop in the air as Trish wrapped herself around my thighs, one shoe dropping to the floor while the other dangled from her toes, the panting, the sighs, the giggles. I remember how the door banged against its frame and–good God–what would the neighbors think?

And I remember taking one quick moment to speak. "Don't want to be a mood killer," I thought I had said, "But there's something you should know. I'm poz."

I did say that, didn't I?

And even if I didn't, I'm sure we used a condom. Didn't we? I remember them spilling out of Trish's purse to the hardwood floor: Magnums. I have always admired optimism in a woman.

The perfidy of memory . . . I remember the brand of condom but can't be one-hundred-percent certain I slipped one on in the heat of Trish and the force of her hunger, so demanding.

I sat down at my desk and held the quote and the short note out in front of me. My hand trembled. I was nauseous.

How did she know it was me?

I glanced down at the envelope and saw her address: somewhere in Streeterville, downtown Chicago. A high-rise. On a high floor. Patricia Ryan.

I turned to my computer keyboard and logged on with Internet Explorer. A quick trip to Switchboard.com gave me Trish's phone number.

Did I have the nerve? It didn't matter. I had to call her.

I began to punch in the numbers.

My hands were sweating so much, I feared dropping the receiver; my heart was hammering in my chest. The phone rang once and I quickly pressed the "talk" button to end the call. I felt like I was about to go breathless.

I could not do it. What would I say to her, anyway? That I wasn't poz? That she asked for it? Echo a sentiment from our time together, this time in an entirely different context: do with me what you will?

I didn't have long to ponder. The phone chirped. I looked down at the display and saw "Patricia Ryan" in block letters, along with her number. I let it ring two, three, four times, then the machine picked up. I was staring at this electronic duo with horror, as if they had suddenly morphed into little killing dolls, spears upraised. I backed away from the small table in my living room that held the phone and answering machine. I wondered if I was going to be sick again.

My voice coming out of the answering machine caused me to jump. Trish's voice following my own made me go cold. "Pick up. I know you're there. You just called."

I scratched at my collarbone, wiped a bead of sweat off my brow.

"I'm waiting," Trish said in a voice that managed to be singsong and incensed at the same time. She began to hum.

I tried to find some breath. "Oh, shit," I whispered, snatched up the phone, and pressed "talk."

"Okay," I said in a breathless rush. *Okay* to what?

Her voice was cold. "You called? I assume you got my note."

"Yeah . . ." I stared desperately at my front door, wishing I had already used it as an escape route. It felt like my nerve endings were on fire. It felt like my face, certainly red, would explode with the addition of even one iota more of blood pressure.

"I have nothing to say to you. I've already spoken to an attorney about this, and he agrees that I have a case."

"How?" This was my life I was talking about here, and I realized I had better straighten up and fight back. The implications of what she was doing were huge.

"What do you mean?" Trish was all business now—the flirtatious, zipless fuck stranger gone, never to return.

"I mean, how do you know I infected you?"

Trish sighed. "Unfortunately, I can't lay claim to a happy marriage. You're the only one I fucked in the past five or six months." She sighed. "I figured someone who would slip a little GHB in a drink and then rape someone would raise that issue."

It felt like my heart, pounding at roughly one thousand beats per minute, stopped. There was a huge inrush of air that didn't even seem like it was from me. "GHB?" I asked; I had heard of the drug, a supposed sexual enhancer popular at raves (and popular among date rapists).

"Gamma-hydroxybutyric acid. Now, I suppose you'll tell me you never heard of it."

"I've heard of it. Never used it. Never seen it."

"Uh huh."

I shook my head. I didn't think this portion of the discussion needed further pursuit. "Rape?"

The line went silent for so long, I feared Trish had hung up. When she finally spoke, I felt ice coming through the receiver. "Tim Bradshaw. That's my attorney. I suggest you refer any further questions to him. I will not speak to you again."

My voice rose an octave. "How can you do this? How can you say this? We both know . . ."

But Trish had already hung up.

She could not do this. Right? Who would believe her?

The sad truth was that many people would. A young HIV-positive guy? Why not? Date rape was in the news all the time, and it was never "innocent until proven guilty" with stuff like this. It was always the other way around. I myself was guilty of immediately taking the so-called victim's side when I read of such accusations in the *Chicago Tribune.*

I sat down in my living room and pulled a pillow to my chest, feeling numb and staring into space for what seemed like hours.

Should I fight her?

Where to begin?

And the questions—and realizations—began firing away in my brain. Even if I did fight her, what would such an accusation do to my life? No one, save for a couple of close friends (and those not even at the elementary school where I taught) knew

I was infected. Would the school rise to my defense when the allegations became public?

I doubted it.

I thought of my classroom: the green chalkboard, the tiny desks, and the fresh faces of twenty-four six-year-olds looking to me, expectantly, to provide guidance. They wouldn't even understand.

But what would their parents think? What would my principal have to say? What about the board of education? Would I be the subject of a specially convened PTA meeting? Would I be put on some kind of hush-hush leave?

I had always wanted to work with kids, ever since I was one myself: a lonely eleven-year-old who found more pleasure from thinking up games and babysitting neighborhood kids and nieces and nephews than I found with my own peer group. How could I let this slide? These kids, teaching . . . these were my life, how I defined myself.

I thought back to when I had heard my roommate from college, Ernie, found out he was HIV positive. Ernie was gay . . . and promiscuous. I thought, unkindly, that those who put their hands into the fire must expect to get burned. But I never let on to Ernie that he had only himself to blame. I was always there for him.

But when I heard his news, eight years ago, I wondered what I would do if I were in his situation. And I thought of things like driving the wrong way down Lakeshore Drive, aiming my car head-on for something heavy that would crush my little Sentra, along with me–a Ford Explorer, maybe. I thought of pills. I thought of somehow finding access to the roof of the Sears tower and flinging myself from it. I knew enough about the pneumonia, the Kaposi's sarcoma, the wasting, and the diarrhea to know that I would want none of it. I would want to go out while I was still healthy, sparing those close to me prolonged suffering and myself the agony of a slow killer that would eat me alive.

By the time I faced my own diagnosis, four years later, my own prognosis was much better than Ernie's had been at the time of his diagnosis. Heroes with names like Sustiva, Combivir, and Viread would allow me to lead an almost normal life. Thoughts of suicide then seemed hysterical.

But now . . . *now* thoughts of suicide seemed neither irrational nor selfish. They seemed sensible. Perhaps the virus would never be the agent of my death, but these allegations could be the agent of another kind of death, a death where everything I cherished, everything that made me *me*, were ripped away by the flippant words of a, of a . . . zipless fuck. How could I have been so stupid?

Three hours—and six vodkas—later, I was ready. I still had a box of razor blades left from when I had painted the bathroom.

And the bathroom was where I would do it. A tub filled with hot water, a little Mozart on the portable CD player on the back of the toilet, a few vertical slashes to my wrists, and all would be over. I wouldn't have to face the humiliation and the crushing loss of everything that was important to me.

I undressed and looked at my body in the mirror: lean, flush, and pink with vitality and health. Who would know that a terminal virus replicated inside my veins? Who would know? Certainly not Trish . . .

I SAT ON the side of the tub, listening to the sound of the flowing water, underscored by Mozart's "Allegretto-Fantasia in D Minor," already in the CD player. I felt strangely calm. The decision to kill myself had been easy, like walking out the door. Final. And with that finality came an eerie kind of acceptance.

I slipped into the water and slid down so that its steamy heat rose up to cover my shoulders. I raised my arms and with three quick slashes to each wrist (the new, and deadly sharp, razors made this process nearly painless . . . a slight tingle, then an almost pleasant burning sensation) cut myself. I lowered my arms into the water, watching as the pump and flow of my tainted blood started darkening the waters. A crimson solution.

I started to feel groggy and lay my head back against the porcelain edge of the claw-footed bathtub.

It was then the phone rang. I could barely lift my eyelids as I heard the answering machine engage after two rings (I had never bothered to clear Trish's earlier message . . . *too late now*, I thought from a cloud somewhere).

"Paul? Paul? Are you there? Pick up–I have something to say." Trish sounded breathless, the halting, hiccupping cadence of sobbing. I tried to rise up on an elbow, to grip the side of the tub, but I felt so tired. I slumped back down, having hardly enough energy to listen as Trish continued.

"I mean, I mean . . . I have something to confess."

There was a pause in which I struggled to keep my eyes open. I would have giggled if I'd had the energy. I knew what was coming.

I could hear her blow out a big breath. "It wasn't true." She let out a sob. "I'm . . . I'm so sorry. See, last week, I found out I tested HIV positive and I knew you were, too. Because you told me, Paul, you told me. I lied. I'm a bitch. We even used condoms, in case you forgot. You were a good guy. Not like the one who infected me." She laughed, a short, bitter bark. "Whoever the hell he is."

She sighed again and I could feel myself fading. I struggled to get up, but was only able to raise the feeblest of splashes and could barely move; it was like strong hands were holding me down in the tub. And in a way, they were: Trish's hands.

"I just wanted you to know there's no attorney. I'm not going anywhere with this. I just wanted to try to get out of facing my husband by coming up with this date rape story. So he wouldn't blame me, you know? And you were the only one I knew for sure who was positive. So it fit. God, I'm sorry.

"But don't worry: I'm going to do the right thing and 'fess up. I'm sorry to have dragged you into this mess. Breathe a little easier, Paul. I promise you have nothing to worry about."

Everything was going cloudy, dark around the edges. *Nothing to worry about.* That was a good one.

Dans le Noir

JERRY ROSEN

MOSTLY IT WAS sunny, but sometimes, heavy gray clouds would arrive without warning to obscure the sky and the ensuing rain drove us inside.

My wife and I hadn't been to Paris in four years. We used to go every summer. Then it slipped to every other. And now, well, a four-year absence is really just too much. Especially when you consider what a fine indulgence Paris is, a delicious dream you walk through awake and wide-eyed. If you've never been there, it's kind of hard to understand. But Paris really gets under your skin. Like a bona fide dream, a night dream, Paris stays with you in unexpected and even mysterious ways, resurfacing in a haunting memory when you're least prepared or expecting it.

This vacation, instead of taking a hotel, we rented a spacious and airy apartment on the rue du Cardinal Lemoine. Not content with just being tourists, it was our goal to casually pretend to live as Parisians. A minor deception, I realize. But basically inconsequential, truly hurtful to no one. Nothing equivalent to the grander, more complicated lies we habitually tell ourselves, or those falsehoods we nonchalantly pass along to others.

Every morning we'd stroll around the corner to our local *boulangerie* on the rue de Poissy to pick up breakfast. We'd get slender cylindrical baguettes or amber-colored croissants, cozy in their waxy paper wrapping, a thin film of butter just waiting for the touch of our fingertips. Sometimes we'd opt for *pain aux raisin*, the doughy bread soft and moist and threaded with pastry cream, the currants plump yet not overly sweet. And perhaps, if we felt especially naughty, we'd buy the small roll known as *petit pain au chocolat*, its delicious warmth gradually softening the nuggets of chocolate snuggly encased within, rendering it even more desirable.

It took only a couple of minutes after leaving the bakery to return to the dim narrow elevator that ascended to our own little sixth-floor slice of heaven. Morning after morning we'd sit in our kitchen, my companionable Lucy and me, eating and drinking coffee, reading the newspaper, maybe struggling with a crossword puzzle. For long stretches at the kitchen window we'd stare in placid dumb contentment at the lazy Seine, at Notre Dame, at the soft Parisian light that filtered gently down on them and on the people passing on the sidewalks below. And every now and then, while Lucy was busy in the bathroom putting on her makeup or fixing her hair, I'd stand in front of the living room window and gaze without restriction into the hotel rooms directly across the street. If I was lucky I'd catch a glimpse of some unknown woman slipping out of her robe or languidly rolling a pair of stockings up her long and shapely legs.

Every afternoon we'd go to parks or galleries. Or we'd shop

or meander through rambling jumbled streets, exploring the neighborhoods. Lost or found, it really didn't matter. A fresh experience always seemed to be waiting around the very next corner. You might stumble upon adventure or romance. You might get laid. Of course, you might also have to step nimbly to avoid a steaming pile of dog shit. For Paris is a city of infinite possibilities.

The majority of evenings consisted of indolent two- or three-hour meals. With mock seriousness we'd analyze the quality of the cooking or reminisce about the events of the day. Mostly we'd intimately gossip, as comfortable married couples do. We heard lots of music too, jazz music, in a couple of very atmospheric local clubs. Then one night we went to dinner at Dans le Noir. It's a restaurant where you eat in absolute and utter darkness, served by waiters who themselves are blind.

"Nervous?" my inquisitive Lucy asked. We were walking in the rue Quincampoix, a previously seedy little street now positively lousy with trendy boutiques, fashionable cafés, and hipper-than-hip art galleries. "Maybe just a little?"

"About being in the dark with you? I stopped being uneasy about that years ago."

"What if it's creepy? What if I feel claustrophobic?"

I placed my hand across her eyes. Gently but firmly I pressed my palm against her face. Her skin was warm to my touch. "What if it is? What if you do?"

Giggling, she swatted my hand away as we reached the restaurant's door. "Behave."

We entered Dans le Noir into a faintly lighted bar area. Two chalkboard menus were posted on the wall to our left. A tall bank of lockers stood waiting at attention in front of the wall to our right. The barman was wiping empty glasses with a towel and setting them down on a narrow shelf. A faint melody of gentle clinks accompanied his proficient handiwork. A slender, eye-catching woman with short-cropped dark hair sat on one of the barstools. Not particularly young, she wasn't exactly old, either. Maybe one side or the other of forty. Tough to tell. Smartly dressed, absentmindedly holding a wine glass by the stem, she conveyed a stylish aloofness that seemed common to many French women. Incongruously, she had a lively and not inconsiderable tattoo on her bare left shoulder. In the dim light I couldn't quite make out the subject of the design. Something oriental it seemed, perhaps a dragon. I thought I saw her cast a perfunctory glance in my direction but immediately dismissed the likelihood.

"We have a reservation for two," I said to the barman in my best tourist French.

A small notepad in a black leather binder rested on the counter directly in front of him. He considered it for a moment with an air of stately gravity. After making sure our name was on the list, he gestured to the menus hanging on the wall. "Tell me what you want for dinner," he said. "If you feel adventurous, choose the 'Surprise' menu. Guessing what you're eating is part of the experience."

After careful study of the menus and a vigorous matrimonial conference, we decided not to take him up on his proposal. "I'm going to have the ostrich for my first course," Lucy said with not a small degree of plucky determination. "That'll be surprise enough."

The barman picked up a telephone and called our order down to the kitchen. "The wait staff is blind," he explained. "But the chef can see. Put your jackets and umbrellas in the lockers. Purse, too. Of course all sources of light are banned. So if you have cell phones or matches or illuminated watches, leave them in the lockers as well. Smoking isn't permitted either. Your waiter will be here momentarily."

And so he was, a short, slight Asian man in his early thirties, with amber-colored skin. He seemed to have materialized almost imperceptibly, from where I couldn't tell. It was as if a translucent shadow had glided soundlessly out from behind a larger sheltering shadow to reveal itself to our still-seeing eyes. The waiter's own lids stretched taut across his shuttered eyeballs. His head tilted slightly to one side.

"I'm Tran," he said. The timbre of his voice was as muted and unobtrusive as his entrance. "Are you ready to pay a visit to the dark? Come close so I can guide you. In this environment it's I who am able to extend a helping hand to others."

He reached out a slender arm. The woman at the bar, already positioned closest to Tran, got up from her seat without delay. She extended her hand toward him. He took it without hesitation, as if he could see. He placed the woman's hand squarely on his shoulder.

"Now you," he said to Lucy with an almost uncanny sense of recognition as to where she stood in the room. She hesitated, though only for a moment. I wasn't sure why. "Don't be nervous. There's really no need. Put your hand on her shoulder so we can form a chain."

Thus, interdependently linked we followed Tran through a doorway, brushing aside several intervening curtains. With measured steps we plunged into an absolute inky blackness. I kept waiting for my eyes to adjust. They never did.

Single file, Tran led us through that unconditional and unforgiving darkness. There were no shapes or forms, nor even any intimation of them. Not even the palest or most obscure contour or silhouette hinted at the size of the room, its configuration, or its contents. There were only voices, some carefree, some louder than what's generally socially acceptable, tinged with faint anxiety.

Soon we paused–on reaching a table, I assumed.

"Sit down," Tran said, the sound of his words directed away from Lucy and me. Then, back in our direction, "No, not you. Not yet. Just a little longer." I supposed the shorthaired woman was being seated. But I really couldn't tell.

"Now you, Missus," said Tran, and Lucy slipped from my grasp. "Do you need any help getting into your seat? Okay, Mister, you come with me. I'm going to put you across from your wife."

It was all we could do to get oriented. We planted our feet squarely on the floor, staking out our territory. We cautiously felt in front of us for napkins and glasses, waiting for the arrival of both water and wine. We caressed the silverware like it was our new best friend.

"How will we ever manage this dinner?" I wondered aloud to Lucy. "It's certainly going to be a challenge."

"Let me pour. I'll keep a finger in the glass to feel when it's nearly full." Smart girl, my Lucy.

"Can you see?" I asked. "I mean anything?"

"No. Nothing."

"Do you think it's true that if one of your senses is taken away, the others become heightened?"

"I guess we'll find out. If you had to lose one of your senses, which would it be?"

"Well, it wouldn't be sight, that's for sure. That would make me feel way too creepy and ill at ease."

"That's because you're such a control freak."

"That's because my heart would ache beyond words, beyond reason, if I couldn't ever again look at your sweet, pretty face."

"Give me your hand." She tenderly brushed the tips of my fingers across her yielding cheek. "This is to help you remember what I look like. For me, deafness would be the worst by far. Never hearing a Brahms trio or a Chopin prelude. Or Sarah doing 'My Funny Valentine.' Feeling left out of conversations. Very isolating. Very lonely and sad."

When dinner came, it quickly became apparent that knives and forks were as useless to us as a Nikon is to a blind man. Since we first had to discover with our hands where our food was located on our plates, it seemed pointless not to just stay put and rip everything apart manually. Was that soft and squishy mound really turnips? How much of my veal had I eaten, and how much was left? Sometimes the sounds in the room seemed uncomfortably near, sometimes faded and far away. Gradually our initial discomfort eased. We began to feel an increasingly relaxed and pleasurable sense of calm and anonymity.

"This place is amazing," Lucy said.

"I'm not sure exactly what I'm eating. But I know it's covered in lots of sauce."

"Which of our friends would we want to be here with?"

"Maybe we should think about who we *wouldn't* want to bring here."

It's no mystery that intimacy, even public intimacy, blossoms a great deal more effortlessly in the dark. After all, who is there to serve as witness? We drank a lot of wine. We fed each other. Before I knew it Lucy was sucking gravy from my fingers. She had three of them deep inside her mouth, going at it with hungry gusto, as if it was her last meal on earth. Finally she relinquished her hold.

"I wish I could suck something else right now," she whispered, her voice suddenly deeper and huskier, urgent. "Something big. Something big and hard."

Where had my predictably modest Lucy gone? Who was the impostor sitting across from me in this impossible dark who had taken her place?

"Don't be impatient, little girl. You'll get what you want, but not until later."

"But I need it now, Daddy."

"Shush. Keep your voice down."

"They can't hear us. And what if they do? We're speaking English. They won't understand anyway."

Gently but firmly I took both of her hands into my own. "You don't know for sure that that's true. Don't get petulant and don't be a brat. You'll just have to wait. That's final."

No sooner had I finished speaking than abruptly and without warning I felt another hand, a fifth, slide onto my leg, just above the knee. Steadily it traveled up the inside of my thigh with all the firm determination of a salmon making its way upstream to spawn. At journey's end, with no equivocation or apology, it pressed directly down onto my crotch. Before I could react, agile, confident fingers began to unbutton the fly of my 501 jeans. The woman with the tattoo who had accompanied us into the darkness? Who knows? Simultaneously my body both tensed and relaxed.

In a blink my cock was free. Slick, greasy fingers wrapped themselves around it with practiced expertise, jerking up and down. My prick stood at wakeful attention, rigid as a slab of granite, a rocket set to blast sky-high. At my age not an everyday occurrence, believe me.

I shifted in my chair to enable more uninhibited access.

Lucy was talking again, but I couldn't quite make out what she was saying. I really didn't care. For all I knew, there were infrared security cameras recording what was happening. To tell the truth, I really didn't care about that, either.

Then she was down in front of me, on her knees, on the floor, her head sandwiched between my legs. Well, I assumed it was a she. Squeezing my knees together with cruel intensity, I locked onto her ears in a vise grip with my fingers. Her mouth pushed down on my dick, consuming it in a gulp. I could feel her chin bounce against my balls. A snug and perfect fit. It was as if she'd finally found her way home after a long and perilous journey.

After getting her initial bearings, she really started going to work with a vengeance. With metronomically precise and faultless rhythm, she bobbed up and down on my cock for all she was worth. She went at it like a heavy-duty suction pump.

The slurping sounds she was making grew louder. So much so, in fact, they were starting to make me feel a bit uneasy, though I realized that in this bleak and utter darkness you couldn't really pinpoint a sound's originating location. *Slurp, slurp, slurp.* Mouthful upon sloppy mouthful.

The hand that had previously been jerking my prick slid down onto my balls. By this time they were coated with a thick glaze of saliva. With subtle but unyielding pressure she began to squeeze. Dexterously, without missing a beat, she simultaneously maneuvered her other hand underneath the sac up along the furrow leading to my ass.

That did it. I was finished. A goner. Harshly pushing her head down as far as it could go, I went off in a rush, shooting a heavy load deep into the most subterranean regions of her throat. My heart thumped away, pounding inside my chest like a madly reverberating kettledrum. I felt great. I felt like shit. What about Lucy?

I needn't have worried. She was still talking, seemingly unaware, unconcerned, as if time had been conveniently suspended.

"Remember that old blues song 'In the Dark'?" she said. And then, with great tenderness, she began to sing, her voice soothing and mellow, "*In the dark, in the dark, it's just you and I. Not a sound, there's not one sigh. Just the beat of my poor heart, in the dark.*"

She paused. The space between us was tranquil and serene, clear and tidy of any discord or friction. The space between my legs had cleared, too.

"Who did that tune?" Lucy continued. "Wasn't that Nina Simone?"

"That's the version you're thinking of. But lots of people covered it. Hadda Brooks. Jimmy Witherspoon. I think it was Lil Green who actually wrote it."

"All finished?" It was our waiter, Tran. He'd materialized beside our table like a ghost. "Are you disposed to leave? Or do you prefer to continue to remain in the dark?"

"I'm ready," Lucy said unambiguously. "How about you?"

And so we left, retracing, I assumed, the path we took on arrival.

Lucy carefully arranged her head so that her mouth was close beside my ear. I could feel her warm breath ebb and flow upon it at regularly recurring intervals. Almost undetectably, her muted voice barely a whisper, she resumed her song from where she had previously left off. "*Gee, but I'm not pretending. 'Cause I swear it's fun, fun to be kissed in the dark. We're gonna find romance in the dark.*"

My impulse was to confess what had happened. But I caught myself just in time. To what purpose, what end? As it does on occasion, and only rare occasions at that, compassion trumps the truth.

"You see," Lucy continued, her singing now at an end, "it's not so very different in the dark."

Isn't it fine for you to think that? I said, but only to myself.

Below the Cut

STEPHEN DEDMAN

I SHOULDN'T BE writing this. I certainly shouldn't be posting it to a site like this one, and I don't know why I am. No one is ordering me to do it: No one gives me orders anymore.

Maybe that's the problem. Maybe that's why.

There's a story by Edgar Allan Poe called "The Imp of the Perverse." It's not one of his better ones, but perhaps you know it. A man knows he has gotten away with a murder but runs anyway, drawing suspicion to himself. Why? Bad conscience, maybe?

Blame this on the Imp of the Perverse.

I KNELT BETWEEN my mistress's spread thighs and licked the plump lips of her golden pussy, smiling as a thin stream of juice came trickling out and ran down to her asshole. She was reclining on the sofa, her eyes closed in pleasure, and she massaged her large, lovely breasts and tweaked her tight nipples as I ate her. Her pussy lips parted like a flower blossoming, and she wrapped her legs around my back as she moaned. When I began circling her clit with my tongue, she pushed her right breast up to her chin and began licking the nipple, a sight that always made my cock swell in my panties, but I knew better than to touch myself.

HE STOPS POUNDING at the keyboard, and though he knows the office is locked, he looks around anyway. He has a perfect excuse for looking at S&M sites and videos and magazines, because tomorrow he will have to make a decision on whether they should be denied First Amendment protection. He has not been ordered to rule that they should, but he knows he is expected to do so. He knows that the people who selected him prize loyalty above all else. And he knows they do not know about his past.

Perhaps they know that other judges, after days of inflicting punishment, go to dominatrices (professional or amateur) to be punished in turn. Lawyers may switch, depending on whether they win or lose, but judges have so much power that they feel the need to submit to someone.

Not him, of course.

Not recently, at least.

WE WROTE A contract. In my mistress's apartment, I would become Clarice, her new femme slave. Clarice didn't have any body hair, and she certainly didn't have a cock; she wore G-strings that hid her crotch but left most of her ass bare for when my mistress wanted to spank or whip it. She was to do whatever housework my mistress wanted done before being allowed to lick her lovely blonde pussy. I agreed to these terms, and my mistress took me out shopping, buying me a short-skirted maid's outfit with stiletto heels, buying me a wig, taking me to a beauty parlor to have my body hair removed and learn to apply my makeup—all with my money, of course. As soon as we returned to her apartment, she ordered me to lie down, then pulled off her jeans and pants and sat on my face until I'd made her come three times. After the first time, she'd removed her leather jacket; after the second, her T-shirt, and after the third, she'd rewarded me by removing her bra and letting me look up at her amazing breasts, watch her squeeze and suck them to stimulate herself.

For the first few nights together, she kept my hands cuffed behind me in case I was tempted to touch my cock, or her breasts, until she was sure I was too well trained to disobey.

HE'D BEEN A young lawyer then. She was two years older and had been with the firm longer. He'd made a fumbling pass at her, and she'd made it clear that that while she'd tried sex with men before, she now regarded that as a mistake; she thought of herself as a dyke, and a butch dyke at that. She liked pretty femmes who enjoyed being dominated, and the only cocks she ever wanted to see in her house were silicone and under her control.

They'd let the matter rest, but she'd surprised him a few weeks later by inviting him over for dinner. She'd just broken up with her girlfriend and wanted someone to talk to. He'd put her to bed after she fell asleep on the sofa; when she'd woken up, she found him tidying the apartment. "You know," she said, sleepily, "it's a pity you're not a woman; I'd really like—" They'd stared at each other for a moment, then he'd asked, softly, "What would you like?"

. . .

My mistress shuddered as she came, but I knew better than to stop. I kept licking her swollen clit until she came again, then wrapped my lips around it and sucked on it to give her her third orgasm for the evening. "Ohhh, thaat's . . . ," she crooned, then snapped back into character. "Not bad," she said, grudgingly.

"Thank you, Mistress."

She nodded. "Is dinner ready yet?"

"No, Mistress."

"Then you'd better keep sucking until it is."

"Yes, Mistress. Thank you, Mistress." I buried my face in her crotch again, lapping up her juices from her warm honey pot, kissing her thighs, and sucking her pussy lips into my mouth before returning my attention to her clit. She sighed with pleasure as I ate her for another half an hour, then tapped me on the shoulder with her riding crop. "Dinner's ready, Clarice," she said. "Have you set the table?"

"No, Mistress."

"*What?*"

I scrambled to my feet.

"Turn around," she snapped. I obeyed.

"Now bend over." I did my best to touch my toes, while she examined my ass for hair. I knew that if she found any, she'd refuse to touch me and would paddle me with a hairbrush while I pleaded for forgiveness. This time, however, she was obviously satisfied. "Over my knee," she ordered.

Eagerly, I obeyed. She spanked me hard, but the sensation of being touched (however ungently) with her hand, and the sensation of my cock rubbing against her thigh (separated only by the satin of my G-string and an ultrathin condom), soon had me on the verge of coming—but I knew better than to let *that* happen.

After a dozen hard slaps, she stopped. "Okay," she said. "I want dinner on the table in five minutes, or you're going to sleep in the bathroom again. Understood?"

I nodded; she was allowing me two or three minutes to go into the bathroom and jerk off. As usual, I came almost as soon as I had my panties off, an orgasm much more powerful than any I'd had during the week. Then I cleaned myself up and went out to serve dinner to my mistress.

My mistress seemed to have something on her mind, though it didn't stop her from enjoying her food. She ordered me to wash the dishes while she watched a video, then permitted me to brush her hair. When the movie ended, she not only let me watch while she relaxed in the bath, but also allowed me to towel her legs and ass dry before ordering me onto my back so she could sit on my face. I sucked avidly on her squeaky-clean pussy until I was almost drowning in her juices and my latex-covered cock was throbbing in sympathy with her pulsing pink clit. "That was very good . . . Clarice," she said, after I'd made her come yet again. "You deserve a reward for being so obedient. Would you like to sleep in my bed tonight?"

I think I stared at her; I considered myself lucky to be allowed to sleep on the bedroom rug rather than on a plastic sheet on the couch. I nodded, not trusting myself to speak.

"You'll have to promise not to touch me, of course," she said. "Can you do that, or will I have to tie your hands?"

"Whatever pleases you, Mistress," I replied, my mouth dry.

I WOKE LATE the next morning, after a mostly sleepless night. My mistress had dressed me in filmy lingerie, loosely tied my wrists to the headboard with silk scarves, then fallen asleep almost instantly. I'd slept on my side, facing away from her, for fear of my cock rubbing against her, and had been driven to distraction by the sensation of her ass rubbing against mine, then her beautiful breasts flattened against my back as she rolled over.

When I finally woke up, I found that my mistress had already gotten out of bed, leaving me alone. Sleepily, I untied my hands and wandered toward the door and the smell of coffee. To my amazement, I saw my mistress sitting on the sofa with a shapely raven-haired woman, her hands cuffed behind her back, kneeling between her legs. The woman was naked but for her cuffs, high heels, and a studded leather collar, leaving me with no doubt about her sex; her pussy was clearly visible, and already glistened with juice.

My mistress quickly clamped her thighs around this new lover's ears and held a finger to her lips to command silence, then pointed back at the bedroom. I backed away, but the woman had obviously heard the door opening, and she glanced over her shoulder. "Who's she?" she asked my mistress. "You didn't tell me you had anybody here!"

My mistress actually blushed, then recovered sufficiently to snap, "I didn't tell you to get here early, either! I said eleven-thirty, remember?"

"Sorry," the woman replied, though her tone was still suspicious, not quite humble enough for my taste. My mistress drew a deep breath. "Clarice, this is Dee; we met a month ago, and she's going to be moving in here, so your services will no longer be required."

HE STARED AT the words on the monitor. They still hurt, more than thirty years later; writing them down at all would have been masochistic enough, without the extra risk of posting them onto a Web site. The knowledge that he could go back to the site at any time and edit or delete the entry was like having stinging ants crawling around in his underwear. He knew he would stay awake all night wondering whether to do it, wondering how many people had ventured past the cut in search of a good sex scene, maybe liked it, copied it, jacked or jilled off to it, maybe even run some textual analysis software over it to determine the authorship...

He shook his head, more at his ego than at his paranoia, and kept typing.

I OPENED MY mouth to protest, then shut it again, and nodded.

"Dee," my mistress growled, "if you ever speak to me like that again, I'll whip that pretty ass of yours until you won't be able to sit down for a week. Understand?"

"Yes, Mistress," Dee replied softly.

"Good. I just hope you can learn to obey me and please me as well as Clarice has. Clarice, go get the toy box," she ordered, "I want a cock."

I stared, then hurried back into the bedroom and returned with the black leather bag that held my mistress's collection of handcuffs, vibrators, and other sex toys. She picked out her favorite strap-on, a fat ten-inch monster, and commanded Dee to kiss it. Dee kissed the tip, then took as much of the dong into her mouth as she could.

"You like cocks, don't you?" my mistress asked.

Dee nodded.

"You've probably sucked as many cocks as pussies, haven't you?"

Dee mumbled something that I didn't catch. "And you want this cock in your pussy, don't you?"

"Yes, mistress."

"Louder," my mistress commanded. "Let Clarice hear you."

"Yes, Mistress," said Dee, sliding the dildo out of her mouth. "I want you to fuck my pussy with this big cock."

My mistress smiled and strapped the dildo on. "And you want Clarice to watch while I fuck you, don't you?"

"Yes, Mistress."

"Good. Now get down on all fours–elbows on the floor, ass up in the air . . . yes, that's good." My mistress knelt behind her, and parted Dee's pussy lips with her thumbs, then slid the thick plastic cock into her spasming cunt. "You may touch your clit, if you wish," she said generously.

Dee, feeling her pussy completely filled, reached back and stroked herself and gasped with pleasure. My mistress spanked her pretty ass as she fucked her, and Dee squealed each time she came.

When Dee was babbling, absolutely incoherent with ecstasy, my mistress commanded me to come closer and crouch down near Dee's ass, then withdrew the dripping dildo and said, "Lick it clean. Both of you."

I began licking Dee's juices off the plastic dong, and after a minute to recover from her orgasm, Dee turned around and did the same. Our eyes met for an instant, then my mistress snapped, "Okay, that's enough." She led Dee into the bathroom, handcuffed her to the s-bend under the sink, lubed up a vibrating butt-plug and carefully inserted it into her asshole, and promised to return in a few minutes.

"Okay," she said softly, after closing the bathroom door behind her, "I'm sorry to do this to you like this. I tried to tell you last night . . . Dee's going to be moving in tomorrow, so I won't be able to see you anymore. You'd better get dressed and go."

I looked at her, thunderstruck, then bowed my head. "Yes, Mistress."

THE NEXT WEEK at the firm was hellish. It had been difficult working with her when he'd been used to thinking of himself as her slave and maid, difficult not to call her "Mistress" instead of "Emma," difficult to ask or suggest rather than beg. But being in the same room as her, being able to see her and hear her and smell her but not touch or taste her, being nothing nothing nothing to her . . . it was worse even than her total absence. And as unbearable as that would have been, he found himself looking forward to the weekend as though the governor was going to phone to grant him a stay of execution.

On Saturday night he was sitting at home watching an old tape of *Wonder Woman* with the sound off, his panties halfway down his thighs, his cock half-hard, a bottle of Johnny Walker Black Label on the floor beside him. He paused when the bottle was half empty, then rather than wonder whether it might actually be half full, set to work on the other half. When the phone rang, he hesitated for a moment before reaching for the receiver. "Hello?"

"Hi," said a vaguely familiar voice. "This is Dee–Emma's roommate? I was wondering if you'd like to get together for a drink sometime?"

"A drink?"

"Coffee? Dinner? Whatever? Look, Emma's told me about you, and I like to fuck men sometimes, so I thought maybe we–"

"I don't know–"

"What I really like," she continued, "is to watch a guy jerk off while I sit on his face."

His cock twitched slightly.

HE LOOKED UP, listened for a moment. Was there someone else in the office, at this hour? Automatically, he hit "Save."

"I REALLY LOVE to watch his cum shooting out," Dee continued. "Especially if he's tied to the bed or something. Then I like him to keep licking me, or maybe eat out my ass, until he's hard again."

My cock throbbed despite my drunkenness; my last mistress had never let me do anything to her asshole, hadn't even liked me looking at it, thinking it demeaned her more than me.

"If he does that well enough, I might even let him fuck me. If not, I'll punish him until he begs for mercy. So what do you say?"

I hesitated.

"I could make it an order," she said.

My cock snapped to attention. "An order?"

"I'll be at your place in an hour," she said. "And your cock had better be hard, or you'll be sorry as hell. You already deserve a good spanking for looking at my cunt without my permission. Do you understand?"

"Yes, Mistress," I said, happily.

HE HIT "SAVE Entry" one last time, then logged out of the site, shut down the computer, and picked up his briefcase. Unusually, he began whistling under his breath and was in the parking lot before he recognized the tune: the Alan Parsons Project's "The Cask of Amontillado." Montresor, he remembered, had waited half a century before confessing his crime. For him, it had been little more than thirty years since he'd last seen either Emma (dead of a heart attack two years before) or Dee (married, a churchgoing grandmother, with almost as much to lose as he had). He'd maintained a thick veneer of respectability for all that time and had worn it like a hair shirt, a form of masochism that was approved of in the rarefied social circles in which he now strutted.

He finally fell asleep at about 3:00 A.M., sometimes walking into his study but never actually logging on to the site to read, edit, or delete his confession. He woke at dawn out of a frighteningly erotic dream and decided to shower and go into the office rather than go back to sleep. To his surprise, his secretary was already sitting outside his office, and he glanced at his Rolex. "Do I have an early meeting?" he asked.

"Your first isn't for an hour," she replied. "The one about banning S&M DVDs and Web sites."

"It's not like you to beat me here."

She smiled broadly, then said softly, "I didn't know you liked Edgar Allan Poe."

He froze. "I haven't read him in years," he replied. "But I was a fan when I was much younger. He invented the detective story."

"I know," she said. "'The Purloined Letter.' I always liked 'The Tell-Tale Heart' myself. How are you going to vote?"

"Vote?"

"On the S&M thing." When he showed no sign of replying, she said, "I think it should be protected by the First Amendment. Consenting adults, and so on."

"I . . ." He rejected several possible replies that came to mind, and began, "I didn't know you were," before deciding that that, too, was just too dangerous a comment to make.

She looked him in the eye unflinchingly, and her smile disappeared. "I *could* make it an order," she said.

You Kissed Mandy

JASON RUBIS

"YOU DIDN'T *REALLY.* Did you? I can't believe you!" Rachel turned her head on the pillow and grinned at Gus, showing every tooth.

"It was just the one time," Gus said, muttering his words at the ceiling. A fly buzzed up there. It was around noon. Lazy Sunday. The *Times* scattered in sections on the bedroom floor, china plates with half-moons of gnawed bagel resting between them on the sheets. On mornings like these Gus often thought, *This is it—this is what we went to college for, this is our reward.*

"But you kissed *Mandy*. Mandy *Strohemann.*" Rachel rolled on the bedclothes like an otter, her nose wrinkled. Something was building in her—a certain feeling, demanding expression. Finally it came, with a massive, giggling shudder, "*Eeuww!*"

"I don't see what's so funny about it. It was two years ago. We were all in college, for god's sake."

Rachel settled onto her belly, dug her elbows into the

bedding, set her chin on her palms, and took up her grin again. Gus was right. It *had* been a while ago. But she didn't share his aversion to nostalgia.

"And you were still with Sharon then?"

"Yeah."

"*God!*"

Rachel and Sharon Siegel and Tina Hess and evil Mandy had, in those days, shared a suite of rooms in Bedford Hall. She had thought Sharon was so lucky that first time she'd brought Gus over. Everyone thought the two of them would get married–it was *inevitable.* Then came graduation; Sharon took that job in Berlin and now Gus belonged to Rachel.

She pressed a finger to the tip of his nose. She did that sometimes, just to see how long it would take before he'd push it away. "So you were dating Sharon and you kissed Mandy anyway." Her voice was lightly accusing, but only lightly. "I don't believe you!" she said again, and laughed.

"Just *once.* All right? End of subject. Sorry I even brought it up." He picked up the sports page and rattled it, trying to get it folded the way he liked.

"Tell me. I want to hear it."

"No."

"Tell me. I'll make you tell me." She wriggled up next to him. This was a game she liked to play–Torture Gus.

An arm over his chest would hold him still; she could then begin sucking his ear, biting it. That was best way to start–you wanted to turn Gus on, you just sucked on his ear a while. Sharon had let her in on that one.

"Tell me," she whispered. Her hand reached for his briefs and peeled the waistband back, uncovering just the head of his dick. He growled, but when she began teasing him with a fingertip, he didn't push her away. He spread his legs instead, just slightly.

More work on his ear, and then she started with the threats, whispering them: "*Torture* you until you tell me. I'll get the honey dust out and lick it off this fat little cock head, off your nippies—I'll lick it right off, you want that? Huh?"

Rachel always called his nipples *nippies* when she was turned on. That was her thing—one of them. She was a tall girl, an inch taller than Gus, and slightly stronger; years of soccer and racquetball had put some muscles on her, kept her lean and hard. When she got turned on, she was difficult to turn off. She wasn't at all sure why the idea of Gus kissing Mandy Strohemann affected her this way, but apparently it did, and apparently it affected Gus as well (his cock was really hard now, his hips were moving just a little), and she was willing to go with that.

But Gus was resisting, too. Being pissy. Eventually, he caught her wrists and held them. "You first," he said, twisting his head to dodge another kiss. "Tell me what you guys had against Mandy. I mean, I've heard all the jokes and the rumors. Give me specifics."

Rachel *tsk*ed. "Well, I mean, you know. I mean, *Mandy* . . ."

"Try harder."

Falling back on the pillow, mock-sulky: "She was just a bitch, okay? A spoiled little princess. She thought her family's money would buy her anything. She went on and on about how she went to school in Europe and all this shit . . ."

"So? Sharon's family had money, too. So did yours and Tina's." His mouth twisted. "And when it comes to spoiled . . ."

"She would talk trash about people. Like all the time. Call them stupid and stuff. Like *she* was some kind of genius."

"Hmm."

"And she was just gross," Rachel went on, seeing an advantage and pressing it. "Just... you know, a slob in the bathroom. Nothing a guy would notice . . . aw, look at you, you're mad! 'Cause I'm talking about your *girlfriend*. You're all embarrassed for her!"

"Quit."

Clinging to his arm, tugging at it: "Just tell me! Why'd you kiss her? Why'd you want to? I mean, Tina I could see, with those tits... but *Mandy?*"

"She wasn't ugly."

"She wasn't *pretty!*"

"She had nice hair..."

"Yeah," Rachel mused. "I guess she did kind of have pretty hair. Should have, she washed it enough. But she was so... so scrawny... no body at all."

Gus inhaled. "Do you want me to tell you about this or not?"

"Yeah! Yeah, please! See, I'll be good." Rachel squirmed under the covers and cuddled next to him, batting her eyes. Gus noticed that one hand was still under the covers.

"Well . . . it was at that party you guys had in your rooms. Remember? Right before graduation. Remember there was all that stuff, that food her Mom had sent over..."

"Oh yeah, *I* remember."

Mrs. Strohemann had insisted on sending a huge raft of deli food for the party, mountains of meats and pickles and breads. People ignored the food at first, then it had become something of a joke. As the drinking progressed, people had started playing with it; slices of roast beef had been pressed into service as hats or odd items of clothing; several olive-throwing fights had broken out.

"I'd been drinking a lot. So I was kind of noshing, you know?

Picking at stuff. And Mandy came in. It was just her and me, nobody else was in the kitchen."

"Naughty." Under the covers, Rachel's fingers began considering the faintly damp crotch of her panties. Skinny little Mandy with her old maid glasses—probably had a book under one arm, she usually did—trying to be all superior to big, drunk, handsome Gus. Wet, Mandy's little spinster *pussy* had probably been sopping. Trying to talk to him about Russian writers or something, eating him up with her eyes.

"Why'd you say 'naughty?' We weren't . . ."

"Okay, okay, you weren't naughty. Yet. So go on . . ."

"So . . . we started talking."

"Oh, you started *talking*, huh? 'Bout what?"

"About nothing. Just small talk, like you do at parties."

Rachel bit his shoulder. "Stop sounding so defensive. You weren't *that* innocent. Get to the kissing."

"She started feeding stuff to me."

"God . . . you're not serious!"

"Yeah. I mean, just playing around. I was drunk, remember? A piece of this stuff, I remember, I asked her what it was, and she said, 'Eat it first,' and then later she told me it was tongue. She said she was afraid I wouldn't eat it or I'd get sick or something if she told me first."

"But she fed it to you—she fed you *tongue*—with her fingers?"

Gus got just a little flustered. "Well, yeah . . . but when you say she fed me tongue, I mean . . . she didn't . . ."

He should have saved it. Rachel wasn't listening. She whispered "Dirty fingers," to herself, staring at the wall, smiling, thinking intently on something. If she hadn't been afraid that it would have stopped Gus talking, she would have thrown the covers back and gone down on him that moment. Sucked him.

She would have so loved to do that. Get that thing in her mouth when it was straight and hard and salt-tasting and close her lips on the root of it. A little vein would pulse there, bumping against her lip.

"So what then?"

"Well . . . it started then. I started kissing her fingers. You know, when she put the meat in. She just let me do it. I remember she . . . she like turned her hand so I could kiss the side. And her . . ." The right word escaped him for a moment. "Her palm. The palm of her hand."

"Slut." Rachel's fingers danced under the covers. She spoke with half-shut eyes, hissing and murmuring. "Playing like she was so pure–she was nothing but a fucking slut, after you the whole time . . ."

She was so loving this. This was beyond price. She couldn't wait to call Tina, e-mail Sharon . . . already forming choice phrases: FED HIM WITH HER *FINGERS*. HOT FOR HIM. PRACTICALLY RAPED HIM.

"So she said, 'You can kiss my mouth if you want.' And I did. I don't know why I did any of it. I guess I . . . when she said *mouth* like that . . . I don't know."

"Oh, GOD! Did she bat her eyes? Did she tell you her toes tingled? I'll bet she ran straight to the bathroom and stuck three fingers up herself . . ."

"No. She didn't do that."

"How'd you do it? Kiss her. I want you to kiss me the same way. Right now." She took her wetted fingers from between her legs. Climax was threatening, and she wanted Gus's dick if she could get it.

Gus moved on top of her, did it quickly. But the kiss was limp; he barely touched his mouth to hers.

"Oh, come on. You kissed her better than that."

"Well, that's the way I kissed her, so I don't know what you want."

"Did you do anything else?"

"No."

"You didn't feel her boobs or touch her between her legs?" She was hoping he would say he touched her boobs. Mandy had little pink boobies—Rachel had seen them once. She wanted Gus to say he'd pinched her nipples, or laid his head on her breasts like a baby and sucked them and then got naughty and bit them. Mandy squealing while bad baby Gus bit her little boobies. For some reason the thought of that really got her going. Her long legs jackknifed under the covers—once, twice, three times.

"No, we just kissed that one time."

"How'd she kiss *you*?"

"Well, like this."

"Huh . . . I don't believe that. I think she kissed you all big and romantic and gooshy, like *this*."

This took a while to demonstrate properly.

"Whatever."

"*I* think she was in love with you. She probably still is."

"Whatever you want."

"What's wrong? Why are you pissed at me? Gus?"

GREEN EYES STARED at him over the chain lock. Not weary, not resentful, not particularly glad—curious, rather. "What are you doing here? It's Sunday."

"I had to get out. Wanted to see you." He touched the chain, set it swinging between her door and where it met her doorway. "Can I come in?"

The door shut, then–not immediately–opened. Mandy was barefoot in a pink robe, a thick green book cradled in her arms, the Diaries of Marie Somebody. She had been reading that one for a while now.

She stood aside as Gus slid past her, looking this way and that, reabsorbing her tiny living room, head tilted up like he was inhaling it. Mandy always joked that the apartment was decorated in Early Graduate Student, but Gus loved it. It was just like her–irresistibly compact, neat, cunningly decorated. It was like a kind of toy.

She shut her eyes as Gus kissed her cheek, and then as he kissed her throat she lifted her chin. Her hand rose up and squeezed his forearm, caressed his bicep, took the measure of it with her small, strong fingers. Every time he came to her she did that at least once.

"How's Jock-Girl?" she asked suddenly.

"Fine." He mumbled it through her black hair. Jesus, but he loved her hair. Two oil slicks, two matching curtains of black, down to her shoulders. Smelled so clean, shampoo and hot water and new brushes. Her little face was clever, vaguely feline–always smiling even when she broke into his kissing with something unpleasant.

"Did you tell her yet?"

He didn't wince. Wouldn't have done any good. Nothing to do but tell her the truth. "I started to. This morning. I started telling her about that time at the party."

"Well, damn. Ancient history. How did she take it?"

"I told her we kissed . . ."

"Uh-huh. So we did." She squeezed his arm again, plucked lightly at the hairs with her fingers. "Nice kissies there in the kitchen. Did you tell her how you took me into the bathroom then and ate my pussy? How you licked my clit? How I had to bite my hand so I wouldn't scream?"

Gus grinned. He liked it when she talked like that. He liked remembering, too. It had been the first time he'd ever done that to a girl, or thought of doing that. With Mandy, it had seemed so natural–he had imagined the smell would make him sick, but it didn't at all. "And then we fucked."

"Twice. Twice we did, remember? Standing up in the bathroom with somebody banging on the door because they wanted to pee. So embarrassing."

Like a little cat, smiling as she told him that. God, but he could have gone for her right then.

"Did you tell Rachel all that? And then did you tell her about six months ago?"

God, but he could have gone for her right then. "I . . ."

"Us running into each other? At the grocery store, of all places? By the produce?"

"No, she . . ."

"You didn't tell her how we hugged, in that 'Ohmigod it's been so long how *are* you' way . . . just before we started kissing? Remember that? Remember how we couldn't seem to stop kissing each other?"

She slid her nails up his arm, as close to his shoulder as she could reach.

"How we still can't?" She leaned forward and bit at his chest. It didn't hurt, but he groaned.

"No. Babe, she wouldn't let me get past that first kiss . . ."

"And of course you didn't press the subject."

"Mandy . . ."

"Shh. Come here, bad boy." She put the book down and undid the sash of her robe, showed him her breasts.

"Booby, huh?" she whispered, backing against a wall. She always got a little babyish when she got excited. "See the booby? Kiss it?" A long purr as his lips found the rose-colored nipple.

She hefted it in one hand, crushing it under his lip. "Lick it?"

He did. Her stiff nipple scraping lightly on his tongue, then forming itself into a little cone as he sucked. His hands sliding under the robe, finding her skin smooth and hot. One hand ventured clumsily down to her pussy and she murmured, "Yeah, do that."

He would have smelled his fingers, licked them, if he hadn't known she didn't like that. But she didn't mind his mouth forsaking her tit for her pussy. For that, she spread her robe and legs both.

Eating Mandy was the best. In a way, he would have loved to eat her for real, swallow everything about her: her brains and her little clever body; her calm, intelligent voice that spoke of books he would never read, strange outlandish films that had no reality outside her descriptions of them. Get all that inside, really *understand* it all for once. He had been to college like everyone else, he wasn't an idiot. He made a hundred grand a year, and there'd maybe be a promotion next September to the tune of twenty more . . . but Mandy knew things no one else did.

She wasn't as pretty as Sharon; his friends wouldn't be as impressed by her, and he knew they wouldn't like her nearly as much as they liked Rachel; same for his parents. But Mandy impressed the shit out of *him*. He still couldn't believe someone like her was into him.

He pursed his lips against the soft place between her legs and kissed there, gently, the way she had taught him.

Her nails in his scalp, like they would drive straight through into his brain. "Come on, Mister."

They would go to her bedroom and fuck long and slow. And then–he knew–she would make him call Rachel up. She had been talking about it a lot the last couple of weeks, how he would have to do that eventually.

She wouldn't play like she was torturing him, the way Rachel would. She would keep her hand on his thigh as he picked up the phone and–the smell of her body still very evident–dialed home. Mandy wouldn't torture him, but she wouldn't let him get away, either. She would rub his back as he spoke to Rachel, but the whole time, he knew, she'd be smiling her little cat smile. He imagined her taking the phone from him at the last minute, just before Rachel hung up (in tears, or cursing him, or utterly uncaring–any of these was possible), and whispering into it: "How do you like me now, Jock-Girl?"

A smile broke on Gus's face as Mandy led him into her tiny, potpourri-smelling bedroom. He thought, *That would actually be kind of hot, if she did that.*

The Blonde at the Caffé Cavour

MAXIM JAKUBOWSKI

1

SHE SENDS ME a photograph in the mail. Together with her book. A collection of her short stories. Published in Florence. Her bare back on Kodak glossy art paper. A yellow glow illuminates her skin, her hair, a darker shade of blonde breaking across the top of her shoulders like a wave on an unknown shore. I think she is looking out of a window. That's where the light is coming from.

Right now, I desire her. Intensely.

I have unreasonable appetites. I languish for the past and all those women, luminous, wonderfully obscene, distant and no longer available, impossible. I dream at night of their vanishing embraces, my heart beats a melancholy rhythm for them all, sad in the knowledge that none will ever be part of my life again. So instead, greedy for more than just memories, I daydream of the future, of the roads still to be taken, of the life still to be loved.

Who cares about the present?

It's too ordinary, so much less glamorous than the republic of dreams.

2

SHE IS BLONDE and a frequent night bird at the Caffé Cavour. Here she whiles away the hours of southern nights discussing The Clash, punk attitudes, the many shades of noir, and drinking Russian vodka and local wine. The debates can sometimes be fierce, and there are times when the bartender thinks tempers are heating up just that little bit too much and is just a word away from demanding silence. But somehow they sense his irritation and the flow of words abates naturally, and they move on to another subject to ping-pong between their fevered minds–whether Chet Baker's 'Almost Blue' is better than Elvis Costello's or even Italian crime writer Carlo Lucarelli's novel partly inspired by the song. She mostly wears black, a short dress that reaches to her knees, or black jeans that mold her delicate rear. Her photograph gives no indication of her height, but I guess she isn't especially tall. Call it intuition. Her nose is sharp, angular.

3

HER EX (THEY lived together five years) is an actor and travels all over Italy for his work. She pines for him. Badly. Which is possibly why she recognizes the same notes of pain in my stories and identifies with the profound sense of yearning I just can't ever shake off, hard as I try. What is this: a mirror image of me? Hell, I'm no blondeblond; my hair has almost turned gray since she-who-must-not-be-mentioned-anymore.

But it's like a hesitation waltz of the damaged as we exchange e-mails, letters, books, song lyrics, and music in quick succession after our initial contact. I follow her online diary, her blog, like a furtive spy, gleaning information, hints, ideas. For what purpose really? Maybe the fascination and the implied unknown promises of the unknown.

I wonder what I should do next.

SHOULD I ASK her for her telephone number? If the answer is yes, go to section 5. If the answer is no, go to section 4.

4

WE KEEP ON corresponding in a friendly manner, one writer to another, endlessly moaning about the pain every word drains in its wake, as you seek to find the right one to express emotion, feeling, reality. It never gets easier even with thousands of pages or more to your credit. You'd think it would, wouldn't you? But she lives much too far away, and anyway, reading between the lines of her online diary, she now appears to be living with another man, so any progress down this particular road is fraught with problems, effort, dangers. Oh, the sheer futility of it all . . .

So instead I fly to New York and meet up with Pilar, the Swiss Spanish academic who believes in the Kabbalah and astrological signs. Her hair falls down over her shoulders, and her breasts are heavy and heavenly. Her skin smells of strawberries, and she closes her eyes when we make love. Pretending I am another? Two can play that game . . .

The sex is wet but hollow, and by the moment I come I already know there will not be a second time with Pilar, whatever her own feelings and desires. She is not what I ultimately seek. But then I don't even know myself what I am questing for, do I?

I return to London. Autumn is flaring, and the cold chills my bones so accustomed to the extended heat of the past summer. An editor in New Orleans is asking me for a new short story. About an erotic woman. I am lost for words, for inspiration. Isn't every single woman erotic? Am I really a man with no discrimination?

I write a vignette that is also a fantasy about the blonde sitting at the Caffé Cavour.

DO I SEND the blonde a copy of the story? If the answer is yes, go to section 6. If the answer is no, go to section 8.

5

HER VOICE IS like a song. With an Italian accent of course. But a song with strong undercurrents of melancholy. Damaged people, those of us who have been through the heart wars, uncannily recognize one another. She tells me all about the sea coast outside the town where she lives and has grown up. Her tone reduces to a whisper when she describes the man she lived with for so long and whose intensity could never match hers, and in a forlorn attempt to console her I lapse into the most abominable clichés of empathy.

I tell her about my own travels and evoke the rain falling on Canal Street and the way the pavement is dry within five minutes due to the tropical atmosphere. I talk of Greenwich Village and the mad way I, on trips to Manhattan, organize my film viewing like a military exercise to maximize the number of movies I can fit into the visit while wasting as little time as possible between performances and theaters.

She laughs.

DOES THE BLONDE respond to him? If the answer is yes, go to section 7. If the answer is no, go to section 4.

6

HER ACKNOWLEDGMENT OF my story is days in coming, during which time I log on twice an hour to check my e-mails, anxious for her reaction. I also shamelessly spy on her diary, but there is no reference to me or her mood, just erotic thoughts on the vampire myth or music she has been listening to. My knowledge of Italian rock music is poor.

Finally, she responds. Her attitude is cool and remote. I realize I have moved too fast, betrayed her confidence. She doesn't say so, but I can interpret her silences. From someone she once admired from afar, I have just become yet another cyber stalker. I have cannibalized her life without her express approval.

Our communications slow down and, one day, just stop. Just another missed connection.

I move on to my next fantasy.

7

SHE SUGGESTS WE maybe should meet somewhere one day. Now the complications begin. Should it be Paris, or maybe Vancouver? We must find neutral ground.

FOR WISH FULFILMENT, go to section 9.

8

I AM A coward and I shelve the story. Write another one that has unbearably descriptive sex scenes, guns, drugs and rock 'n' roll and in which every female character is a brunette and has a heart of ice. The protagonists race across the world from American highways to late-night bars near the Sicilian coast and leave a path of bloody destruction in their wake. The story is full of sound and fury but of course means nothing. It is a pure work of my imagination at its most commonplace and clichéd. The principal heroine is eroticism incarnate, with porcelain skin, lips that are made for kissing, and the obligatory shaven pudenda, and her shapely ass as observed from the rear evokes nothing less than Nicole Kidman's in the opening sequence of *Eyes Wide Shut*. But despite those inherent attractions, it is a tired story and I know it. Crime and sensuality by numbers.

9

AS EVER, IT'S a hotel room, stuffy and overheated when they arrive and before he switches one of the radiators off.

He craves the feel of his fingers caressing her pale shoulders, the sensation of his fingers combing through her short blonde hair as a pockmarked moon ascends into the sky outside the window.

This is a moment like no other.

Decisions have been made. Both parties have resolved to go through with this. But he doesn't want it to ever end. Sure, he wants to undress her with all the agonizing slowness he can conjure up until she is finally fully nude, innocent, helpless, arrogant, so totally exposed to his prying gaze.

But what of the smell of her body, the fragrance of her fear, her sweat? He cannot know them.

Will her breath still carry the combined echoes of stale cigarettes and vodka? Will her skin remind him of rough silk. What of her breasts (B-cup he estimates), what of her cunt?

Will she ever be a vulnerable body in an anonymous hotel room in another city, another land, another time and life?

Every road in his past has been leading him here, every intersection and side road ignored, like abandoned branches on a tree with a million ramifications. The worlds of *what if* magnified to the *n*th power.

As much as he tries to imagine the moment, he just cannot guess what her first words will be, how she will sigh and moan when he touches her. She is just another blonde in a universe of women he cannot know, and he sadly realizes the sheer obscenity of his imagination as it illegally brought her to this room in this city and land. *Shame on me*, he thinks.

He closes his eyes and keeps on typing, ever a slave to the tyranny of words.

10

THE BLONDE TURNS her gaze away from her laptop screen. She sighs. For a moment, she is still entrapped in the story she is writing. She is still flesh and blood, the incarnation of both her female characters in their doomed odyssey. She looks up to the window. A moonless night. She feels like having a beer. But she would rather go out and have it at a nearby bar. And maybe a Chinese meal. That would be a treat.

Her life, she senses, is at a crossroad.

Somehow her mind keeps going back to that book she read the other week, about the landscape after the battle, the life one is left with after the emotions have taken their bloody toll. She wonders about the character. She just knows the English writer had based her on a real person. It was unmistakable.

She goes online and calls up a search engine and enters his name.

There: an e-mail address.

Maybe she should write and ask him what happened to the woman in question?

She smiles. No, why would he respond?

What the hell, she goes on typing, the beer and the Chinese meal can surely wait.

Phallus in Wonderland

R. JOHN CALLAHAN

I DATED A girl in college who wanted me to rape her. This wasn't some innocent rape fantasy or role-playing fetish. This was an overwhelming desire to be taken, unwilling, and desecrated. She would not be happy, she told me, until I pinned her down, maybe uglied her up some in the struggle, and eventually forced myself into her, dry as a bone. The hard rub, turned to chafe, turned to burn and blister, was essential for the full effect, she explained.

I should mention that she was my first, that since then I've been exposed to all manner of vile, smutty proclivity, and that if she'd asked me now, I might just have obliged. As it was, though, naivety fostered some misguided notion that the man must always be gentle, that the woman must always desire and deserve respect. I promised I would, eventually. I promised it would happen when she least expected, that it would be everything she'd ever not wanted, and then I put it off. My hope was that she'd outgrow it, or at the very least give it up, if only I held out long enough. My hope was that each passing anticipatory day would bring her a little closer to the realization that she was, without a doubt, far too fucked up to be left to her own whims. It didn't work.

I learned then that there's a time for deprivation and a time for depravity, and a missed step in either direction is a step on the path to tragedy. It didn't take long for her to get tired of waiting, give up on me, and move on. When I saw her a few months later, half her teeth gone and a nose like tapioca, if I thought I recognized anything at all in that bruised and twisted face swollen on her skull, it was an ear-to-ear smile of total enlightened bliss.

Okay, it was an ear-to-the-other-side-of-the-head-where-another-ear-used-to-be smile of total, enlightened bliss. I keep thinking about her. I keep thinking that if she'd only stuck it out, if she'd just given me a chance, she would have learned the truth. I'm thinking maybe that would have been enough. Maybe she wouldn't have needed the abuse to get off. Maybe my dirty little secret and the deviance thereof would have sufficed, but we'll never know now, will we? I suppose there was a lesson to be learned from all of this, but I think I'd rather just flunk out and move on . . .

A LIE IS like a tightrope. Lose your balance and you fall to your death. It helps, though, that I've got the greater good to hold me steady. I'd have been just another stain on the big-top floor a long time ago if not for that driving force. As it was, years ago now, after I'd expended every possible benefit of every last doubt, I realized just how repugnant people truly are, and how much more so than women are men.

Men are despicable things, and the more I came to see this, the more I understood the ex who thrived on rape. No man was perfect, and she knew deep down that as long as her outlook stayed positive and she kept hoping for just a little bit better, the more disappointed she would be in what she got. If, on the other hand, she kept striving for something worse, she would have to find him. There may be a romantic plateau that's as good as it's ever going to get, but you can always throw a rock in the air and hit something worse. He'll probably even hit you back twice as hard. That was her reasoning. As long as she was looking for something worse, she could always find what she was looking for.

I had the opposite response, for as long as men were so horrible, my efforts to be that much better than the rest could only take me higher. As such, I vowed to become the perfect man, the greatest lover, friend, provider, and protector the world has ever known, and after all this time, effort, and failure, I think I'm finally getting close. I think this might be the one. I think she completes me, and I think I complete her, too.

We've flashed forward to present day now, and I should apologize for any confusion this may cause. I'm telling the tales of many of my loves, and in none of them will I mention names. This is my confession, not theirs, and it wouldn't be fair for me to tell you who they were, so pronouns will have to suffice. One can be only so detailed using *her* and *she* as their only descriptors, but this is as far as I'm willing to go on their behalf, so I hope you'll understand.

As I was saying, I think this one's the one. Sure, it's only been a short time, but there are those times–and you know the ones I mean–when you just know from the start that everything is right. Everything is perfect. This is one of those times. We like the same things, hate the same things, and share the same indifferences. We compliment each other in every possible way. We're each other's emotional, intellectual, and spiritual mate, and the sex . . . the sex! Well, how can I describe perfection in mere words alone?

When I'm inside her, when she clings to me warmly, wraps me tightly within her, I'm keenly aware that this is just one of the many ways we're a perfect fit. This isn't like anything else I've ever known. I've had the guesswork, the awkward fumbling over unfamiliar parts, the learning which button does what and which not to push, maybe for hours before we reach our anticlimactic end. I've been through the cycle of mistakes, outcomes good and bad, and I used to thrive on the excitement, the nervous tension over whether either of us would get anything of it right, but now that I know this is how good it can be, I don't miss any of that. I've played into the lie, that it was still good anyway, that the orgasm wasn't the most important part, and why not? So much of sex was about deception, why not revel in the occasional harmless little lie? Why not, if it doesn't hurt anything? Why not, if maybe it even makes things better?

With her, though, there are no additional lies necessary. Whether it's a slow, gentle night spent basking in each other's soft caress, washed and cooled in the warm, sweet breeze of a partner's staggered breath, or we're pounding, pulsing, and panting ourselves into exhaustion, it just works. Even when she's screaming, gasping, clutching my back, extracting skin souvenirs with razor-fine fingernail blades, marking me as hers, now and forever—no, especially then—it's the most romantic feeling I've ever had. Each time I go to bed with her I know that the hours ahead will be hours of pure, uncut bliss. We're each the other's better half; she completes me and I, her. Together we're perfect, and while this isn't all we have together, at this particular moment it's all I can think of that matters.

The best part is that it's been this way from the start. We both knew it right away, that first night spent together swapping horror stories of love's labors gone horribly wrong. We nodded and gazed at each other with an unspoken understanding, as if it were our mutual destiny to date the same or similar kinds of total creeps, to nearly resign ourselves to lonely lifetimes of celibacy, and then to find each other just when we'd each been about to give up.

Her biggest fear that night had been more of the same, that I was just another in a long series of pretenses to really identifying with her, but I assured her otherwise. It wasn't that we'd miraculously had all the same bad luck in love, I explained. It was that the same bad luck was the only luck in love most people ever had, so it was natural that we'd keep running into it. The miracle was that we identified with each other, for real, no pretense necessary. Given our situation, there were no broken hearts lurking in the future behind the veil of that particular deception. We had nothing to look forward to that wasn't better, nowhere to go but up. She sighed after my speech and asked me how any man could treat the woman who loves him like other men did. I told her it was because the women who love them let them. I asked her never to let any man lie to her, ever again, and she promised she wouldn't. I empowered her, built her up and made her invincible, just like you'd expect the perfect man to do. That night we shared our mutual tales of terror and tumult.

She told me of her high school sweetie and how he got her too drunk to enunciate any semblance of the word "no" on graduation party night. I had no high school stories to tell.

There were no good options for me then. It wasn't until I got to college, after I moved away from home and had an opportunity to truly reinvent myself, that I started dating. I told her about the masochist, and she followed up with her number two, as sadistic a beast as could be allowed by law to roam free. When her account was finished, I spent an hour just holding her, comforting her against the pain of that memory, and then it was my turn.

My number two was sweet and pristine, the kind of girl who would flirt with you until you offered a ride home, then make out with you until the sun came up, but would go no further. If I were any other man, I might have complained about her all-night teasing and taunting of genitals that had done nothing to deserve it, her sending me home at dawn with testicles that felt like they'd been run over by a steamroller made of brown dwarf matter, but being who I was, I only found it more endearing than anything. She had her feet planted firmly at second, and she explained her repeated foiling of my attempts to steal third as an issue solely of self-consciousness.

She was afraid, and as the man, I was responsible for quelling her fears. She couldn't stand the possibility that she might not be good enough. The idea that she might not be enough for me, or that I might think she looked ugly naked, or any number of other things that could go wrong, was simply too daunting a barrier for her to pass. I overcame her objections, of course, promised her that she had nothing to worry about, and after countless unsuccessful attempts I finally found myself rounding another base on my way home.

I stopped once I got a hand inside her panties, though, as soon as the realization hit me that spelunking those new and unexplored depths had me coming up with a fistful of penis in my grasp. As it turned out, it wasn't that *she* wasn't enough for me, but that *he* was more than I'd expected. Although that night didn't end well, I did eventually forgive him. I even empathized a little. With men being the hateful creatures they were, who would want to be one? That I chose to set a new standard for males and he chose to aspire to the standards of females were just two different reactions to the same underlying problem, and I couldn't hold that against him forever.

Of course, there's some deception in every encounter. Take now. She and I share our own unspoken lie with every tryst and turn of our relationship. When we're together, she's as beautiful and thin as she wants to be, not that she isn't already, but one's own mind's eye is easily the most critical. As for me, she makes me the man I dream of being. In those passionate moments of transformation, my arms are thick and toned, my otherwise small, flat chest is a perfect symmetry of pecs resting over Adonis's own abs. My body is the shape of a mighty *V* when she's wrapped around it, not the frumpy, unripe pear it is at all other times. I'm taller, stronger, better. The small, effeminate me dissolves within the illusion of our mutually assured deception, and I am all man, in all ways. Such is the way of the good lies, no matter how ephemeral.

The ephemeral lie of our perfection–hers, mine, and the combination thereof–isn't without its snags. I know her past, even if she knows only enough of mine to keep it going. I know how much easier self-deception is than the other kind. In all her past exploits, it's apparent to the outside observer that she wasn't always entirely the innocent victim. I can discern the truth from others' perceptions. There were times when she brought it on herself, or made a bad situation worse. To hear her recall it all from her perspective, one need only read between the lines to see what she doesn't, but this alone does not a bad person make. There are those who would call me anything from pessimistic to downright evil, but I'm sure they simply don't understand me as well as I do, and even if they did, the interpretive fissures within the foundations of perception are what bring subjective realities crumbling down to make way for the objective. If one were to ask all of her past nightmares for their sides of the stories, they would undoubtedly sound the victim each and every time. No matter the wrong done, it is a rare breed of bad guy who does what he does without seeing himself the hero. I've been forced to feel the pain of said bad guy plenty of times, and to all those who've done the forcing, I only ask if theirs would have been a different path, knowing what I know, sharing the same motivation.

It's funny how one who has been wronged forgets his or her own wrongdoings. After the cross-dresser, for instance, I fell in with a spoiled rich girl who could do no wrong. Being raised within a stone's throw of the fulfillment of all her desires and wants, she was oblivious to the concept of going without, and soon after I met her, her loving parents took it upon themselves to teach her what it is to work toward meeting her own needs. In order to retain their good graces, she was forced to take a part-time job at the local grocery, and while her weekly paychecks were but a drop in her weekly buckets of allowance money, she was expected to soak some responsibility out of her surroundings. She took the notion that she should be working instead of going out to satisfy her desires as the greatest of all possible insults, and eventually she conceived of a way to retaliate and satisfy herself, all in one great, disgusting fell swoop.

On nights after closing, she masturbated with the fresh produce. There wasn't a carrot, cucumber, celery stalk, or even eggplant upon which she didn't drip her vengeful honey. She submitted to her every irresistible urge and took revenge against the whole of society on whom she was forced to wait and serve, and when Dick and Jane Suburbanite tasted the tang of her deep fried discharge, she felt they got what they so rightly deserved. It all came out when the locals were stricken by an unknown plague, later classified in medical journals as a never-before-seen social disease. Intestinal herpes was to be her legacy, and after it was all over, she clung to the fact that it wouldn't have happened had she not been forced to deny her natural urges. She was a monster, but merely a monster of society's creation, and it was no good of them to whine or break out the torches and pitchforks the second she started on her first rampage.

I don't condone what that girl did, but I understand it. Whether for revenge or reconciliation, we all go to extreme measures to meet our goals, and while I'm fully aware that the goal in her case was ignoble, it was what that girl thought was right. There have been those who discovered my secret and been understandably repulsed, but even after all the doubting moments of my past, I know now that what I was doing was the right thing to do. The end has truly justified the means, and I see my affirmation reflected in her beautiful, loving eyes every time we share an infatuated gaze. Others have found me out to be a monster, and I nearly gave up because of it. If not for this one, the one wonderful and perfect completion I share with another living soul, I might have already. Thank God I was willing to give it one last try.

I could go on about others. There was the unemployed actress who thought faking orgasms was a perfectly good way to better her craft. There were the tamer deviants with their handcuffs and edibles and sodomite sex aids. There were many more who didn't come close to the level of perversion experienced with veggie-girl, penis-girl, or rape-girl, but I've made my point. What I have now is everything I've ever dreamed of, and everything I never expected. The ocean of dysfunction through which I've waded to reach this island of perfection was deep and wide, but it's behind me now. She and I share what neither of us ever thought was possible. If there's such a thing as true love, this is it, and for as long as I can keep up my end of the lie, it will remain so.

And as I've said, while the sex isn't the only thing we share, it is the most tangible that I can speak of. If I have any worries at all, it's that our love life will continue to improve, that it will one day be so good that I can no longer hold out until she and I come together upon the elusive and legendary shared orgasm. With every moan, with every gasp, clutch, scratch, and bite through which she tells me just how good it has gotten, I am that much closer to male perfection, and this is ultimately what moves me closer to bliss. There is the physical aspect as well, the feeling I get when I'm working her from the inside, and this is what's in most need of suppression, but ultimately it's the atmosphere and not the act that brings us to our climax.

It's during climax that I'm most vulnerable, and that's why I can't finish first. I lose control then, and if she weren't similarly wanting for awareness, she might notice things. One slip, one crack of my voice, that's all it would take. If I drop character, she'll be on to me. She'll know the secret of her man's perfection, and in an instant she'll understand how I know exactly what it takes and what it is to please a woman. In that instant she'll be as disgusted with me as have been all the rest. It's the smallest of lies that I lead, but with some of the direst consequences, so it is essential that it be maintained.

AT NIGHT, AFTER the lie is born and died, after she's fallen asleep before me, I excuse myself to be alone with this dilemma. I creep quietly out of bed and into the less forgiving light of the bathroom. I sit and contemplate upon the open toilet seat, peel away the condom and drop it in, watch it swirl and disappear as I flush the lie away. I hold my manhood in my hands and examine it. This is the focal point of both my ultimate perfection and the lie by which it is achieved. The phallus resting within my fingers is the tool by which I perform my trade. When all is said and done, this is what makes me the man on his quest to attain perfection.

After some reflection, I take it off and go to the bathroom. I hold it in my hands, turn it over in the light. I examine every ultrarealistic vein and ridge upon it. It's the best that money can buy, yet it's still not good enough. The inside, where it touches the skin, rubs and tickles my clit just right, makes it hard for me to keep from cumming first. I should try some kind of padding or cream. There's got to be something out there to keep the physical part of my climax out of the equation. If I can keep it purely emotional, purely spiritual, I can keep up the charade. As long as I can keep up the charade, as long as I can keep her shrouded in this tiny little deceit, I'll still be the perfect man, and she'll never have to know otherwise.

The Third Confession

BRYN COLVIN

"COME BACK TO bed."

There was a tone of command in his voice that Gemma found irresistible. She turned from the window and from the squirrels cavorting in a tree at the far end of their narrow garden. Her dressing gown discarded, she slipped naked under the duvet, snuggling up against Victor's warm body. Sunday mornings were usually deliciously indulgent, with a few extra hours just to lie in bed, make love, and talk. With Victor's workload, time like this was something they could seldom afford during the long and busy week. In a little while, she knew he would have to rouse himself and get back to his books. He was researching something new, but it was still a fledgling project and he was not ready to talk about it.

"What are you doing today, my beautiful girl?" he asked.

"I don't know."

She let her fingers stray across his flat stomach.

"I thought I might cook for lunch, and maybe, if you can spare a few hours before it gets dark, we could go out for a walk or something? It looks like a nice day."

"If I get up now, I could probably get enough done. Okay."

She watched him dress. He was neat in everything he did. Attiring himself in a loose shirt and corduroy trousers was a process of assuming his working identity again. The naked man she shared a bed with was a playful, affectionate being, soon disguised by the sensible persona of his academic, professional self. He turned and smiled at her, his expression utterly captivating. She loved these private moments, and the parts of him she never had to share with anyone else.

When he had gone, Gemma dressed slowly, pulling on a close-fitting dress and stockings, and brushing her curly red hair back into a simple ponytail. There were things they were going to have to talk about. She had been stalling for a while, fearing his reaction to the confession she had to make, and wondering if their relationship was strong enough to survive it. He was a lovely man, but his world was an ordered, well-planned one, and she was about to turn it upside down again.

It would not be the first confession she had made, although the previous two had been difficult in their own ways and, she supposed, just as life altering. He was frequently stern, such that owning up to anything always made her feel like a delinquent schoolgirl; but then, that feeling had a certain allure of its own. She started to peel potatoes, experimenting in her thoughts with what she might say and trying to guess how he might react. She was very much afraid that he would be angry; he had made it all too clear before that it was not the sort of thing he wanted. At least if they were out in public when she owned up, there was every chance he would be moderate in his reaction. Victor had a temper—one that he seldom aired, but that nevertheless terrified and excited her when it was released. Currently she was feeling far too fragile to be able to enjoy a serious outburst.

The very first confession to him was one she had made nearly two years ago, not long after she got her results for her master's degree. Victor had been her tutor—she had come to Birmingham expressly for the purpose of studying with him. His books had been the basis of her dissertation; his reputation was international and his work inspired her. She had not known what to expect of him in person, but he had not betrayed her sense of awe in any way; he was a tall and intense man, with a way of looking at her that had always made her feel very small and unknowing. Under his direction, she had worked as never before and she had achieved more than she would have thought herself capable of. Praise from his lips was rare and utterly addictive. She passed with distinction and had gone into his office especially to thank him for all of his good advice and support. He seemed very surprised to see her.

"I wouldn't have expected anything less," he said, when she told him her results.

"I just wanted to say thanks."

"And now you've said it."

He was slightly impatient; everything about his tone and body language told her that he really did not want to be wasting any more of his time with idle chat. She took the plunge.

"I was wondering if I could take you out for a drink, or a meal, or something?"

He raised an eyebrow, eyeing her quizzically.

"Did you, now?"

"Well, you're not my tutor anymore, so I thought it would be all right, and I thought it would be nice."

Victor made her nervous, and so she did not risk saying any more.

"I accept. How do you wish to proceed? Do you want to pick me up here after work, or from my house?"

Victor did not have a car, she knew that much.

"From your house, if you like? I'll get a cab."

It gave her an excuse to have his home address.

She had no idea what his tastes were–probably expensive, as seemed to be the case with everything else in his life. Not being someone who normally ate out, she had been short of ideas and had flicked frantically through the Yellow Pages and called several friends in search of inspiration. They had ended up in a small Italian restaurant on the outskirts of the city, and it had proved to be a very good evening. At first, talking to him had been a bit of a challenge, given that their shared interest in her course was over, but he was much more relaxed and friendly when outside of a professional situation.

She could have driven, but the use of a taxi meant she was free to drink, and she thought she would probably need the confidence alcohol gave her. It was half past ten when the conversation turned to arranging transport home.

". . . unless you want to come back to mine for coffee, or something."

He looked at the face of his wristwatch, his expression thoughtful.

"I tend not to be too late on weeknights."

He had missed, or ignored, the implicit suggestiveness of her offer. She leaned across the table, touching the sleeve of his jacket, hoping she was not about to make a total fool of herself and knowing that she was a dangerously long way from sobriety.

"Look," she said, "I think this is probably my last chance to say anything, so I'm going to say it. I think you're great—always did—that's why I wanted to study with you. I've been really good all the way through, haven't I? I've never said anything. But the thing is, Victor . . . the thing is, I really, seriously like you."

She had never seen him look surprised before, and the expression on his face made her giggle.

"You're teasing me," he said dismissively.

She leaned closer to him, sliding over on the seat so that she was much nearer and pressing her mouth against his ear.

"I know you're straight, and I know you're single, you've said as much. So, if you want me, if you want to come back to my apartment and make love with me . . ." She could not think of a good way of finishing the sentence, and simply pressed a kiss against his neck.

"You're drunk," he said.

"Maybe a bit. Look, if you don't want me, just say so, okay? I'll live with it. I'm not just asking because I'm drunk, I'm asking because I've been in love with you for ages and I want to go to bed with you."

She had not meant to tell him that she was that besotted-crazy about him, but somehow it had come out all the same. He looked at her for a long time, his expression thoughtful and intense. She waited for his response, her stomach turning and dancing with fear.

"You can come back to my house, if you're serious," he said. "And that way I won't have to worry about getting my things for work tomorrow."

He was coldly deadpan, and she almost lost her nerve then, but a flicker of intuition told her that he was testing her, ascertaining that she was not saying more than she meant while seeking to safeguard his dignity. She reached across the table again, placing her hand over his, then lifting his fingers to her lips and kissing his knuckles. The smile that touched his face was like no expression she had seen him wear before; he looked surprised, certainly, but also delighted in a remarkably innocent sort of way.

"I really would like to go home with you," she confided.

"I'd like that, too." His tone was conspiratorial.

They held hands in the back of the cab, and kissed for the first time outside his house. It was an uncertain, questing sort of kiss, and afterward he cupped her face between his hands, looking at her as though he still was not entirely sure she was serious. Much to her surprise, Victor proved to be ever so slightly shy, and Gemma rapidly discarded her fantasy of enjoying some furious and wildly charged sex. What happened, instead, was a slow and sensual mutual seduction that began as soon as the door closed and lasted for nearly an hour as they gradually made their way through the house toward his bed.

It had been a gentle, erotically charged coming together, rich in pleasure and joy. Afterward, they had sat together in the semidarkness, and he had finally told her, "I've wanted you since the first time I saw you."

"Really?"

"Yes, I remember the dark green skirt you were wearing that first day, and your tight, black top that showed off your chest so well. You had your hair tied back, and I just wanted to pull the band out of it and let it tumble down round your shoulders."

She moved, brushing her curls over his chest, letting him feel the softness of them against his skin.

"I was hoping you'd notice the tight tops."

"I did."

He reached down to caress her breasts, touching each in turn, his fingertips barely skimming across the surface of her tantalized skin.

"What else did you want to do?" she asked.

"This," he kissed her lips, "and this," as he licked each nipple in turn, "and I'll admit I spent rather a lot of time thinking about this." He slid his hand down across her stomach and began to gently tease between her thighs.

"Believe me, it's no easy matter trying to correct an errant student when you'd much rather be touching her."

He paused, and his voice took a more serious tone.

"I never for a moment thought you might be interested in me. I mean, I'm a good few years older than you and . . ."

Gemma did not allow him further time to express why he was surprised, but wrapped her arms around him, pulling him down onto her and silencing him by slipping her tongue between his lips.

"I'm very interested," she told him, when she surfaced.

"I'm starting to realize that."

She never spent another night in her apartment after that, and within a month, he had suggested she give it up and officially move in with him.

THREE AT THE little table in the kitchen. The dining room always seemed too big for just the two of them, and the kitchen was a far more relaxed and cozy place. Gemma picked at her food delicately, trying not to raise his suspicions with any odd behavior but aware that she was not all that inclined to eat. She did her best.

"Did you want to go anywhere in particular this afternoon?"

"I don't know. We can't go too far, we'll lose the light."

"Malvern would take too long, wouldn't it?"

"Yes."

"A pity. Maybe we could take some time for that next weekend?"

"How about Tardebigge? We could go and walk along the canal, that'll be pretty."

He nodded approvingly, giving Gemma a warm feeling of satisfaction that offset her nervous anticipation of the conversation she could no longer avoid.

All previous confessions seemed modest, if not trivial, in comparison to the one before her. The two great confessions—those she remembered and was especially conscious of—had, retrospectively, been all too easy. Since then there had been countless sessions of kiss and tell, and tell some more, with scenes played out in the comfort of their bed, or curled up on the sofa with wine to smoothe the way. These were games, almost—exchanging past histories, secret fantasies, and evidence of mutual obsession. The third confession, the one she could no longer avoid, was not so innocent or free from consequence. She simply had no idea if Victor would understand what the urges of her young body had prompted her to do. At the time, driven by need and potent hormones, it had seemed like a good plan, but afterward, realizing the consequences and the way she had misled him, she felt far less certain of herself. More than anything, she needed his acceptance and support, but had no idea if he would be willing to give either.

The second confession had seemed absolutely terrible before she had voiced it but afterward had melted into something far more palatable. It had troubled and embarrassed her for weeks, becoming an ever-present source of self-doubt and unhappiness, until eventually he had challenged her one evening.

"Gemma, something clearly is bothering you, we can't go on like this. I need you to tell me."

She had hung her head and looked away, fiddling with the remote for the VCR. He took the device from her hands.

"Now."

It was just the sort of tone he had used when challenging her over her work, or suggesting that her research had been lacking. It was the tone he always used for telling her off, on those rare occasions when he felt the need to, and it sent a shiver of delight through her body; but then, that was rather the problem.

"It's stupid really," she said, even though lately it had taken over her life.

"Tell me."

There was no refusing his order.

"I think I'm a submissive."

It was said, and, terrifying though the words sounded, she was relieved to have aired them.

"What precisely does that mean in this context? I've seen precious little sign of your being tame or docile."

"It means I like you ordering me about–which, frankly, doesn't sit very well with my feminist ideals."

"You very seldom do anything I tell you to."

"I kind of like getting you cross."

He laughed at her then, shaking his head like a bemused adult faced with the incomprehensible logic of a child.

"Were you hoping I might put you over my knee and spank you?"

"Maybe . . ."

Gemma looked up at him from under her eyelashes. He seemed entertained. She had owned up to the thoughts that had been eating away at her, she had bared her psyche, confessed to her newly discovered fetish, and the whole thing was being met with mild amusement.

"You are a funny little thing," he said.

From anyone else the phrase would have sounded patronizing, but Victor's saying it made her feel protected somehow.

"Does this mean you want me to order you about and tell you off more often?"

"I don't know."

"Come here."

He pulled her across his lap, stroking her back and bottom. He tapped her lightly a couple of times, friendly pats on her soft rump that made her realize she would very much like an awful lot more.

"I'm not going to spank you," he said. "I'd worry I might hurt you."

"Oh, spoil sport!"

She wriggled provocatively and he patted her bottom again.

"Listen here, Little Miss Submissive, I'm not going to paddle your bottom, and that's my final word on the matter, understood?"

"Yes, Victor."

After that it had seemed all right, as though merely airing the issue had made it manageable. He had not minded, or been cross, or put out, or any of the other unpleasant consequences she had imagined. He was amused, nothing worse than that. The inclination remained very much with her, but she learned to live with it, relishing those moments when he did forget himself for a while and act as though he was the tyrannical lecturer and she his misbehaving pupil. She learned that the tabloid images of power play and the Internet stories of slavery were not the be-all and end-all.

The whole thing had been set in motion by her accidental discovery of the term through a comment on an unrelated Web site. Intrigued by a glimpse into an otherwise unfamiliar world, she had set forth on an electronic quest, reading stories of increasing extremity and power imbalance on dedicated sites. It was easy enough to do while Victor was working in the evenings, which he often was. She had been disconcerted to discover that these images and tales of bullying, dominant, and sometimes downright abusive men gave her something of a thrill. Victor had always been physically gentle, but he had a very strong will and could be utterly commanding when he wanted to be. She had pondered and agonized over the nature of her relationship with him and whether she should even be feeling this sort of thing at all. For a while she had no idea what she wanted, or how she wanted him to treat her. Dominance and submission were very much outside the world she had known, and she had nothing to guide her in trying to find her way through this fascinating and dangerous sexual playground. The extremities of slavery frightened her, but at the same time the mere thought of such total surrender turned her on.

After the confession it began to occur to her that she could very quietly enjoy being very occasionally dominated by the man she was in love with. Having surrendered control of her condition by admitting it to him, she had become free to get on with her life. He teased her about it sometimes, but that was no great hardship. She did not need chains in order to be ruled by him; he could do it by force of will alone if he wanted to, although he seldom bothered. He had to be utterly focused on her in order to do it, though, and that, she realized, was the attraction. During the days of her master's degree, she had felt herself to be the center of his attention only when he was in the process of telling her off for something or demanding that she do more. Even then, she had often found herself wishing he were demanding that she did entirely different things, things that would not count toward her final mark in any way.

THEY WALKED ARM in arm along the towpath, enjoying the autumn colors and watching the waterfowl bobbing about in the canal. This late in the year, there were very few people taking narrowboat holidays, and they passed only one of the brightly colored craft as it made its way up the long lock-flight. There were occasional dog walkers, but for the greater part they had the narrow pathways to themselves.

"Victor," she began tentatively, "there's something I need to talk to you about."

"Go on."

She knew from his tone that he had not yet guessed the seriousness of the topic she needed to broach. She swallowed hard, finding that her mouth had become hopelessly dry and that her tongue no longer seemed to work properly.

"I've done something . . . I've lied to you; I've gone behind your back . . . I can't offer you any good excuses, except I wanted it so much and I didn't know what else to do."

Her voice was tremulous, and she knew that it was coming out garbled and incoherent. This was not what she had planned to say at all. Everything seemed to be making her cry lately, and she fought to regain control of herself. Victor stopped walking and turned to face her.

"What are you saying?" he asked. "Is there someone else?"

Gemma laughed hoarsely.

"In a manner of speaking."

He sighed, his expression crestfallen and his shoulders

slumping somewhat. Realizing what he must think, Gemma felt a wave of guilt and pity. She reached her hand out to touch him, needing to reestablish contact.

"Don't," he said, "just don't."

"It's not what you think."

"No?"

"I'm pregnant."

He covered his face with one hand and turned from her. Even through her own fear, she realized that he was still thinking along totally different lines.

"I haven't been seeing anyone else, love."

He remained still, and she was frozen by uncertainty, not knowing what else to say or how to reach out to him.

"I know you said you didn't want children, but I was so broody all spring, I was starting to feel like I was going to go totally nuts if I couldn't have a baby. So I stopped talking the pill. I didn't ask, and I didn't say, and I know that wasn't fair of me, but all I could think about was how much I wanted to have a child–for *us* to have a child."

He neither moved nor spoke. When something troubled Victor, he tended to fold in on himself, becoming distant and silent until he found his own way through things. It could be very isolating–left on the outside when he barricaded himself away. Gemma brought a hand up to her mouth and bit down on her fingers, one after another, needing the small amounts of pain to stop her from being overwhelmed by panic and despair. His silence seemed to go on forever.

"You're pregnant?" he said slowly, as though he was still struggling to come to terms with the notion.

"Yes, about two months along, I think."

"Oh, god."

"I'm sorry."

"Don't apologize for something you clearly intended to do," he snapped.

She recoiled–startled by his anger even though she had almost expected it. Gemma felt as though she was standing on the edge of an abyss, and that any moment she would start to plummet. Her mind raced: Would Victor ask her to terminate the pregnancy? Not that she would, not even for him.

"I'm sorry," he said, his tone repentant, "I shouldn't have said that."

He turned so that at least she could see his face.

"You're pregnant," he said again sounding marginally more confident about the fact. She smiled wanly, glad that he was at least still talking to her. He shook his head.

"This is going to take some thinking about."

"If you don't want to see this through with me, I'll understand."

His eyes widened in an expression of pure dismay.

"Gemma? How can you even suggest that? Of course I want to see it through with you. I love you, and you're carrying my child."

There was a note of real pain in his voice, and instinctively she moved closer to him, putting her arms around his waist and resting her head against his shoulder.

"Of course I want to see it through," he repeated, "I didn't mean you to think otherwise, I'm so sorry if . . . it was just so unexpected, I hadn't planned on doing this with my life."

He stroked her hair, falling silent again until a couple out walking with a dog had passed beyond earshot.

"It frightens the hell out of me. I mean, parenthood. But I suppose we'll manage, most people do, don't they?"

"I get that impression."

He squeezed her shoulders.

"I wish I'd known."

"You said you didn't want children."

He chuckled. "I did, didn't I?"

Gemma risked looking up at him and found that he was smiling down at her, his expression as bewildered as it was joyful. He kissed the tip of her nose.

"We're really going to have a baby?"

"Yes."

He buried his face in her hair.

IT WAS ALMOST dark by the time they got to the car. They sat in the relative warmth of the vehicle, sharing tea from a thermos and watching the last of the light fade from the sky.

"It's strange to think," Victor said suddenly, "all those times over the summer when we were making love, and I never thought anything like this would happen. Every time I came with you and I never thought. One of those times must have done it, and I had no idea at all."

"I felt really guilty at the time, not sharing that with you, but I was so afraid you would have said no."

"I'm starting to feel glad you didn't give me the chance to be so stupid."

"Really?"

"Yes."

She smiled, touched once again by the sense of just how deeply she loved this unpredictable man. Reaching across, she stroked the back of his hand, and he pushed his fingers back, lacing them through hers.

"Do you remember back in July, that really hot weekend when we just lounged about the house naked all the time?" she asked.

"Yes."

"And it got really cool in the early hours of the morning, and we were both so awake, and we went out in the garden and made love in the moonlight?"

"I was afraid we'd be spotted."

"Me too, but it was seriously hot, me in just that little dress, you with your shirt open and your shorts . . ."

She smiled, remembering the encounter. They had been under the trees in the long grass, the moonlight filtering down between leaves and branches to partially illuminate them. At first they had just lain together, holding hands and gazing up at the sky, but his fingers had started to caress her palm, then her wrist, and she had rolled over to kiss him, feeling his hand slide over her bottom and up the back of her flimsy summer dress.

"Anyway, I'm not a hundred percent certain, but I thought at the time it had probably happened, and it was the following week that I started feeling queasy."

"That was a memorable night," he said, "You looked so beautiful in the moonlight, so mysterious. I think I fell in love with you all over again. It seems like a good way to have started a whole new person."

He touched her cheek, his fingers straying over the corner of her lips.

"I thought so," she said, kissing his hand and remembering the feel of night breezes on her skin as she had wrapped her thighs around his slender body and teased his tongue with hers.

He gazed at her, love and wonder evident in his face, as his fingers trailed down over her coat and flicked the buttons open. She felt his hand upon her stomach, questing for the new life that had only barely made its presence felt.

"How do you feel?" he asked.

"Right now? I want you."

He smiled–that innocent, surprised expression of delight that she loved so dearly.

"You had probably better get us home then, little minx."

"Your wish is my command."

Gemma fumbled with the ignition key, starting up the car and getting the small heater going to alleviate the chill.

"Before we go . . . look, this isn't quite how I'd planned to do this either, although I promise you, I was going to do it anyway. But if we're going to have a baby, I really think we ought to get married first."

"Are you proposing to me?"

"Yes. I mean I wanted to do the whole down on one knee with a ring bit, but this has rather come out of the blue."

"And you'd have asked my father's permission first, no doubt."

"Well, yes, maybe that, too."

She smiled at him.

"So?"

"What?"

"Will you marry me?"

"Of course I will."

She leaned across to kiss him, and his hand roved across her breasts, cupping each in turn.

"I'm not fragile, I won't break."

His fingers worked eagerly then, rubbing at her nipples through the heavy fabric of her dress until she was alternately fighting for breath and burying her mouth in his.

"Home," he ordered.

She scowled at him and ran a hand over his thighs.

"Come on, drive."

"Oh,"

"Don't 'oh' at me little Miss, we're going home–either you drive, or I will."

As Victor had never been behind a wheel, this was a considerable threat.

"It's far too cold and cramped in here. The sooner you get us home, the sooner we can ease your frustration," he told her.

"Promise?"

"You just try and stop me."

Good for the Soul

KIT

"PHIL, THERE'S SOMETHING I need to tell you, to show you."

He looks up from a stack of papers that he's brought home from work–some rush job apparently. There's an annoyed expression on his face, and his words are abrupt.

"Can't it wait?"

I shake my head.

"What is it? I'm really busy, baby. This has all got to be done by Monday, and I don't want it to take up all of our weekend."

"Follow me," I say and turn away. He sighs. As I walk away, I hear the sound of his pen being slammed on the table, the scrape of the chair legs on the tiled floor.

I lead him to the living room. In the doorway, he tries to take my hand, but I slip out of his grasp and move aside to let him through.

"Sit down," I say, pointing to the armchair where he always sits to watch television. I've drawn the curtains against the sun, to cut the glare so he can see the screen. The curtains are a pale shade and unlined; there's still plenty of light, so I can see his face, which is all I'm interested in watching.

Across the room, the television is already switched on, the sound muted. Football players run around, their lurid red tops in sharp relief against the green grass.

He sighs again. "Oh, Christ, this isn't going to be another of your accusation sessions, is it? Fuck, Julie, I don't have the time for this."

I meet his eyes, say nothing. He stands in the doorway, torn between going back to his paperwork and resolving the issue.

He stalks over to the chair and throws himself into it, frowning ferociously.

"Look, baby," he says, in a tone that suggests he's just managing to humor me, just hanging on to anger. "What can I do, what can I say to convince you?"

When I don't react, he goes on.

"Listen to me: I . . . am . . . not . . . seeing . . . anyone . . . else. Get it? I . . . am . . . not . . . fucking . . . anyone . . . else." He's slowed his words down, as though this will help me understand, help to convince me; but as he speaks, his frustration breaks through. His voice becomes louder, and by the end he's shouting.

There's silence for a moment. Then he takes a breath.

"Look, Julie, I love you, I want to be with you. But, babe, you are going to have to deal with this, get some professional help maybe. These suspicions are eating you up, they're eating both of us up."

He sounds righteously indignant; he always sounds righteously indignant and this time the righteous indignation has some validity. You see, it's true: he isn't fucking anyone else, isn't seeing anyone behind my back.

Not now.

I wait, still silent. At last he shrugs, and his eyes are drawn to the screen. I perch on the arm of another chair so I can see his face. I can see the screen if I turn my head a fraction, but I've seen this tape before, several times. It's his reaction I want to see.

I pick up the remote and press "play."

PHIL HAD BEEN living with me for eighteen months when one day I suddenly knew he was cheating on me. There wasn't anything obvious, no working late, no chunks of time unaccounted for, no lipstick on his collar, no change in his sex drive, no suspicious behavior–just an instinct.

I asked him, "Phil, are you fucking someone else?"

We were doing the early morning waltz around the kitchen, boiling the kettle for instant coffee, browning toast for me, pouring cereals and skimmed milk into a bowl for him, unplugging cell phones from their chargers, getting sandwiches out of the fridge. The sun was shining, the birds were singing, and Phil didn't miss a beat.

"Eh?" he said, his hand on the handle of the kettle, waiting for the whistle to die down. "What are you talking about?"

He poured water into his mug carefully, stirring as he poured.

"Why would I want to fuck someone else when I live with the best lover in the world?"

It's something I'd been wondering, though I hadn't put it in those terms. Not the best lover anywhere–just the injured party.

I said coldly, "Variety?"

He poured water into my mug, then turned to face me, meeting my eyes in the way popular wisdom says the best liars always do.

"Baby, baby, what are you saying?" He gave me a mock leer. "You complaining you aren't getting enough?"

I looked at him, the open body language, the disarming grin, the blue eyes I used to trust.

"No. I just think you're fucking someone else."

I buttered my toast. Phil picked up the mugs, walked to the table, and plonked my coffee in front of me.

"I don't understand you," he said, looking down at me with an expression halfway between hurt and quizzical. "We've got something really good going here, you and me. A comfortable lifestyle, a good social life, great sex. Why are you trying to rock the boat?"

He shook his head in apparent confusion as he sat down to his cereal. He ate a few crunchy mouthfuls, then his blue eyes met mine again and he grinned.

"Oh, I get it—your period's due, isn't it? Oh, baby, are the hormones kicking in hard this month?"

Sometimes I feel sorry for hormones. They get blamed for so much. I won't say I don't get a little moody on a monthly basis, but I wasn't hormonal then. I just knew he was fucking someone else. But I didn't have any evidence. And what do you do when your unfaithful partner won't confess, even when you offer him a clear opening?

I shrugged—let it drop, let him enjoy his puzzled expression and his air of injured innocence while he could. He kept talking and acting as though hormones were the issue. That night he was especially painstaking in bed, doing all the things he knew turned me on the most. My body responded and I came like Pavlov's bitch, but I knew that in his mind he was fucking someone else. I could almost see him overlaying her features on my face, her body on mine. I could almost see her, even though I didn't know who she was. Not then.

I WAITED A few weeks and tried again. This time Phil lost his temper. He left the much-maligned hormones alone; now he said I was being irrational, stupid. His self-defense mingled spirited rebuttal with the air of confused innocence he'd performed so well before.

"Do you want to stop seeing me?" he said at last. "Do you want me to move out? I mean, I'd hate to lose you, baby, but I can't cope with these accusations."

I still didn't believe him, and yes, actually, I did want him to move out. But I didn't want him to move out as the injured party, protesting his innocence and denouncing my irrational accusations to everyone we knew.

"Really, baby, you need to get some help. This is paranoia. You can get help–pills, a counselor. Talk to a doctor. Get these delusions out of your system. Go private–we can afford it."

I wanted him to confess. I needed him to confess. It was becoming increasingly clear, however, that he wasn't going to. I would need proof of his infidelity.

THE TAPE STARTS with white noise. Then there's a blank screen. No titles, of course. I turn up the volume to maximum using the remote. There's not much sound on the recording, and it's not very good quality, very quiet, but what there is adds to the ambiance.

I watch Phil. He's flicking his eyes between me and the television. He starts to speak, but stops when I put my finger to my lips. I point at the blank screen and he looks again. When the picture finally starts rolling, there's no reaction for a moment, then he does a double-take that almost makes me laugh out loud.

Smile! You're on Candid Camera.

It's our bedroom, filled with the sharp light and dark shadows of the mid-afternoon summer sunshine. The walls are pale, and the light bounces around the room and makes one feel full of spring and desire just looking at it.

It's Phil, but the woman he's dancing with isn't me. It's immediately obvious she's not me: She's blonde, I'm dark; she can dance face-to-face with Phil without tipping her neck up, where I'm a good half-foot shorter than he is.

And he's never danced with me. Not even with clothes on, in public.

In the living room, I watch his face dispassionately. His mouth has dropped open. He glances toward me, but looks back at the screen when I shake my head and point.

I watch the images in my head as Phil watches them on the screen. I'm image-perfect now. I've watched the tape again and again. Take the tape away, give me two actors and a cameraman, and I could reconstruct it perfectly, even the first time.

I watch on the screen in my mind as they smooch, watch his hands smoothing over her back and the curve of her buttocks, watch her nails slide gently down his shoulders. He pulls her closer into him and they kiss, open-mouthed. For hours it seemed, the first time I watched it. He lifts her against him, cupping her buttocks so that she stands on tiptoe. He grinds his pelvis into hers as they circle around the floor. And still they kiss.

I watch as he breaks off from the dance, picks her up, and places her gently on the bed. *Our* bed. She lies on her back, her legs slightly apart, one knee bent, trailing one hand low across her stomach. Her breasts, a little younger and smaller than mine, have gravity on their side. Her nipples are erect, hard little points. I'm not sure of the color—the tape plays in black-and-white—but they look very dark against her all-over tan. Phil stands for a while looking down at her as she preens the thin line of her pubic hair with her fingers, his cock pointing toward her like a compass needle toward magnetic north.

He slides onto the bed beside her and they kiss again, their hands stroking each other's skin. He covers a breast with one hand, lowers his mouth to its sister, and flicks the nipple fast with his tongue. If you listen hard, you can just hear her moaning on the tape.

In the armchair, Phil is motionless, his face expressionless.

On the tape, his fingers slide lower, moving in circles down her stomach, over her hipbones and her thighs. She shifts her legs wider and his hand disappears between them. From the way she arches her back and the shrill cry that comes from the speakers, I judge he's pushed a finger or two inside her, though from this angle which hole he's chosen to penetrate is anyone's guess. She moves, riding his hand; tight around his cock, her own hand moves in rhythm with her hips.

When I watched the tape the first time, something struck me as familiar. The second time I realized what it was: The lovers onscreen fuck like we used to fuck, Phil and I. Intimacy, care, focus, leisure, driven by urgency.

After a while, she pushes him onto his back. You can tell she's saying something and laughing, even though you can't hear. She pulls his legs wide, straddles him, dips her head and laps at his cock, and then she sucks it deep into her mouth. He lies there and lets her lick dick for a while, his eyes closed, his fingers digging deep into the duvet when she makes a particularly good move.

Then he reaches for her hips, pulls her legs back and lifts his head. She sucks him sensuously, one hand around the base of his cock, the other wandering over his thighs and balls. From this angle you can't see him licking her, but it's clear from the positioning of her body and his head that what we have here is a full-on *soixante-neuf.*

In front of the television, Phil stands up abruptly.

"Turn it off, Julie."

I press "pause," glancing at the tableau. The tape doesn't freeze well, and the onscreen licker and sucker still seem to be moving in a rhythmic pattern.

"Watch," I say. "You had your chance to talk, to tell me. Now I'm telling you. Watch. Enjoy the show. You certainly seemed to enjoy making it."

He steps over to the television and switches it off. He hits the eject button on the player and jerks the video out. He lifts the flap and begins to pull at the flimsy tape, ripping it out of the casing viciously. When he's pulled it all out, he throws the tape and the casing on the floor.

Then he looks at me.

"No more," he says. His face is livid red. He's very angry, though I'm not sure why—after all, he was happy to do the fucking.

He starts to move toward me, shouting.

"You spying bitch!" he yells. "You fucking spying whore!"

Ah, I understand. He's not in the wrong for fucking her; I'm in the wrong for collecting evidence of something he denied. I'd half-expected something like this, and the moment he touches me, seizing my upper arms in a strong and angry grip, I call out, "Mr. Robinson!"

Phil looks startled at my words, but that's nothing to his astonishment when Mr. Robinson comes in through the hall door. Phil drops his hands, steps a pace or two backward. Well, you *would*–Mr. Robinson is very well built.

I take a deep breath and drop back to my perch on the chair arm. For a moment, all you can hear is breathing.

Then I look Phil straight in the eyes and say, "You can't say you didn't have every chance to tell me about"–I pause for effect–"Fiona, can you?"

Phil's mouth drops open again. It's not an attractive look for him, and I'm glad I won't have to worry about seeing it again.

He says, "Julie, I–"

"I what?" I say. "Can explain everything? No, this is my moment. It's my turn to explain, my turn to confess, if you like. Sit down, make yourself comfortable. This may take a few minutes."

Phil flops into his chair, still gawking.

"Yes, I taped you. Well, actually Mr. Robinson did. It's one of the things he does in his job. I found him in the Yellow Pages, and I think you have to agree he's done really well. I'm sorry you didn't want to see the rest of the tape; you might have kept it as a memento."

I smile at Phil, and I'm afraid it's not a nice smile.

"Phil, I knew. I told you that I knew and I gave you every opportunity to tell me, to confess. May–was that when it started? Or did I just not realize it until then? I tried again in June and July–twice in July, I think. And you kept on denying it. We might have been okay, weathered it out, if you'd told me about her, if I'd known she was just a fling, a squeeze. But no, you had to lie to me and bitch at me and act injured at my–what was it?–*irrational and hormonal accusations*. I knew I was right, and you weren't going to confess, so I decided to prove it. It wasn't hard, really. Mr. Robinson here fixed up some clever gadget. I only had to switch it on before I left for work, switch it off when I came home. While it was switched on, any movement in the room would start it recording. And then I only had to wait."

Phil opens his mouth as though he's going to start protesting, so I continue quickly.

"Morally reprehensible, perhaps, but no worse than what you were doing to me. Remember? You said I was paranoid. You tried to send me to a doctor. And all the time I was right, all the time there was Fiona."

Phil flinches at the sound of her name.

"She might be great at sucking cock," I say. "We can all see that, can't we? But she's not very bright, is she? When I sent her a text message last Monday evening from your cell phone, she just fell for it. Panting for it, I suppose. *Afternoon off Tuesday. Julie working late. Two P.M.?* She didn't text back, but she turned up on the doorstep at two o'clock next day, meek as a lamb, and hot as a hot, hot thing in a miniskirt like a belt and a top she might as well not have bothered with. She was surprised to see me, tried to make out she was canvassing for some charity. Dressed like that! That made me laugh. But I recognized her, even if she didn't recognize me; she'd forgotten we met at your firm's Christmas party last year. Not very flattering, but I suppose she only had eyes for you. Well, not only eyes, as it turned out. Tits and ass as well."

A discreet smile flickers across Mr. Robinson's face, but Phil doesn't seem to think it's funny. He looks pretty bleak, as if what's happening has just hit him. Mind you, fucking your boss's wife is not something you want generally known, never mind recorded for posterity, so I can see why he might not appreciate the joke.

"Anyway, she agreed to come in and talk to me. We had a long heart-to-heart, and after a couple of vodka and tonics, she saw sense. Well, it might not have been the vodka; it might have been the tape that did it. She agreed her husband probably wouldn't want to see it."

I pause again, enjoying the memory of Fiona's shocked face as I played her the tape. I didn't go from the beginning with her; instead, I'd positioned the tape at a great shot of Phil giving her a facial, his back to the camera, her face in full view, easily recognizable despite the spurting spunk.

"You were up in Richmond on business. Tuesday. The day you got the text message from her saying she couldn't meet you anymore. I wrote that. She handed over her cell phone without a protest."

I look Phil full in the face. "Understand this. I don't care anymore. I don't care why you fucked her, why you lied, why you wouldn't confess to me. I watched you and Fiona fuck on my bed in my bedroom in my house, and I stopped caring about you." I grimaced in disgust. "You didn't even change the sheets, you dirty bastard. You just flipped the duvet over and let me sleep under your mess."

I stand up again.

"I'm going out," I say. "Mr. Robinson will supervise your packing. He might even help you. He has a van outside and will drop you and your stuff wherever you want. Take all the time you need—he's yours for the rest of the day." I pick up my purse and walk to the hall door.

I turn back. "Oh, I nearly forgot. Mr. Robinson will give you his invoice, too. I think you'll find his terms reasonable. Don't think of not paying—he knows where you work, and that tape you destroyed wasn't the only copy. I'm still sure Fiona's husband would be fascinated by her performance."

I nod to Mr. Robinson. "Good-bye, and thanks for everything," I say to him. "Please leave Phil's house and car keys on the kitchen table. A pleasure doing business with you."

He nods back. A man of few words.

I take one last look at Phil and say, "Good-bye forever, and thanks for very little." And I go.

THEY SAY CONFESSION is good for the soul, whoever "they" are. It certainly did mine some good. It felt great to regain some power, to claw back control over my emotions. My glee, as I skipped down the path to the car, punching the air, was pure, empowering, and amazingly horny.

I still have a copy of the tape. For a while after I threw Phil out, I watched it over and over. The first time I ever saw it, I was filled with cold horror to be confronted with the truth I'd tried to make him confess. The second time, I was calmer, taking in the details of the woman, the patterns of sex. After Phil left, my relationship with the tape changed. It became a kind of ritual. I'd draw the curtains, take my jeans off, sit down in the armchair where he used to sit to watch television, throw one leg over the chair arm. Get comfortable. Then I'd start the tape running, and soon I'd slip my hand under the waistband of my panties and massage my clitoris as my eyes drank in the images of Phil and Fiona. I'd come, gasping, as she came howling on the screen.

Yet another confession. That one's just for you.

You Think You Know a Person

CHRIS BRIDGES

IT WAS A nice little café, perched on the waterfront and open to the sky. Kind of an old Italian style, or as close as could be managed in Fort Lauderdale. Simple white furniture and ivy all over everything, with small tables stretched along the ocean shore, roasted garlic in the air, and the hinted suggestion that any second now the Pope might stop in for a bite. I had never been here before, which was fitting because I was here to meet the love of my life, whom I had never met before.

Currently she was a four-hundred-pound wolf woman with knobby knuckles and a single eyebrow that was well on its way to becoming a beard as well. In my mind, anyway.

I had made the mistake of getting here early, which gave me far too much time to drink cup after expensive cup of coffee and dream up nightmarish first-date scenarios that were each worse than the last, some of them with sound effects. I knew,

I just knew that any second now I'd look up and suddenly have to keep a straight face and not scream or wet myself, and I was dreading it. It's probably a pretty common blind date fear. I wouldn't know.

However, if anticipating your date's probable disfigurement was also a common blind date thing, I was well along the curve. So far I had pictured Charlene as a fifty-five-year-old divorcée serial killer biker with a scar across her face and only one ear, a plucky double amputee who liked listening to show tunes while setting fire to municipal buildings, and a fat male comic store clerk. And I hadn't even touched on the potential twisted sexual hang-ups yet.

I set my cup down as carefully as I could, despite the shaking, and took a deep breath. Then I slapped myself hard across the face. People at the tables around me looked up, startled. "First date," I said, and they smiled, nodded, and went back to their conversations.

Let's be honest here, I told myself. The problem isn't that I might not like how she looks. The problem is that Charlene might not like me. And who could blame her? A twenty-two-year-old computer geek with a dead-end job and no real interest in anything that couldn't be downloaded? Not prime stud material, I'm thinking. What if she panics and flees as soon as she sees me? What if she leaps over the railing and disappears forever? Was that why she had picked an outdoor café? Had she already planned her dramatic helicopter getaway? Would it be able to lift her if she really did weigh four hundred pounds?

Great, now my insecurities were surrounding me and calling in air cover. I shook my head and tried the opposite approach, just to balance things out.

She had hair like flowing caramel–I had seen it in my mind

a thousand times. Skin like cream, probably. Clover green eyes weren't out of the question, maybe a button nose, and even, white teeth beneath lips like the first spring wine, almost certainly. I smiled. I had been doing that a lot for the last few months. Smiling.

We'd met in a science fiction chat room during a spirited discussion about the *I, Robot* debacle. I think I fell in love right away, with her sensible attitude; her adorable, self-effacing charm; her sweet sexiness; her usage of complete, correctly spelled sentences; and her Tank Girl avatar. We argued for hours that night on every topic anyone could think of: science fiction, fantasy, science fantasy, comic books, movies, science fiction movies . . .

I'd never met anyone with whom I'd bonded so quickly, or at all. Maybe most guys could pick up girls the same way they picked up library books—casually, with the mutual understanding that everything would be back on the shelf in two weeks, slightly worn. Didn't work that way for me. The idea that someone was interested in me was . . . interesting.

Then she made her move.

We were arguing over whether *Firefly* was better than *Babylon 5* when she went private and came on to me. "Do you have a girlfriend?" she'd typed.

I admitted I didn't.

"Would you like one?" she'd asked.

I admitted I would.

"Would you like one like me? I might come off as pushy, but I'm very biddable. Try me. Bid something."

We stumbled through some virtual foreplay. She quickly realized it was my first time, although I somehow failed to mention it was my first sexual interaction of any kind, and she led me through it with tenderness and more than a little simulated hunger.

"Have I been a good girl for Daddy?" she'd asked.

"Well, you have been kind of naughty . . . But please, call me Chet. Nothing personal, the Daddy thing just creeps me out. And I like it when you say my name."

"Say my name!" she'd typed immediately, over and over. "Say my name! Hee!"

"Fuck you. You know what I meant."

"Sorry, sorry, couldn't help it. You make me giggle a lot. I bet you could make me moan, too. You want to teach a girl some tricks?"

"You probably know more than I do. What if I touch you . . . here?" I had typed, inordinately proud of myself. I had moves! Who knew?

She had typed back, "Ohhhh . . ."

Ultimately it developed into very detailed oral sex being performed on me for almost an hour, during which time she had used some very descriptive, very eager language to tell me exactly what it felt like, until I was forced to rethink my whole "masturbating in front of your computer is pathetic" theory. I described to her just as carefully what it had felt like to me, to her delighted response, and afterward I felt warm and loved and virile. Sitting there with my eyes closed in the Florida sun, I remembered that incredible feeling, of being powerful and masculine and–

And suddenly a very large man in a black suit and sunglasses was looming over me, blocking out a sizable portion of the sun. "Mr. Gellert? Chester Gellert?"

Oh, crap. Suddenly my heart was pounding faster, for entirely different reasons. Okay, yeah, I was aroused in a rather pronounced fashion, but surely that couldn't be bothering the other customers unless they were hiding under my tablecloth. "Yes? What's going on?"

He sat down as if he'd been specially trained to do so. It didn't reduce his height by much. His craggy features stared at me over tented fingertips, grim and professionally serious, like Tommy Lee Jones dropping by to tell you your dog is dead. "You were waiting to meet Charlene Davies. I regret to inform you that you will not be meeting Ms. Davies here today. Or any day."

"What? What have you done to her?"

"You were asked to come here, Mr. Gellert," he said, in a tone that brooked no disagreement, "because we felt that you deserved an explanation for Charlene's disappearance."

"You're damn right I do." I jumped to my feet and backed away, keeping the table between us. That bulge in his coat could be a gun, or a detonator . . . Images from thirty years of Bond movies flashed before my eyes. "Why can't she tell me herself? Where is she?"

"Please, Mr. Gellert, you're making a scene–"

I kept backing away, bumping into tables and stumbling over the legs of the other patrons, who were either trying not to notice or were staring openly. Suddenly the quaint little café seemed awfully enclosing. Where was Charlene? Did this guy have her somewhere? Was she hurt?

"Come back and sit down, Mr. Gellert. Let me explain–"

I turned and ran for it, throwing chairs behind me as I passed. With any luck, he'd trip on a few of them and sprain his trigger finger before he could shoot me in the back of the head. I spun around a surprised waiter and ran into the cool interior of the café. Front door or back? No time to decide. I saw daylight and dove for it, causing a few customers to scream and one unfortunate woman to spill a pitcher of beer over both of us that hastened her trip to the floor and my trip to the outside world. My mind was spinning with plans of derring-do and personal heroism. Get to the police, get out an APB, and save the girl I loved in a daring rescue. I had just enough time to imagine the grateful look on her face—which was now perfect and scar-free—before I slipped on a puddle of beer and heroically smacked face-first into the doorjamb.

THERE WAS A distant voice, a female voice calling me through the darkness, and a cool cloth pressed against my forehead. "Chet?" the voice asked.

I opened my eyes and sat up suddenly, causing more sharp pains. In front of me was a vision, finally my glorious vision of honeyed hair and clover-green eyes and . . . well, a few more crow's feet than I expected. In fact, she was probably a good twenty years older than I was, but she had a lovely smile and there seemed to be a lot going on behind those eyes, and that was more than enough for me. "Charlene?"

Her smile turned sad, and that was bad. You'd think, *hey, smile, good,* but I've gotten a lot of sad smiles from women in my day, and I've never liked any of them. "My name's Agent Stark, Chet."

"Oh, crap," I said. Now that I could see a bit more clearly, I noticed the name badge.

A gravelly voice next to me said, "We just want to talk to you, Mr. Gellert." The big guy was right there, holding me up. We were inside the café now, in a booth around the side of the bar by the window. Agent Stark appeared to be kind and friendly and feminine and was very effectively blocking my way out.

"Where's Charlene?" I asked, trying to sound a lot more

forceful than I felt. "Are you her parents? Did they call you? Did she call you? What? I demand to talk to her right now or I'm calling the police! Now!"

The guy slumped, as much as he was capable, and sighed. "You *are*, Chet."

"What? Talking to her or to the police?"

"Both." And then he did an amazing thing. He took off his sunglasses and he smiled at me. Suddenly he looked like a person, instead of a Terminator, and I was completely unprepared for it. "I'm Agent DeCarlo. We're with the FBI. We work online to catch pedophiles, people who prey on children to feed their perverted needs."

"I've seen the after-school special. But Charlene is over eighteen, I asked! A couple of times!"

"We know. Don't worry–you're not in any trouble here."

The waiter showed up with drinks for everybody. Apparently, commerce had occurred while I was away. He left, looking back at us warily. I wondered what he thought was going on. For that matter, I wondered what *I* thought was going on.

"You see," DeCarlo said. "Sometimes a guy will talk up some teenybopper online, get her all hot and bothered, convince her that he's the only one who really understands her, and then ask her to meet him somewhere. That's where we come in. When he shows up to collect his jailbait, we show up with handcuffs. The kind that aren't fun."

"Charlene's parents called you? But she's over eighteen, why–"

For the first time, the agents looked uneasy. "Responding to parental reports is only part of our job," Stark said. "Sometimes the kid is the one to call us." She shifted her feet uncomfortably. "And sometimes we go online ourselves."

Sitting there, I could feel my testicles crawling up into my body. "Oh my God. You're telling me that you're–"

"Yeah," she said. "Surprise. Nice to finally meet you, Chet." She held her hand out and I shook it limply, trying to grab on to some part of my functioning brain for long enough to form actual English words. "We realize how awkward this must be for you."

"Awkward? No, no, 'awkward' is when you walk in on your sister when she's naked, holding her schnauzer and a big bowl of peanut butter. I just found out the love of my life is really an FBI agent. There's gotta be a new word for that."

DeCarlo had the grace to look embarrassed. "Two FBI agents, actually," he said. "We work together."

"Oh, God. Look, can I have a few minutes? This is very . . . I don't know what this is, that's what I need the minutes for." They nodded but kept looking at me, which didn't help any. I put my face in my hands and rubbed. "And here I thought I'd planned for everything."

Stark said quietly, "It was a mistake."

"You meant to seduce some other Chet?" I said.

"After we determined that you were not a pedophile," DeCarlo said, with all the tender emotion of Joe Friday, "we had no right to continue pretending. I take full responsibility."

Stark glared at him. "The hell you do. It was *my* decision to seek you out again after the first contact, Chet."

"Why?"

"Do you remember when you stayed up all night comforting 'Charlene' when her cat died?" she asked.

"Yeah, the second time we talked. Great, it's good to know that treasured memory of mine is backed up at Langley somewhere–"

“That was me,” Stark said. “My youngest was very sick, in the hospital. I was terrified I'd lose her. My husband was flying back, but there were hours to wait and I needed some blind sympathy from someone with the time to cheer up a total stranger. You kept me sane that night, Chet.” She looked up at me with moist eyes and smiled. “Okay, you kept telling me I could always go buy another one that looked like her, but you didn't know I wasn't grieving for a pet. You helped me a lot.”

“Is she all right?” I asked. Stark nodded happily and wiped her eyes. “Okay, I gave good chat. And after that?”

She shrugged. “I told you things that night I had never told anybody, not my husband, not even this lug. You're easy to talk to. It got to be a habit.”

“Also one hell of a security risk, and a violation of I don't know how many regulations,” DeCarlo muttered.

“Like you were any better,” she said.

“Yeah, well . . .”

Stark grinned. “He chewed me out for being unprofessional, then went online to break things off with you and ended up chatting for six hours about major league baseball.”

Pissed and confused and upset as I was, I still laughed out loud at that. “The World Series! She . . . He said he couldn't watch the game, so I typed a play-by-play for her. Him. You. God, what a night!”

“See? I was at my desk, dreading what he'd say when he came back to work, and he comes in all embarrassed and goes, ‘He's a great guy, isn't he?’ So we kept on talking to you.”

“I guess that's why we only had sex that first time,” I said. For a brief second I had a flash of Agent Stark in some improbable lingerie, typing away to send me into online orgasmic glee. It wasn't a bad image, especially when I imagined her snaking a hand between her legs to join me . . . "I met your basic 'not-a-pedophile' condition. Jeez, that's a relief, sort of. I was sure I'd done it wrong or something, I didn't want to push. Do you get, like, special training for that?"

They exchanged glances, looked at me, and then did it again. Finally DeCarlo coughed. "Um," he said. "Usually I, ah, I do that part."

Suddenly we all became very interested in our drinks.

I looked at him–huge, husky, five o'clock shadow and all–and tried very, very hard not to remember Charlene telling me, approvingly, what my penis tasted like. I swallowed hard and made a mental note to boil my keyboard when I got home.

DeCarlo turned away, blushing like a rosy sunset over a rocky ridge. "I got a good imagination," he muttered.

"He does all our sex scenes," Stark said. "He's got a gift. I never know what to say."

"You're gay?" I asked.

"No!" he said, shocked. "I mean, no, I just . . . I got a good imagination. You were pretty good, too."

"As God is my witness I have absolutely no idea how to answer that." I frowned. "Wait a minute. 'All our scenes?' So you're saying there have been others?"

"Well, yeah, we do this for a living," DeCarlo chuckled. "We've got a pretty good arrest record, if I do say so myself."

"You slut," I said, startling them both. "So the girl I'm in love with has been taking on the whole Internet?" Without warning I found myself getting choked up. Bad enough that my lover didn't, technically speaking, exist, but she was unfaithful too? This was too much. I would have been better off with the four-hundred-pound wolf woman.

Both agents reached to touch me, comfort me, but I pushed

past Stark and stood up. "Look, I need to think about this, all right? I need to . . . I have to . . . I want some air."

Stark stood up and brushed her hands across her slacks. DeCarlo unfolded himself to stand next to her with an expression that suggested that my going anywhere wasn't a good idea, but she stopped him with a glance. "You do what you need to, Chet," she said. DeCarlo scowled but remained quiet.

I walked to the front door and turned back to see them in the same positions, waiting in the dim and smoky light of the café. "You're taking a hell of a chance here, right?" I asked. "Couldn't I file charges against you or complain to your mysterious and shadowy boss or something?"

DeCarlo's scowl deepened, something I would have bet money wasn't possible. Stark pressed her lips together in a thin line and nodded once.

"So why meet me at all? Why not just stop writing me, or change names?"

This time DeCarlo answered. "We didn't want you to always be wondering if it was your fault she left you."

There was a long pause. Then I stepped through the door and into the real world, which was much brighter and didn't smell like garlic. Fresh air didn't help much, my head was still spinning. God! My daydream of meeting my dream lover and spending the beautiful spring day making love in an elegant hotel surrounded by chocolate and champagne was getting dimmer and dimmer. That had been the best-case scenario, the one without the disfigurements.

What the hell should I do now? I felt mildly violated, but not in a sue-the-bastards way. More like waking up to find that someone had slipped me roofies and then repainted my apartment. Stunned and confused, maybe.

And betrayed.

They took her away from me. Okay, yes, she was imaginary and everything, but she was mine. Charlene was my friend and they took her away, and the sudden sense of loss was almost overwhelming. I staggered over to my car and leaned against it. Charlene was gone.

No more late-night bull sessions on the nature of God, man, and Texas Hold 'em poker.

No more watching the same late-night movie while messaging each other with comments on the plot and suggestions for better dialogue.

No more giggly messages popping up at all hours of the day and night.

No more heart-to-heart talks with someone who was really interested in me.

No one to fill a giant void in my life that I hadn't even known was there.

I leaned way over to the side until I could see them through the café window. They looked pensive. Professional, dangerous, probably sudden death on four legs, and they were clearly nervous at the thought that my feelings were hurt. And they were right–I could really mess up things for both of them. I don't know what the punishment was for FBI agents who flirted with their case studies in off hours, but I was pretty sure it didn't involve candy and backrubs. And they still told me anyway.

It was just the sort of thing Charlene would do.

I WALKED BACK in and slid into the booth. "I think this is the 'we can still be friends' part of the date," I said carefully.

DeCarlo's eyes widened. "You kidding? Seriously?"

"Yeah," I said. "Relationships take a lot of work, you know. I don't want to give up on this one just yet. Besides, I'm pretty sure you guys are both armed, and I've heard about you jilted girlfriends."

Both of my new friends smiled; Stark patted my hand and DeCarlo sighed happily. We ordered some food and relaxed, finally at ease with each other for the first time.

"It's not going to be easy," Stark said, trying for sincere soulfulness and missing it completely. "You like *Babylon 5*, we like *Firefly*." Her lips twitched upward. "These mixed marriages rarely work out."

"Actually, I liked *Farscape* better than either of 'em," DeCarlo said.

"God," I said. "You think you know a person . . ." DeCarlo grinned and went for his first sip of coffee. I timed my words carefully. "And hey, who knows?" I said, watching him. "Play your cards right, you might get lucky again." Suddenly Stark and I were laughing and wiping coffee off our shirts, while DeCarlo coughed like he was trying to bring up his own foot. "See, I knew you were lying," I told him. "You *are* a spitter."

"I've still–*cough*–got my handcuffs, you know," he wheezed. Agent Stark smacked him on the back while trying to hide her giggles with the other hand. I did my best to project cherublike innocence. And life went on.

So it wasn't young love. But it was new friends, and a new level of trust, and no one got shot. And isn't that all a first date should be?

Exit Interview

PAULA L. FLEMING

"HEY, NICK. GLAD you could meet with me today. We got a pile of applications for your assistant manager job." Katy stood up to lift several bulging file folders off the top of a precariously balanced stack. Her sable brown jacket was unbuttoned, and her generous breasts pressed firmly against the deep gold silk of her blouse. I caught a glimpse of one bas-relief nipple before she found the file she was looking for and the jacket fell closed. She pushed her long, dark brown hair away from her face and opened the file.

"Most of these are crap. You're welcome to look through them if you want . . ." She glanced across the desk at me, eyebrows raised in a question.

"That's all right. I'll take your word for it," I said.

"But there are three here who might have what you're looking for." Katy took the three résumés off the top and pushed them across the desk at me. Her fingernails were close-clipped and plain, except for her left pinky, which was long and painted bright blue with a gold ankh in the middle. It seemed like a radical statement from someone so buttoned down.

I glanced through the three résumés she'd culled for me. The first two seemed promising: The applicants–both men, I noticed in passing–had plenty of marketing management experience. One was even going to night school to get his MBA. The third looked like a dud, though: Heather Colby had been an assistant manager at several fast food places and a couple of clothing retailers, never staying anywhere more than a year. She'd taken some college classes in business but didn't have a degree. I was looking for someone committed to a career in marketing and someone who'd fit in with our corporate environment–a power-suit kind of person.

"I'll interview these two but pass on this one," I said, handing Colby's résumé back to Katy.

"How come?" she challenged. Her hazel eyes locked with mine. I sensed a fight brewing, though I couldn't imagine why.

"She just doesn't have the kind of marketing background I'm looking for."

Katy shook her head, as though she was a teacher and I, her student, had just given the wrong answer. "We don't have enough women in management at this company. We look bad to the EEOC. We look bad in magazine surveys of woman-friendliness. Give her a chance."

I could have argued that interviewing Heather Colby would just be a waste of both my time and hers, but I had a feeling from Katy's tone of voice that I wasn't going to get out of her office until I agreed with her. You've got to choose your battles, as the saying goes.

"Okay." I took back the résumé. "I'll interview her, too."

. . .

THE MBA-GETTER didn't impress me in the interview. He was very bright, but only in a book-smart way. He studied the carpet while answering each question in agonizingly methodical detail. I needed someone who could influence people and push through ideas. The large tomato sauce stain on his tie didn't help his cause, either.

The other guy clearly viewed this job as merely a stepping-stone to greater things. There's nothing wrong with ambition, but I wanted someone who'd look at this job as a real opportunity and give it his or her best shot, not be looking around for something better from day one. Frankly, I had the feeling he'd be gunning for my job. He also wanted more salary than I was ready to pay.

So when the receptionist told me that Heather Colby had arrived—ten minutes early, a good sign—I was really hoping that she'd show me something in the interview that I couldn't see in her résumé.

Oh, my. She probably wasn't going to show me nearly as much as I wanted to see, but I was sure glad for the chance to look. Heather was petite but, even under the severe navy blue suit, obviously well curved. Her skirt stopped several inches short of her knees, which was fine, because her legs were perfect. Her face was a little girl's face, with dimpled chin, upturned nose, and big eyes, but she wore just enough makeup to show she was a woman. Her golden-blonde hair was artfully tousled to fall in sweeping curves around her shoulders.

"Good morning, Heather. Thanks for coming in," I said. I stood to shake hands with her and was glad I'd kept my jacket on. I had a boner worthy of a sixteen-year-old.

"Good morning, Nick." Her hand was small, the bones fragile, but her handshake was nonetheless firm. She wasn't wearing any rings. Her nail polish was the exact shade of her lipstick. She met my eyes, and her smile seemed warm and sincere.

She'd impressed me immediately as composed and confident. That impression didn't waver a bit as the interview went along. She acknowledged her lack of experience–and I couldn't help wondering how experienced she was in other ways–but gave several examples of how she'd proven herself a quick study. She explained her job-hopping by saying she kept feeling frustrated by the lack of challenge in her jobs, that each job she'd taken had been talked up as a real opportunity for career growth but turned out to be more of the same old, same old.

She came across as bright, motivated, and persuasive. She'd need a lot of training to get her up to speed, but surely, if I was any kind of manager, I could do that. Especially, I admitted to myself, if it meant working closely with her every day.

I concluded the interview with the standard, "I'll be in touch soon and let you know my decision." We shook hands again. This time, she took my hand in both of hers and just held it for an instant. My cock–I swear it has an imagination of its own sometimes–jumped back to attention.

"I'll walk you out," I said.

As I opened my office door, my boss walked by. "Hey, Nick, I've been wanting to talk to you about . . . Well, hello." He didn't quite blurt out, "Hubba-hubba," but it wasn't far from his lips.

"Jim, this is Heather Colby. She's interviewing for the new assistant manager job."

He turned on his best shit-eating grin. "I'm very pleased to meet you, Ms. Colby, very pleased. I'm sure you have impressive qualifications."

"Thank you, Jim." She extended her hand for a handshake.

He looked at it for a moment as though it were a rare hummingbird hovering in front of him, before seizing it in both of his mitts and raising it to his lips. "I'm *very* pleased to meet you, Miss." He'd already forgotten her name.

"I was just walking her out. I'll catch up with you later, Jim."

"Sure you will, Nick." And he gave me a wink that she must have seen as well. I could feel my face turning red in embarrassment for her. She didn't deserve to be treated like a walking piece of T&A.

After seeing her into the reception area, I didn't feel like dealing with Jim right away. He reminded me too much of the jocks back in high school: tall, wide, and smirking. I worked too hard and produced results too good for him to pick on me the way he did with some of his weaker managers, but he seemed always to be probing for an opportunity for bullying. I'd thought I was over all those high school insecurities, but Jim never failed to bring them right back out of the gym closet where I'd stuffed them.

I went to the men's room. It was empty. I washed my hands in cold water and rubbed them down my cheeks. To get my mind off Jim, I reviewed the three job applicants in my head.

Tomato-stain guy was definitely out. Mr. I-Want-Your-Job would probably do well, but I already had Jim to deal with. Did I want another hyperaggressive male ego around the office every day? If those two bonded, I had a feeling *I'd* soon be looking for another job.

That left either going back to Katy and saying, "Try again," or …

I remembered Heather coming into my office: the warm smile curving her generous mouth, her skirt riding up on her thighs as she sat down, her breasts defying the nearly military cut of her jacket. My groin hummed like a power line with a sudden surge of desire. I touched myself through my slacks and imagined her hand there–imagined how big and heavy I would feel encircled by her delicate fingers–and my cock started to throb as though my heart was in it. I took two quick strides and got into a stall, where I undid my belt with a quick jerk and got to work.

AFTER A FEW weeks on the job, Heather seemed to be working out okay. She certainly worked a lot. She was almost always in the office when I got there in the morning, and she often stayed late and came in on weekends. I asked several times if I'd given her too much to do, and she just said, "Oh, no, Nick. It's not that. It's just that I have so much to learn. I want to read through the old focus group feedback on our products so I don't reinvent the wheel," or, "I've never worked with spreadsheets before, so I'd better double-check these numbers."

She didn't contribute anything to product development meetings, and she couldn't direct a design team when I was tied up with another project. However, her coworkers seemed to like her, and she seemed to be fulfilling my hunch that she would quickly grow into the job.

I stopped by human resources to thank Katy for finding her. She was in her office, riffling through dog-eared folders and chucking them into a large plastic bin.

"Hey there, Nick!" When she smiled, her whole face lit up, and she looked a lot younger. She was wearing black boots, black jeans with red flowers embroidered down the sides, and a red sweater. Sure, she was a little generously filled out through the butt and hips, and her stomach probably hadn't been flat for twenty years, but those breasts! I could have just lived between them.

She dropped a heavy stack of paper into the bin and grinned at the loud thump it made. "It's clean-up day. I can spend the whole day just getting rid of stuff. Maybe the best day of the year!"

"I just dropped by to let you know that Heather is working out very well. Thanks for making me interview her."

Katy looked puzzled. "She *is* working out?"

"Well, yeah." *Now what?* "She has a lot to learn, but she's working hard, and I think she'll be up to speed soon."

"That's not what I've heard."

Shit. "What have you heard?"

"Maybe I shouldn't tell you this, but . . . come on in and close the door." I did and sat down.

Katy perched on the corner of her desk. The dark brown faux wood jutted between her thighs. I could have lived between her thighs, too. I caught myself staring and made myself look at her face. Since when had I become such a lech?

Since I'd started working day-in, day-out with Heather, that's when.

"Jim has talked to me a couple of times about your hiring decision."

"He's talked to you?" If he had a problem with *my* fucking hiring decision, why hadn't he talked to *me* about it?

"He says she's useless. Can't contribute a damn thing. That her only 'qualification' is a great body and a cute smile. Oh, and a willingness to fuck anything with two legs."

She hadn't fucked *me!* I felt my face heat up. I hoped like hell Katy assumed I was embarrassed by the general smuttiness of our conversation, or that I was reddening in anger at Jim's accusations. She couldn't guess that during dull meetings, I fantasized about Heather standing on the conference table in nothing but her high heels and silk panties. She couldn't guess that when I walked out to my car, I imagined Heather waiting for me on the hood, wearing her suit but nothing underneath. She couldn't know that I was jacking off two, even three, times a day in the men's room, as if I was back in high school again—could she?

The best defense was a good offense. "Jim is a dirty-minded, sexist fuckhead. I don't know anything about Heather's sex life. It's none of my business. I know that I've only seen consistently professional, hard-working behavior from her. She hasn't made much of a contribution yet, but she's only been here a few weeks. I have no doubt that I'll be giving her a four-star annual review."

Katy just gave me a long look, her mouth twisting a little at the corner. Finally she slid off her desk, walked past me, and opened her office door. "Just remember, Nick, you didn't hear it from me."

After that conversation with Katy, I became paranoid about Heather's job performance or, more precisely, how her performance *looked*. If Jim had said those things to Katy, then he'd probably told most of the management team, too, and from there the gossip would trickle all the way down to the janitorial staff before you could say "rumor mill."

I started looking for a project that Heather could shine at, something I could document and put up as concrete evidence that she was doing a good job in the face of whatever innuendo might circulate. Office politics are potent in making someone's life miserable, but if it comes down to firing a person, facts usually have the edge.

It wasn't just a question of being fair to Heather, and it wasn't about defending my hiring decision. Fact was, I didn't think I *could* fire Heather. She'd seized my imagination the way no woman had since . . . well, since I'd been a sex-obsessed teenager. She reminded me of the super-popular girls with the perfect bodies on the dance squad. They'd never go out with a nerd like me–and I knew that, so I'd never asked them–but I sure could look at them and dream. That's how it was with Heather. I wasn't going to sleep with her. She was my subordinate, for crying out loud! I knew the company policy about that, and I knew how the sexual harassment laws worked. What I might think was consensual, she might view as something she had to go along with to keep her job–and sue the pants off me afterward. Nope, I was in no more position to sleep with Heather than I was to sleep with the whole dance squad in high school.

But just like in high school, I could still obsess about her. And how on earth do you fire a woman you've been fucking a dozen times a day, in every possible place and in every possible position, even if it's all been in your head?

A year ago we'd acquired a company that made packages of shrimp cocktail, plastic-wrapped slices of bruschetta, and other "high-end" appetizers for the lunchboxes of discerning parents' kids. Despite putting a lot of money into advertising, sales had remained flat, so we'd decided to extend our successful, frozen diet-food brand to the lunchbox product. That way, the theory went, we'd make a logical connection in the minds of dieting moms between the food that was good for them and food that would be good for their kids.

Extending a brand is fairly straightforward: Take off the old brand name, put on the new brand name, and tell your retailers and end-customers about the change. I put Heather in charge of the project but checked in with her almost every day to give guidance, usually after five o'clock, when the office quieted down and I wasn't being interrupted every ten minutes.

As we sat in my office together, reviewing the project rollout and discussing our next steps, I'd try to turn the conversation to more personal subjects. I was frankly curious about the "slut" reputation that had come to Katy via Joe. Locker room fantasy or truth? I mentioned that I had thought about getting a dog but decided I wasn't home enough to take care of it, but Heather didn't have any pets. I talked about my last vacation, a road trip touring Civil War sites, but Heather had never traveled outside the state except once to Los Angeles for a friend's wedding. I said my favorite kind of food was Thai, but Heather said she just nuked frozen whatevers in the microwave. She elaborated on that answer, adding that she'd tried our brand of frozen diet dinners and liked them.

I couldn't find the least hint of sexual wantonness. I couldn't even find much of a personality. And I was beginning to doubt her aptitude for the work. The more time we spent together, the more I realized that while she kept the project documentation very organized and asked intelligent-sounding questions, she could never actually push the work forward on her own. She never knew what to do next unless I told her, and sometimes I had to tell her twice.

She often didn't get my jokes.

My ardor for her was cooling. She'd make a great centerfold to jerk off on, but actually rolling around in a bed together wouldn't be much fun.

As our deadline neared, I got more and more nervous. The day before the brand rollout, Heather had to attend a mandatory, all-day diversity training workshop. I started checking with our graphics department, our sales group, the factory. Had Heather contacted them? Were they changing the packaging? Informing the stores? Preparing an ad campaign? Yes, she'd called them and talked generally about a brand change. But no, no, and no. They had no idea what they were supposed to be doing–or even that they should be doing anything.

Frantically, I went through Heather's file cabinet and her computer, pulling together our notes on the brand extension. It wasn't hard–she *was* organized. I began making calls, sending e-mails. The responses were outraged and disgusted. *You want us to do* what? *On what kind of deadline? Are you crazy?*

The next day, Heather called in sick. An ad campaign for our frozen diet-foods line, initiated six months ago and never canceled, started on billboards and TV. It didn't mention children's lunchboxes. The factory shipped product to the stores in the same old packaging. Our sales force gamely tried to get the message out that stores should put the lunchbox treats on more visible shelves because we were repositioning them and they would become a hot product, but the stores–seeing no evidence of any "repositioning"–ignored them.

I sat in my office, trying to rehearse what I was going to say to Heather when she came back. Joe walked in. He wasn't even bothering to hide a smirk.

"So, how's that rebranding going? Gonna have those kids' snacks flying off the shelves today? Gonna add ten percent to our bottom line? That was your goal, wasn't it? Ten percent?"

I tried to keep my cool. "It's not happening, Joe. Which I

suspect you already know. Heather dropped the ball. She's not working out."

"Whoa! Blaming a subordinate? That's not cool, Nick. Leaders have to take responsibility around here. Who was responsible for monitoring Heather's performance?"

Since when had Jim taken responsibility for anything? *Just suck it up, Nick*, I counseled myself. "I was."

"And just who assigned such an important, bottom-line-impacting project to her?"

"I did."

"And just who hired her, when she has no marketing experience and no college degree?"

"I did."

"Well, there you go, Nick. And that's why I'm going to have to fire you."

I let his words just sit in my head for a while. The funny thing was, they didn't hit me like a ton of bricks. I didn't feel bad. I actually felt a little relieved that Jim was finally getting to do what he'd long wanted to do . . . and that I was finally getting out of here? How long had I wanted that?

"I brought Katy from HR along. She'll supervise you while you clean out your desk, make sure you don't take anything you're not supposed to. Your computer access has already been revoked, so don't bother trying anything there. Then she's probably got some HR crapola for you."

He stood up. "This office will sure look a lot nicer with Heather in it."

It was as though a flashbulb had gone off in my face. I could barely see. My heart pounded as if I was running up stairs. "Heather? You're not firing Heather?"

"Fire Heather? That delicious little peach? I think that with the right guidance, from a man like me, she'll be able to turn her performance right around. I'm going to start by fucking her right here in her new office."

He walked out. "Hey, Heather," he called, "you want to say good-bye?"

She came in, looking as poised and confident as she had during her interview.

"Close the door," I said. Joe could fire me so the office could hear, but I wasn't going to act just like him.

Instead of sitting down as I expected, Heather walked around to my side of the desk and perched with one hip up on the corner. "You wanted to say something to me?" she asked.

"I'm not saying this out of spite or anger, Heather. I really want to help you. I think it's important for you to know that Joe is only keeping you around because he–" *Because he wants to fuck you* was too blunt. "–because he finds you attractive. You're not up to this job, Heather. You won't be successful at it."

She snorted, her pert little nose flaring and her wide lips forming a rosebud pout. "As if you hired me for my 'qualifications?' Look, Nick, I'm not delusional about myself. I know what my 'qualifications' are. And I'll go as far as I can with them. Right now, that's this office, and you're in my way."

Now I was done with civility. "Right, I need to move so he can fuck you on this desk. Is that the picture? Or will he just do you up against the wall?"

"Whatever he wants, baby. He's the boss." She unbuttoned her gray jacket, then her white blouse with the Peter Pan collar, and finally unhooked her lacy white bra in front. It fell away, showing me her perfect breasts. They didn't drop a millimeter as they lost their support, instead maintaining their perfect, perky C-cup shape. Fake, I realized. Implants. Despite my loathing, my hand moved toward them, as though of its own accord.

"Don't touch," she snapped. "You can look, but you can never touch. Boys like you can never touch."

I went cold. "I think you should button your clothing, Miss Colby. You're sexually harassing me."

The look on her face was priceless. While she quickly buttoned, I grabbed my few personal belongings, opened the door—I didn't care who saw her fumbling with her clothes—and met Katy in the hall.

"Hi, Nick," she said. "I need to do some 'HR crapola' with you, but there's no rule saying we need to do it here. Want to go get coffee? Or something stronger?"

She walked me about seven blocks across downtown. I felt the scene back in my office falling away from me a little with every step, so by the time we reached a dark little hole-in-the-wall bar and went in, I was feeling almost normal. I ordered a dark German beer; she got coffee. "I have to go back to work this afternoon," she said. "So I need your access key and company ID card."

I pulled them out of my wallet and handed them over.

"And I'm supposed to do an exit interview," she continued. "There's a whole bunch of questions on the form, but I didn't bring it with me. Okay if I fill it out for you? You were satisfied with your job duties, with your pay, with your benefits, with your hours, blah, blah. You thought your manager was a jerk, blah, blah."

"That sums it up."

"So there's really just one thing I want to know." She studied her left pinky, looking at the long, bright blue fingernail with the gold ankh in the center. "Why did you make such a stupid hiring decision?"

"You told me to."

"Bullshit. I told you to interview her. I hoped maybe there'd be more to her than she'd managed to get across on her résumé. I *am* trying to get more women into management. But I didn't say you should hire someone entirely unqualified."

"I guess I was smitten."

"Well, that's obvious." She arched her eyebrows and twisted her mouth impatiently. But I mean, why *now*? Surely you've worked with attractive women before and haven't gone completely stupid."

Katy was an attractive woman. She'd be great fun to roll around in bed with. A high four-poster with a canopy, in a hotel overlooking the Mediterranean perhaps. To be followed by nude sunbathing on the beach. Then a fresh seafood dinner and wry conversation, spiced with lots of laughter. And more tumbling about in bed for dessert.

Her question deserved an answer. It was the right question. I needed to answer it. "She took me back to high school. I was recast in the role of class nerd. And I behaved just as nerdily now as I did then."

"I didn't know you in high school, but I've seen you manage projects, manage people. You're an adult, Nick. Of all the many employees we have here who act like children, I've always been able to count on you to be an adult. So why the sudden self-sabotage?"

Self-sabotage? Had it been? And Heather just a convenient vehicle? I remembered her bared breasts, just a couple of feet away, at eye level, and I felt nothing. I didn't want them anymore.

I had what I wanted. I'd gotten out of the corporate rat race. *Thank you, Heather. Thank you, Jim.*

"Question for you, Katy."

"Shoot."

"What's with the fingernail?"

She smiled and lifted it up so it caught what dim light there was and glittered just a little. "It's my reminder at work that, despite the suits, despite the words like *synergize* and *leverage*, despite the politeness we fake even when we're furious with each other, we're still real human beings. We have real feelings. We have real lives that maybe are only interrupted by a need to make a living."

I took her hand in mine, lifted the golden ankh in its blue sky to my lips, and kissed it.

Love and Lies

MADELINE DE CHAMBREY

IF I COULD only see you tonight I would tell you this tale in person, but it's bad luck for the bride and groom to be together the night before the nuptials. And I've only just now decided to tell the truth before you legally bind yourself to me. It's the right thing to do.

You believe I am good. I *am* good, so that's okay. You believe I love you, and I do. You think I always tell the truth, and I do—about today, about tomorrow, about forever. But everything I've told you about my past has been a lie.

My parents didn't die when I was thirteen, only my mother did. Before then she was just always very sick. My father was and still is very much alive. The situation after my mother's death wasn't a good one for me. My dad missed her, so he started to drink. In short order I became his provider in all ways. I left when I was fifteen, not to attend a boarding school paid for by the generous provisions of my dead parents' will, as I have always maintained. I left for the street.

I lived on the streets of downtown for four years. First I was protected by the other homeless kids because of my youth. Then I tried to protect the newcomers because of their youth. That's how it works. We were a family of sorts, and since I'd once been part of a family, before my mother died, I didn't sink as far as some. In that sense I consider myself one of the lucky ones. This is a long way of saying that of course I sold myself for sex, but I didn't get too far into drugs. No needles. I guess that's the good news, Darling.

Anyway, this isn't the part of the story that needs telling; it's already been told. If I know you, you're already forgiving me for the 'I'm a virgin' lie. Do you forgive me? I felt like a virgin with you, because you were the first man I *gave* myself to, and surely that counts for something. I know you love me. I imagine you're already leaping into action, maybe clutching this letter in one hand and keyboarding madly with the other, searching for the best abuse therapists in the country. Please don't. Please focus on my words.

And yes, my past is part of why I became a nurse, but not the main reason. The main reason for my career choice, for being in the situation I find myself in now, for *being*, came after.

It's odd because all the tall tales I've told you about my life, all the lies, sound pedestrian compared to the truth. The truth is I was standing at my usual spot one day when I was taken away by a john and never returned. I was kidnapped from life on the street!

First he said he just wanted me for the night and he'd pay for the pleasure. I hadn't turned that sort of trick in a while. It can be dangerous. But he said he wanted me to come to his house, and no one had ever offered to take me home. Of course, I needed the money, or thought I did. Anyway, he had the kindest eyes you've ever seen. I know, you think my eyes are the kindest eyes you've ever seen, but they are merely a reflection of his. I'm the moon to his sun, you see, and that's the thing I must confess.

He seemed ancient, but he was just sixty, which is still forty-one years older than I was at the time. That also made me want to go with him, because older guys like a lot of talk, and then once the action starts it's usually over pretty quick. So it would be an easy trick. Anyway, that was my thinking. I said yes.

He drove to a lovely house surrounded by trees. It wasn't isolated. I knew I could scream loud enough to wake the neighbors, for sure, if necessary. But he was behaving like a gentleman. He even came around and opened my door for me! I laughed, which I hadn't done in a long time. I thought it was going to be fun.

He told me to heat up some food, and while I did that he sat at the kitchen table and asked me questions. It was sort of the way it had been with my dad, except this man wasn't drinking or yelling. But I still figured I had everything under control. I knew what was coming and it was okay by me.

He told me to set the table, which I tried to do. Darling, at that time I didn't remember what a real place setting looked like. Wouldn't your mother be shocked? Are you? Silly me, I'm sure my history as a hooker is more shocking than my confession that I was once socially inept. These details all seem one and the same to me–simply the bad luck to have had an unfortunate childhood.

Anyway he kindly showed me how to set the table properly. That was the first of many lessons I was to learn from David. His name was David Palmer. As I've said, he was sixty when we met. He had a gorgeous mane of silver hair, which he was rather vain about. He had a slight paunch. He was barrel-chested, with powerful arms and legs like tree trunks that held him firmly rooted to the ground. He was clean-shaven and not very wrinkled. His mouth was mild. He had unkempt eyebrows above gentle amber eyes. I thought he was okay-looking at the time. Later I would consider him the handsomest man on earth. But really he wasn't so much handsome as beautiful, in the same way a saint is beautiful. I mean that.

After we ate, he cleared the table and washed the dishes while I sat at the table and talked some more. I didn't care about my past, so I was straight up about it, which saved us time later. He didn't say anything much about it, just listened. After that he pulled up a kitchen chair and sat down opposite me. I slid to the floor and put my hands on his belt. Time to sing for my supper.

But he stopped me. Darling, I swear. He put his hands over mine and drew me back up to my chair. He said he was lonely and he needed help, for which he would pay. He was offering me a job.

You probably think I jumped at the chance, but it wasn't normal and that made me suspicious. It occurred to me that he might kill me in my sleep or sell me to slave traders or a big-city prostitution ring.

Anyway I said okay, I'd spend the night and we could give it a try. I figured he probably wouldn't kill me or anything, and if he did, so what? I was world-weary, my love, at the age of nineteen.

He showed me my room (!) but wouldn't let me go inside until I'd cleaned up. David ran the bath, and while he did I stripped down. I figured the sooner we got on track, the better. But he barely looked at my naked body, just took my filthy clothes and left me alone.

It was obvious he'd planned to bring someone home that night, because there was everything there that a girl would need to get gloriously clean. My God, it was marvelous! He'd even laid out a fluffy towel and satin pajamas. They were huge on me, but you know what? They were new. And that's the first time I really thought I might have lucked out big.

When I came out of the bathroom he was in his room, reading in bed. He called me over to his bedside. I was all ready to give him a big, sexy good-night kiss, but he told me to turn out his light and go to my room. So I did.

That was the beginning of my life with David.

For the first few months, the routine didn't vary much. In the morning I'd dress in a shift and cook breakfast while he read the paper. He'd read aloud the things he wanted me to know. Then he'd wash up the dishes while I did the rest of the housework.

He'd been a professor before retiring earlier in the year, so he had a lot of books. From that first day he told me I could read any book I wanted from his library. But my job was to organize the books alphabetically, by subject. David showed me exactly what he wanted me to do and how to do it, and that's what I did until lunch.

At lunch he would work on cryptic crossword puzzles while I cooked. He taught me how to make everything he liked and let me prepare things I liked, too. I didn't have to eat everything on my plate if I didn't want to, but I usually did.

In the afternoon his friend Rosa, a psychiatrist, would come over to talk to me. She helped me understand that what had happened to me wasn't my fault. Usually, after Rosa left I cried and had a nap. Then I'd make supper, and David and I would talk and watch TV or play a board game and go to bed.

After a while Rosa didn't come every day. David had other

friends come and teach me or talk to me about things. He had an amazing group of friends. I know some of them didn't entirely agree with what David was doing. One accused him of being a "Svengali" and "Machiavellian" and "Pygmalion," but I didn't even know what those words meant, and once I did, I didn't care. I was legal.

So I learned a lot. I talked with a clergyman about God, and I talked with a historian about the world, and I talked with an oboe player about music, and with the curator of a museum about art. David never touched me in all this time.

Sometimes I'd go to his room at night and try to crawl in beside him, but he'd say no. Sometimes I'd cry and say he must find me repulsive, but he'd just send me back to my room. Sometimes I'd throw myself at him and say that I was in love with him and would kill myself if he refused me again, but he would just gently loosen my grip and order me not to hurt myself.

I always did everything he said. That was solid between us—if he told me to do something, I did it.

Then one night I went to his room, knelt down by the head of his bed, and whispered, "Thank you, David." He said, "You're welcome. Now turn out the light." And I did.

The next morning all the shifts were gone from my closet. In their place hung suits. So I put on a suit. There were stockings and high heels, so I put those on, too. When I came out of my room, there was a hefty woman already mopping and dusting. I had been graduated.

I went to David's study and he told me to "Take a letter." I didn't know how. He said to try, so I did. Then he told me to type it and print it and bring it to him. I did my best, but it was a real mess and I knew it. I wished I hadn't thanked him the night before. Now that he knew I was grateful, he was humiliating me. As far as I was concerned, we were always engaged in a power struggle. I knew he expected something in return. It had to be sex, that's the only thing that made sense.

I made a show of presenting him with the letter. I'd wondered if he was going to put me over his knee sooner or later. Lots of older guys are into that. So I leaned down close to his noble silvery head and whispered, "I hope I didn't make any mistakes, Sir."

He glanced at me, and I turned so that my rear was under his nose. I wiggled it provocatively and gazed over my shoulder, pursing my lips. This was the first time I ever heard him make a noise when he laughed. He chuckled at my presentation!

David looked the letter over. I was so embarrassed, I started crying and yelling and trying to stamp my feet, although that was hard to do in heels. I told him I could do some things really well, but he wouldn't let me show him! I started teetering and he steadied me with a gentle hand. David said the letter wasn't bad for the first effort. Then he sent me to my room.

I know now that any item that ever touched my body was made of the finest material. Pure cashmere, pure silk, pure cotton. My sheets were of luxuriously soft Egyptian cotton. Darling, my room was so cozy! Truth be told, I could have lived in there, as in a cocoon, but I was too driven to relax. I needed to prove myself indispensable to this man, so that he would never be able to be rid of me.

For a few months I wore suits and played secretary to the best of my ability. Ladies came and taught me how to do my makeup and hair. They flirted with David, which he enjoyed, so part of me hated them, but most of me wanted to learn how to look just like them, so that he'd enjoy flirting with me.

Those times, the "secretary times," were good ones. We had fun, the two of us, playing board games and watching TV and talking at breakfast and working on the daily crossword at lunch.

I made him laugh a lot. When I first moved in, he was a silent laugher. It was during the "secretary days" that he started to chuckle. That's one of the reasons I remember that time so fondly.

After a while I became as proficient at writing as I'd become at reading. (Although I'd laughed at David when he told me to borrow anything I wanted from his library, I'd done so.) I was as happy typing as I'd been sorting books and as I'd been dusting. It was all one and the same to me, you see. I was still waiting for the real reason for my presence to surface.

One morning I went to my closet and in place of my suits and blouses and high heels were hip minis and belly shirts and chunky shoes. Belts almost as wide as the skirts they were meant to go over. Kilts. Blazers. Shrugs. Jeans. It was glorious!

I dressed up and clomped down the hall to David's office. A woman sat in the chair I was accustomed to and David was dictating a letter to her! I couldn't believe the betrayal. I screamed at the top of my lungs, louder than I'd have screamed if he'd tried to murder me that first night, louder than I'd ever screamed in my whole long nineteen years. Louder than I screamed the day I'd been born into this sordid life.

Ms. Cool barely looked up from her notepad. Oh, she was a special one. I took a deep breath. As she crossed and uncrossed her legs, her stockings whispered to David. He had yet to look at me, yet he glanced at her legs! I couldn't bear it! I screamed until my face was purple and I was exhausted. My eyes bulged from the pain of shedding boiling tears. My howl was an incomprehensible endless noise that finally, mercifully, faded to a whimper. He sent her away.

"Go stand in the corner until I say that you may come out," he said to me. His voice was shaking. It was the first time that had ever happened, and it scared me, but it was thrilling, too. I was finally getting to him.

It was weird, stuck in the corner like that. For a long time he ignored me completely. I was afraid to be sexy, because that had never worked in the past, but then I'd never been in this situation in the past. Maybe this was the prelude to our lovemaking? Anyway, standing in the corner in chunky shoes is hard to do. So I started wriggling. David left his desk and came up close behind me. I was woozy with excitement! I thought he might take his belt to my ass, or maybe shove the back of my skirt up and fuck his little tramp long and hard, or maybe even spin me around and take me in his arms, but he didn't. He just sighed in my ear and whispered, "What am I going to do with you?" Before I could answer, he said, "That's a rhetorical question. Go to your room." And I did.

I remember my "teen years" fondly. I got to do whatever I wanted, pretty much. I took advantage of it, too. I played my music loud and often. No more Piaf and Big Band sounds for me! I stopped reading good books and disappeared into turgid romances and fashion magazines. I wore lots of makeup and accessorized to the max.

David was a little preoccupied during that time. He and his new secretary worked hard, sometimes late into the night. I thought he was fucking her, and I still think so. But I never actually caught them doing anything. I was living in my room more and more, partly because I had so few duties now, and partly because I was exhausted. I slept most of the day away, sometimes only getting up to throw together a meal. David never complained, of course, just ate what he was given and washed up the dishes and went back to work in his office.

One night I snuck into his (locked) liquor cabinet and got drunk. I put on a show for him at bedtime, mock-begging him not to fuck me (in case that was what he was waiting for) and then throwing a tantrum when he put me in the corner (instead of spanking me, which was what I suspected he wanted to do). Dawn found me down on my knees, not submitting sexually, but with my head in the toilet, vomiting and peeing myself while he held my hair back, murmuring comfort.

Another night I cried and begged until he took me out to the movies. I flirted with all the young guys, but David didn't seem to notice, or if he did, he didn't care.

The "teen years" might have lasted indefinitely had I not heard David showering one morning and decided to take matters into my own hands. I was horny. Life with David was getting kind of dull. I still saw Rosa regularly, but I'd decided I'd rather sleep than meet with David's friends, and David had agreed. I think I was just looking for a little action that didn't originate with my own fingers, so I impulsively slipped into the shower behind him.

It was the first time I saw David angry. I guess I really did surprise him. He spun around, slipping a bit. His arm was raised, and his eyes were the cold, dark color of petrified wood. I shrunk away from him, losing my balance. I slid between his legs and ended up prone, staring up at his balls and dick.

David slapped the shower curtain open and left me there, the water filling my mouth as I tried to scream. That was the end of my "teen years."

What came next is something I'd hoped never to share with

you, Darling. I believe you can accept everything you've read so far, I really do. I believe you love me that much. But will you accept this?

The next morning all of my junior miss costumes were gone. In their place were frilly little tops and big puffy bloomers. Baby dolls, Darling, but not the kind a woman wears when she wants to be sexy. The kind babies wear.

They were made of cotton and soft lace. There wasn't a scratchy neckline or tight bit of elastic anywhere. No labels, of course. These were baby clothes made for a woman. They fit perfectly.

So *this* was his kink! He wanted me dressed as a baby. At last it all made sense. I doubt I'd have agreed to it that first night. "Dress up" is fine and dandy, but this verged on creepy, so he'd taken his time before introducing it. Still, I was legally of age and this would surely make him keep me forever. So I did it, I put on the baby clothes. I was sorry to find my makeup missing. I'd had in mind to do my face up like a little porcelain doll. It'd go perfectly with the white-with-pink-smocking dress and frilly pink bloomers I'd chosen.

On that morning there was no portly cleaning lady in the house, no sexy secretary. No Rosa, that's for sure. Just David and me.

I toddled into his office. He turned his big leather swivel chair to face me. David laughed! He laughed with glee at my pretty little self, and I laughed right back! David opened his arms. "You are adorable!" he said. I knew it to be true. I toddled toward him.

And I started to get scared. You see I'd always played the part to match my outfit. I really tried to be his secretary when I wore the suits and heels. I really was the teenager in the minis and belly tops or schoolgirl kilts and blazers. So I really felt like an adorable baby, and it just seemed wrong that David should use me in that state. It sort of disappointed me to think that that was what all this time and effort were about. David wanted a variation of "sex with baby" that he could consider ethical. Part of me hoped he'd just spank me, and part of me thought that would be even worse than sex. Poor baby!

But if David wanted me to say "Goo goo goo," I would. After all he'd done for me, I felt compelled to pay him back in whatever manner he chose. And the darker the secret, my Darling, the tighter it bound him to me. That was my thinking, at the time.

I toddled to him. I gurgled with joy at the sight of him! He scooped me up in his arms and cuddled me on his lap. That's all, Darling, I swear. He cuddled me and it was heavenly. I curled up against his barrel-chest as he praised me to the skies. "The sweetest, the prettiest, the goodest!" (This from a man who never misspoke!) He kissed me all over the top of my head and held on to me as tightly as he could without hurting me.

I was speechless, and not only because I was lost in baby land. I didn't have a clue what to do.

When he rubbed his cheek against mine, I discovered his was wet. David was crying. This was something I had never imagined. I burst into tears, which made him laugh through his. He laughed and cried and cuddled me, and I laughed and cried and let him cuddle me.

Eventually he crooned a little lullaby and I fell asleep, right there in his arms in his office chair.

The "nursery days" were beautiful, my Darling. So beautiful I never wanted to speak of them to anyone. I never *imagined* trying to speak of them until recently. It's obvious to me, now, what David wanted from me all along. He wanted me to understand that he didn't want anything at all. You see, already I'm jumbling my words. I'll finish the story.

For the next while, I was David's helpless baby. (Well, happily I was a precocious child who'd learned to use the potty at a very young age, so I wasn't completely helpless!) David tended to my every need. He spoon-fed me the sugary cereal I'd demanded during the "teen years." He bathed and dressed me, and he tucked me into bed at night.

I was a very good baby. I didn't feel inclined to tantrum, probably because I'd done so much of it during the "teen years." Because I didn't have anything to do, I could hardly do anything wrong, had I wanted to test his patience. Anyway, by now I knew that David's patience was limitless. He didn't want to screw or spank the baby that was me—he just wanted to pamper me. I gave in. I couldn't help it. I was little.

We didn't talk much during those days, because the baby I'd become didn't know how to say much more than "I wuv you," which she said a lot. He said it right back, too, without a moment's hesitation. "I wuv you too, baby," he'd say. We said it back and forth, back and forth, all the time. I think we both knew the "nursery days" would not last a week, and they didn't.

David had never hidden anything from Rosa, or from any of the other visitors to the house. He believed in full disclosure. So once he'd run out of excuses to keep Rosa away, she showed up, and once she showed up, all hell broke loose.

She'd seen me in my shifts and my suits and my teenage clothes, although all of them were more outfits, really, than costumes. She must have known that David was trying to nurture me back to wellness, so to speak. I guess the baby duds were just too far over the top.

She stormed into David's office, and a real screaming match ensued. I listened shamelessly at the door. Rosa yelled "infantilism," and David yelled "age play" right back. Rose screamed about "manipulation," and he screamed about "unconditional love." That sounded right to me. David and I unconditionally loved each other!

I knocked at the door, but they wouldn't let me in. Rosa started yelling about "professionalism" and "decency," which was crazy, because David was without doubt the most decent man I'd ever met. He yelled back about "personality integration" and "ethics." Then Rosa called David selfish, and he didn't reply.

Not long after that, David sent me away to college. I didn't argue. I wanted to do everything I could for him, because it was obvious he was sad. I was terrified, but at the same time, I was looking forward to being with people my own age—for that matter, *being* my own age.

I studied nursing, as you know. The rest—my college friends, my work at the hospital, my love of music—the rest you know, my love. Except for this . . .

I hadn't been home in a while. I'd spent the summer working and Christmas and New Year's skiing with my gang. David and I talked all the time, of course, by e-mail and telephone.

One night on the phone he sounded weary. I realized after we hung up that he'd sounded that way for quite a while. I flew home.

David was dying, and he had been for more than a year. He'd already had surgery, chemotherapy, and radiation. He was sprouting tubes and high on morphine by the time I showed up. It was stupid of me not to figure it out earlier, but at least I figured it out in time. I wasn't angry, I just said I wished he'd told me earlier, and he said that now I'd arrived he was glad to see me, and we left it at that.

We had six wonderful weeks together. I was David's primary caregiver. I sponge-bathed him, changed his pajamas, administered his medication, took him for walks around the house, and made all his meals. He wouldn't let me spoon-feed him, but he did let me guide his wrist so that he could get the spoon to his mouth. When he stopped being able to feed himself, he stopped eating. Five days after that, he passed away in my arms. David died with dignity. That's what they always say about the dead. As a nurse, I know it's a lot easier said than done. But we pulled it off. And we were damn proud of ourselves, too. We said "I love you" and "I wuv you" back and forth, back and forth, until he didn't speak anymore, and then he didn't breathe anymore and it was over.

Please forgive my lies, Darling. Now you know why my eyes are kind and my spine is stiff and my heart is soft. How it is I can roar like a lioness and cuddle like a kitten. You know when my passion and my joy were born. You know why I am "your angel."

Now you know what I mean when I say that I love you. If you still want me, I will love you until death do us part.

Lifers

ANN REGENTIN

JIMMY REECE KEPT a bottle of ammonia on the dresser in his room, and when things got a little dicey, he'd take a good whiff of it. It helped, at least it fucked up his nose so badly that he couldn't think about anything else for a while, and when he got his breath back, he was back on planet Earth again.

He didn't know which was worse, the first day of prison or the last. Both were like walking through a door into an alien planet. Going in was scary as hell, because he knew he'd get his ass kicked and worse, but by the time he got out, he was just as scared. His family hadn't even bothered disowning him; they had simply vanished the day he was arrested. His divorce had come through while he was inside. He had a degree, but it was useless now. He had no place to go, nothing to do, and nobody waiting for him.

The Department of Corrections helped him find a job as a

janitor, a night job, and he was grateful. Very few people would hire someone like him, or rent to him either. Home was a single room in a building filled with men just as unsavory as himself. Some of them were even worse, men who had committed crimes even he thought were unspeakable, although sometimes he wondered what had stopped him from going down that road. Then again, he wasn't really a violent man. Just a sick one. A sick man with half his life ahead of him and no future.

Don't project, Jimmy, he heard his therapist say, a stern, astute man who pulled no punches. *You're not psychic. Let the future take care of itself. Take it a day at a time.*

The problem was that there was nothing in his days to take. He spent them going from one place to another, always on time, always careful, always doing what he was told, weeks drifting aimlessly into months before even he noticed. He did his job, paid his rent, went to work, went to see an occasional midnight movie, living in a world that held as little danger for him as possible. He made friends, the only friends he could make and still be honest: the other men in his building, men who were in the same boat. He cracked jokes with Anita, who owned the place and whose blunt honesty was refreshing. She didn't like what he'd done, but she could find a way to like him, to like any of the guys who didn't get in her face, and most of them didn't. They all knew it was either that place or no place. Homelessness was always right around the corner.

He went into work one night to find a woman on the crew. He didn't expect that. He knew without asking that they were all ex-cons, all on probation—that was who did those jobs, cleaning up after people were gone in places where there was little trouble to be gotten into. Her name was Darla. She looked to be in her late thirties, short and curvy with her hair dyed a bit too blonde. It clashed with her tired brown eyes. When she wasn't smoking, she was chewing gum, and the polish on her nails was chipped. He did his best to ignore her.

She did not ignore him. He liked to take his break at a table in a quiet corner of the courtyard where no one else went and he could eat in peace. She found him there one night and sat down across from him. "Got a light?" she asked.

"Yeah." He pulled out his lighter and set it on the table between them. He was no gentleman and wasn't about to start pretending. She had a sexy voice, he thought, then he wracked his brain to see exactly why he thought it was attractive. It was contralto, raspy from years of heavy smoking. Not something to be worried about.

She lit her cigarette and took a long drag. "Where are you from?" she asked.

"Livonia," he said. Once upon a time.

"You married?"

"Not anymore."

"Any kids?"

"A son." Unlike most fathers, he prayed night and day that his boy wouldn't take after him. Best that the kid forgot he had a dad. "What about you?" If she answered wrong, that would fix it right there.

"Two daughters. Court took them years ago." Voice flat; unable to care anymore, because caring didn't do a rat's ass worth of good.

"Do you miss them?" he asked. Try some salt in the wound, maybe that would make her leave.

"All the time," she said. "What about you?"

Return volley. Wrong target. "Not anymore." *Go away*, he thought. *You will anyway. Everyone always does.* He barely dared to look at her, didn't dare let himself think that underneath the exhaustion and resignation, she had been pretty once.

After work, Jimmy lay on his bed, chain-smoking and watching the sun come up. It was Saturday. No Darla for two days. That was the best news he'd had in a long time, but he still couldn't get to sleep. There was so much that he wished were different, but it was no good wishing. Wishing never got him anything. It was a long time before he stubbed out his last butt and pulled the covers over his head, trying to block out the sunlight.

Naturally, Darla was there on Monday and inclined to be social. He was resigned. If there was a devil, she was possessed by it, or maybe she was his own personal demon.

"Good weekend?" she asked.

He nodded. Actually, it had been. He'd gone to see a movie, pretended to be a normal human being for a few hours.

"Gonna ask about mine?"

"How was your weekend?" he asked, a bit sarcastically. The woman could not take hint.

"Shitty," she said. "My ex-husband showed up. Not at the house–I've got a restraining order on him–but at the grocery store. I mean, Jesus, you'd think he'd leave me alone now. He got what he wanted out of me. Why does he have to come around now and fuck everything up?"

"What happened?" he asked, curious in spite of himself. He was starting to care. Not good.

Her ex, it turned out, was a drug dealer. She loved him, would have done anything for him, even though he abused her regularly and hooked her on heroin and crack. But she stayed and did his dirty work, acted as a courier, even turned a trick or two when things were tight, and eventually she got caught with enough cocaine to put her away for a while. Because they were married, she could not be forced to testify against him, so he got off with a slap on the wrist and she ended up in prison, divorced and deprived of her parental rights. He'd heard this a thousand times from the other side, from men serving light sentences while the women they suckered did hard time. He'd hated them even as he envied them, envied their confidence, their ability to do whatever they wanted while he chased his own tail until he was too dizzy to do anything at all.

"So," she asked. "What were you in for?"

Jimmy's head dropped. The inevitable question. He'd known it was coming. He could lie, but it wouldn't help. If she spent any time around him, she'd find out. His parole was too strict, too specific. Shit! He knew the words, knew them all too well, but he couldn't say them to her.

"Oh, my God!" she said softly.

He didn't look at her.

"I sure know how to pick 'em," she said, mostly to herself. "A drug dealer and now a child molester."

Anger flared hot and sharp. "I didn't ask you to sit here," he said.

She flinched. "I'm sorry. You seemed like such a nice guy."

Yeah, well, he'd heard that before. Such a nice guy. How could he do such a thing? "You can't judge a book by its cover," he said harshly. *Go away! Just go!*

"I'm sorry," she said.

He kept his head down. *Fuck off!* he thought.

"Can I ask you something?" she said.

"I can't stop you," he said. He knew what it was, the question everyone asked him.

"Why?" she asked.

Why? All of the things that he had gone over with his therapist went through his mind: the ADHD and depression he had unknowingly struggled with all his life, his insecurity and self-loathing, his difficulties relating to women in general and his wife in particular; but none of it fully explained why, when it came down to the wire, he had turned to the nine-year-old daughter of a neighbor, a girl from a deeply troubled family who had needed someone to talk to. None of it explained why he had felt so much more comfortable with her, so much stronger and more competent. None of it explained why he took a chance without even realizing what it was, before he even knew what he was doing, when fantasy turned into reality and he became a monster.

He'd never meant to hurt her.

He was on Ritalin and Prozac now, helping him concentrate and think clearly, leveling him out considerably. Ironically, he was more functional than he'd ever been, not that it was going to do him any good. The Prozac had the added bonus of taking a bite out of his sex drive, although not as much as he'd hoped. He'd been in an inpatient treatment program, undergone intensive therapy, and he still not only had to avoid being around children, but also had to avoid the kinds of stresses that made him most likely to offend. One of those was women. Jimmy had sworn off them altogether, not that he'd held out much hope anyway. Sex offenders weren't overwhelmingly popular with the ladies, and it was just as well. It was more trouble than he needed.

The problem with Darla was that he couldn't avoid her. Children were fairly easy to dodge, especially if one were nocturnal, and he lived and worked far away from them by choice as well as by law. He was not about to tempt fate. Women, however, were fifty percent of the population. His therapist was right. He couldn't avoid them indefinitely.

Why? Should he answer her? Why not? Maybe then she'd go away. "I don't know."

"You don't know?"

"No," he said.

"That's pretty lame," she said.

He shrugged. If it had been that simple, he wouldn't have done it.

"Can you help it now?" she asked.

"Yes," he said firmly. He could. If the ammonia failed, he could call his therapist or find someone to talk to. The men in his building supported one another and watched one another like hawks; they all knew exactly what to look for. If he showed any sign of deviance, someone would report him to Anita, who would report him to his parole officer, which was enough to keep him in line right there.

"Are you sure?"

No. He'd done time, been through treatment, he took his meds like clockwork, and he still had to be his own thought police. But Christ, once a door is opened, how do you close it? He knew what was possible, what he was capable of, and nothing would ever be the same. Would he ever be able to trust himself? "I don't want to do it again." Which was only half-true. What he really wanted was to be the sort of person who didn't want to do it again.

Stripped in therapy of his delusions of consent, he considered his crime just as loathsome as everyone else did, and he fell over himself trying to avoid a second offense. The truth was, very few people were happy about being pedophiles. The hardest part was breaking through the denial, but once they got past it, most would do whatever it took to stop, even going on Lupron, which killed the sex drive altogether and had some nasty side effects. Once he accepted the reality of what he'd done, he'd wanted to kill himself, but his therapist had assured him that he had a very good chance of leading a normal life. The recidivism rate for men like him was low. He was a situational offender, not a predator: disorganized, rather than one who planned. His was a lesser offense–no violence, no penetration. He had that. At least he had that. He hadn't done worse.

Not that what he'd done was anything to brag about.

"I just don't understand why anyone would do something like that in the first place."

"I don't understand you, either," he shot back, defensive and angry. Why wouldn't she just leave him alone?

"What do you mean?" she asked.

"Your ex-husband." The anger shifted ground. "Why would you stay with a man who beat you, for Chrissake? And hooked you on drugs? Why didn't you testify against him? Legally, they couldn't make you, but you could have done it. Why didn't you? Why did you take the fall for him?"

Tears welled up in her eyes. "You don't understand," she said. "I loved him so much. He was my life."

Aw, shit! It seemed like no matter what he did or said, every interaction he had with the human race went straight down the toilet. It was a catch-22. In order to stay sane, his therapist said, he had to cultivate social contacts. The only problem was that every time he tried, something went wrong, usually badly, and it left him feeling worse than before. He'd gone through life-skills training, but he never seemed to be able to apply any of it to real life. He had ten minutes of his break to go, and a crying woman sitting across from him. Now what?

If you think you owe someone an apology, give it right away. It's easier if you do it sooner, and it can ease a lot of tension.

"Hey," he said softly. "I'm sorry."

She just sat there, curled up in a ball on her chair, sobbing into her arms. What else had his therapist told him to do? *Don't assume that you know what someone else is thinking. Repeat back what the other person has said, and make sure you have it right. Don't give your side until they know that you understand theirs.* "You're right," he said. "I don't understand." And he didn't, but he didn't always understand himself, either.

"I didn't want to love him," she sniffed. "I just couldn't help it."

He wanted to reach out, comfort her, but the last time he had done that . . . he wasn't going to think about it. No, he had to, he had to, had to make sure he stayed on the right side of the line. But that's how it had all started, with comfort and reassurance, with him telling someone she was better than she thought she was. It had been true then, and it would be true now if he said it to Darla. She had so much to give. She could do so much better.

You'll do better someday, he heard himself say in another lifetime. *It won't always be so bad.* And in the gratitude in her eyes, he had seen something else, or thought he had, wanted to, and he'd been horribly, disastrously wrong.

Darla was an adult.

You can't trust women. His father. *They're lying, sneaking bitches, and they'll rob you blind if you don't watch them every goddamn second.*

Jesus, Jimmy, you can't even do the simplest things. Why do you have to fuck up everything you touch? His wife. Or his mother, he wasn't sure which. Sometimes their voices were interchangeable.

Had it been wrong of him to want more?

That was the thing about children. You could trust them. They were kinder, more open, more loving, so beautiful . . .

No! No no no no! Ammonia. Dammit, where was the bottle when he needed it? On his dresser, of course. He put his face in his hands, inhaled hard, smelled the cleaning solutions that soaked his skin, tried to make himself feel the burn, both a distraction and a deterrent. Almost. Almost. Right. Where was he?

Darla. Back to square one. He looked at her. She, too, was fighting for control, wiping at her face with her sleeve, smearing her makeup. She was too sensitive. That was her problem. She needed to toughen up.

Let people be who they are. When you start picking away at someone, most of the time you're projecting your own self-hatred onto them. You want to change them because you want to change yourself. Start by forgiving them and see if you can forgive yourself, too. You have some serious problems, Jimmy, but other parts of you are just fine.

Right. She was sensitive, end of story. Let it go. "Are you okay?" he asked. "I'm really sorry." He reached across the table, set his hand down near her, not touching, not daring, but wanting to so much.

She covered it with hers and sniffed. "You know, you really are sweet," she said a bit ruefully. "The sweetest guy I ever met, and he turns out to be a child molester." But she did not let go of his hand. "How bad were you?"

How to answer that? "I'm a Level One," he said. Not deemed a serious danger to society, not considered likely to reoffend. Although law enforcement would keep track of him, he wouldn't end up in the public registries as long as he toed the line.

"I guess it could be worse," she sighed. She squeezed his hand.

He squeezed back, breathless. So good to touch again! Her hand was smaller than his but just as callused and work-roughened, and so warm, so alive. His face hurt before he realized that he was smiling.

Work became something to look forward to for a change, but taking it out of work was harder. Really, it was up to their parole officers. His had to do some checking, make sure that Darla really had lost her daughters, and hers had to make sure he was clean. Like him, she had to sign in and out and she had strict curfews. Bring Cinderella in late and the coach turned into a paddywagon. Neither of them had a place of their own.

But when the time came, there were other places. The hotel wasn't great, but it was the best he could afford. They couldn't spend the night there, but they could have the afternoon. No wine. She couldn't go near the stuff. Flowers, though–roses, something to tell her she was special.

"Oh, Jimmy!" She threw her arms around him and he heard her sniffling into his neck. Darla, it turned out, cried when she was sad, happy, frightened, or angry; in other words, at the drop of a hat. It had driven him nuts at first.

Just let her cry. You don't have to do anything about it. Be responsible for yourself, don't take responsibility for her.

It was surprisingly good advice.

So he just held her, and after a minute she calmed. "They're so beautiful," she whispered in his ear.

He squeezed her tighter and kissed her.

She tasted of cigarettes and peppermint as she always did, but still this kiss was different. Her body melted into his, her bones dissolving into a soft, languid drape. There was no one watching through a window, no minutes to count, just the two of them and the whole afternoon. He started to panic. He was on Prozac. What if he couldn't function?

Take it a step at a time, Jimmy. His therapist's smooth voice in his head steadied him.

Luckily, his body was a few steps ahead of his brain. He was hard, good God, yes, he was hard. Darla had dressed up for him in something stretchy, and he dug his fingers in, feeling it cling and pull against her skin. Her heels put her almost at his eye level, which made it easy to kiss his way down her neck, lingering at the collarbone her ex-husband had broken, kissing the old hurt away as if she were a . . .

No! Fuck! He was still for a moment, his mouth resting on her neck, wishing for the bottle on his dresser. He inhaled instinctively, smelling her perfume.

There are similarities between how lovers interact and how adults interact with children. Don't be surprised if they scare you a bit. You've broken some boundaries, and you're going to have to work to put them back together again.

Right. Could he let himself enjoy this, or was he crossing the line?

Keep your mind on your partner and you should be okay. As long as you're thinking about her, you're safe.

Not difficult. Darla burned through him like a brush fire. She was not still, her hands slid over his chest and shoulders, up into his hair, and her body arched into his. He responded instinctively, pulling her even closer, kissing again, back up her neck to her mouth. Only one sensible place to take this: bed.

Her dress came off over her head in one smooth pull, and underneath she wore black, delicious against her olive skin. Her breasts were small, with dark nipples peeking through the lace. He pushed the fabric out of the way, not thinking, just a blind need to suck, and she moaned and snapped open the clasp of her bra as he worked her nipple with his tongue. Her fingers fumbled with his shirt buttons, and he let go of her just long enough to shed his own clothing, then lay back down beside her, bare skin to bare skin. How long? Too damned long, too many barren years. He pulled her close, wrapped one leg over hers, felt her moving against him, ran his hand over the curve of her ass, felt his calluses catch on the lace. Pretty panties, but it was time for them to come off now, he wanted more skin. She wore no stockings or pantyhose, because she didn't need them. She still had fantastic legs.

So she shed her last scraps of seduction and rolled on top of him, hugging him hard and then leaning up, sandwiching his cock between their bellies. It felt so good that he started to laugh, and she joined him, echoing his giddy joy. He ran his hands down her back, all the way to where her legs parted around his, his fingertips lingering just inside her thighs. Oh, she was marvelous, and he couldn't believe she was here with him, couldn't believe she really wanted him. He tipped her back onto her side, cradled her head on his arm, and covered her breast with his hand, her nipple like a pebble in the center of his palm. Her fingers played in the hair on his chest, her fingernails grazing his nipples, making him groan as she tangled her legs in his. Then her hand slipped down over his belly and wrapped around his cock.

Cold fear drenched him, making him think for a minute that he'd lose his erection. He'd never been good at this, never quite at ease with it except once, and he was keeping his mind as far away from that as possible. Darla. Safe in one way, dangerous in another.

Oh, God, Jimmy, you're useless! His wife. He had never been able to figure out what she needed, never been able to please her.

No matter what your penis does, you can still satisfy her. His therapist.

How? Jimmy's whole body had burned with shame.

His therapist had scribbled a few titles on a piece of paper and told him to go to the library.

He hadn't checked them out. Not with a woman at the counter, although a man wouldn't have been an improvement, to his mind.

When it came to what people thought of him, Jimmy had always tended to imagine the worst. After his arrest, the problem started gobbling steroids, to the point where he preferred not to deal with people at all. Anyway, he couldn't bring books like that home, not to a building inhabited by thirty-odd sex offenders of various stripes. Nothing explicit could cross the threshold. So he found the quietest corner he could and read, torn between embarrassment, fascination, and arousal.

I don't know if I can go down on her, he'd said the following week.

You don't have to. Stay within your comfort zone, especially the first time.

How do I find her . . . ?

Clitoris? His therapist made the word sound normal somehow. *Ask her. Chances are good she knows exactly where it is. She can show you.*

I can't ask her. She'll think I'm an idiot.

You're projecting again, Jimmy. You can't know what she'll think. I know it feels awkward to you now, but there are some approaches you can take to make it feel more natural. Communication is even more important in bed than out.

Communication was not his strong suit.

Jimmy rested his hand between her legs, feeling her pubic hair against his palm and sinking his fingers into a wonderland of soft wet. It made them both sigh, and her hand tightened on his shaft. He felt around in her slippery, swollen folds, looking for something, anything, that might be a clitoris, but there was a huge difference between a picture and a live woman, and one thing just seemed to flow into another until it all became cunt. The sounds she made were encouraging, but after a minute he realized it was hopeless. He had to ask. Fuck. He buried his face in her neck, hiding his fear and hiding from it. Deep breath.

"Show me what you like best." If he hadn't been whispering, his voice would have cracked.

She said nothing, lay still for so long that he wondered if she'd heard him at all, then she rolled to her back, one leg at an angle, and covered his hand with hers, cautiously, tentatively, and he wondered if she'd ever been asked before. He still didn't dare look at her, but he kissed her neck, unable to speak, trying to encourage her, hoping she wasn't angry, and her fingers guided his, up a bit, farther than he would have thought. Yes, there seemed to be a particular spot she wanted touched, a bump or something under sliding skin, and she liked tiny strokes just above it.

When you find it, be very gentle. It's incredibly sensitive. And remember that a change in pressure or rhythm will throw her off, just like it throws you off when you're masturbating. Stay as steady as you can, and don't be surprised if it takes a while. Women warm up a bit slower than men do, but it doesn't mean she won't get there. Be patient.

But she kept her hand over his, and that made it easier, they were both gaining confidence. She was making tiny, anxious noises, and he lifted his head finally, looked down at her, and found her eyes closed and her face flushed. Her breath caught, then she tensed, a thin, high wail escaping from her throat. Was this it? Her body arched against his hand, her legs were rigid as steel, her eyes flew open, and in them was a familiar ecstatic panic. He'd done it. He'd actually done it. He'd made her come. It was breathtaking, achingly beautiful.

Then it was over, and she let go of his hand and pulled him down hard, wrapping her legs around him, murmuring happy thanks, kissing him wildly, and it took an effort of will to untangle himself long enough to find and put on the condom. *They're not optional, Jimmy.* In the wake of her orgasm, she was like velvet soaked in thick cream, sinking into her was unbearable bliss. He tried to go slow, but she dug her nails into his ass, pulling him in hard, and he let himself get lost in it, in the friction and in the woman who writhed beneath him, her low, sweet voice filling his ears. Knowing his meds, he wondered if he'd be able to come at all, but orgasm became possible, then inevitable, and he pressed his forehead to hers, anchoring himself as she took him in as deep as he could go, holding his shuddering body in the cradle of her thighs.

Afterward, he lay holding her as they shared a cigarette, gazing out the window through the cheap blinds as she ran her hand idly over his chest. In a while, he'd take her back to her halfway house and he'd go home to his leper colony, back to the real world. He kissed her hair and she snuggled closer.

He was a child molester, and she was a professional doormat with old needle tracks on her arms and between her toes. He may have done his time, but in truth, his crime always carried a life sentence whether he served it behind bars or not. He would never pay his debt to society. She had, but then again, she'd lost her children, a life sentence of its own.

He pulled her up and she looked at him, wondering, drawing hard on the cigarette and inhaling up toward the ceiling. He ran his hands through her hair; at her scalp was about half an inch of dark brown, her natural color. If he asked, she'd probably let it grow back.

Take her as she is, or let her go.

Right. He was what he was and she was what she was, but their sentences might be easier if they served them together, at least for a while.

Birthday Suit

FLORENCE HOARD

HE CHECKED INTO the resort at Mystic Beach just as the chaises began getting scarce, about 9:00 A.M. Already, the sun asserted itself on the horizon, warning the bronzed bodies what was in store for them.

Nude beaches were not new to him. His family had spent their summers at Cap d'Agde, where he matured among naked bodies of all shapes, sizes, ages, and muscle tone. He was grateful for the early exposure, for it enabled him to grow up with no inhibitions about his own body and no fears about women's.

He slipped out of his clothing quickly and headed for the bright expanse of sand. Even at fifty, his six-foot frame and seven-inch penis turned heads. He kept himself firm and tan, and knew that his lustrous, full head of dark brown hair didn't hurt, either.

He took the first available lounge, nodding to the man next to him. "*Bonjour,*" he said politely.

“Hi, there,” the older man said. “I’m Bill.”

“Jacques,” he replied, leaning toward the man to extend his hand. “*Enchanté*.”

The older man’s pubic hair had been shaved, revealing a smooth groin and sleek balls. His cock was an average size and certainly seemed to loll happily in the warm sunshine. The French would have called Bill *sympathique*. Basically, a nice guy.

Jacques settled into his lounge, enjoying the warmth from the sky as it soothed his grateful body. He wore darker sunglasses than Bill—no eye contact was made between the men, but an easy silence transcended as Jacques stretched his long legs out before him. He felt Bill’s eyes assess his soft but sizable package and smiled to himself. Men never ceased to find the comparison of their genitals a highly engaging activity.

He let him look, completely unthreatened by the man’s gaze. He was accustomed to being watched but spent little time watching others. Why watch when there was so much to do?

“You’re here with French Telecom, I guess,” Bill ventured.

“Yes. French Telecom. Just for today,” Jacques replied without turning to his neighbor.

“Good, good. What studio are you in?”

Americans. So inquisitive. “Fourteen,” he said.

“Oh! Here comes my wife.”

Jacques glanced in the same direction as Bill and one eyebrow shot up involuntarily. Ever since Jacques was an adolescent, his eyebrows usually went up just before his cock did. He sometimes wondered if they didn’t actually cue it somehow.

The woman appeared to be considerably younger than her husband; Jacques guessed around fifty. Her body, a study in controlled voluptuousness, instantly triggered the circuitry between his legs. Her skin dripped with salt water and glowed with health.

"The water is fantastic!" She exclaimed, eyes ablaze with life. Her breasts were full and remarkably high, with pretty pink nipples that reveled in their freedom. She looked ripe and succulent, as if she'd ooze sweetness if he bit into her. And he did want to bite into her.

"You look very refreshed," he heard himself say.

His words forced her to look at him, and as she did, Bill stepped in with introductions.

"Lillian, this is Jacques. He's with French Telecom, working on that project near the aqueduct. Jacques, my wife, Lillian."

Now her eyes danced. She did not hesitate to take his outstretched hand. Her grip communicated as much as her eyes. This was not a shy woman.

"Hello," she said. "And yes, I am refreshed." A sly smile crept across her face. No matter what this woman said, it would sound sexual–and he liked that very much.

A subtle breeze swirled itself around his stirring cock, as if to announce his imminent erection. His sense of decorum would not allow him to get hard for a woman in front of her husband, so he abruptly but politely got to his feet.

"I think I'll enjoy some of that refreshment myself," he explained, and headed quickly toward the sparkling waves.

He'd seen her eyes linger on his swelling cock. She probably knew that his escape to the ocean was an excuse to hide his arousal, but what of it? If there was one thing he'd learned about women, they liked a long, slow flirtation. She saw what he had. Now he had to make her wait for it.

As he floated in the cool water, he imagined how her eager pussy had already begun to cream with anticipation. She'd be talking to Bill right now, but her cunt would be thinking about being fed by this mysterious, foreign stranger. He had to confess that he liked the waiting, too. The delayed gratification that resulted in rock-hard cock and drenched pussy, the prolonged explosion of fantasy into reality. With the right woman, the process was unforgettable. Older women knew how to pace themselves without holding back passion. As he swam, his penis thickened with every stroke. When he was ready to come out, he forced himself to wait a little longer, secure in the knowledge that the more time he took to return to his lounge chair, the hungrier she'd be. Few things turned him on more than a hungry woman.

Finally, he emerged from the sea with his semi-erection leading the way. As he walked toward the couple, his rod swayed, lightly slapping one thigh and then the other. The subtle friction merely served to harden him further. By the time he was close enough to Bill and Lillian for them to recognize him, his seven inches of manhood had puffed up to eight.

Lillian didn't even pretend to look anywhere but his crotch. Bill looked on with bemusement and a thinly veiled awe. Jacques found himself developing a certain manly respect for the guy. There weren't many husbands, especially American ones, who would be secure enough in their masculinity to allow their wives to enjoy the sight of another man's goods, let alone the possibility of what those goods could deliver.

Jacques prepared himself for some awkwardness. He was clearly hot for Lillian, and Lillian hardly seemed opposed to the idea of him, but there was the complication of her husband. Jacques decided to let Bill determine the course of the action.

"Welcome back, Jacques. I see the water is fine. Think I'll jump in for a bit myself." And he ambled away toward the shore.

"Your husband is a brave man," Jacques commented behind his dark glasses as he made himself comfortable in his lounge chair.

"Brave? Why? Are there sharks in the water?" She chuckled at her own wit.

"No, but there are a few here on the sand." He would have winked if it weren't for the glasses.

"Is that supposed to scare me?" Her smile was constant now. Their sexual swords had been drawn and the battle of innuendo begun.

He laughed. "When was the last time you were scared? I cannot picture it."

"It's rare," she confessed. While he'd been swimming, she repositioned her lounge so it sat at an angle, half facing the water, half facing him. As she opened her legs ever so slightly, he understood her motivation for the new arrangement. Like her husband, her privates were completely free of hair. Even without the gap that now existed between her thighs, the folds of her labia and the curves of her mons were obvious and more than a little beckoning. With her knees apart, the smaller pink and pinched folds were on display. He looked but did not linger long enough to be accused of ogling, even though that's what she wanted him to do.

"Are you and your husband here for a while?"

"We spend a few weekends here every summer, and we also try to squeeze in a full week or more as time allows. How long are you here?" The question had none of the coy pseudo-innocence it might have had from a younger woman's lips. Her directness captivated him.

"I fly back to France tomorrow."

She grinned. "So much to do, so little time."

"*C'est vrai.*" He grinned back, still under cover of his Polaroid lenses. He watched her search his face for clues that only his eyes could give.

"And yet you picked a good day to be here."

"Oh? I think any day seeing you would be a good day."

An uncertain breeze tousled Lillian's light brown hair slightly. The ocean was reflected in her eyes as she smiled with the right side of her mouth. She drew her knees up to her chin and hugged them, still keeping her smooth pussy lips in clear view–in fact, in better view, now that they were framed by her thighs.

"You know, most women say they don't trust charming men, but personally, I think they're fun. What I meant about this being a good day was that it's my birthday."

"*Mais, non!*"

"*Mais, oui!*" She laughed. "Bill has promised me that anything goes today. Whatever I want." Her eyes penetrated him without wavering.

"And have you decided what you want?" He was hard now and let his erection speak for itself. It rose to signal her, but she'd long ago established communication with it. Now she assessed it as if she knew that she was responsible for its growth.

"Yes, I think I have."

"Will your husband let you have it?"

"He said 'anything goes,'" she repeated.

The juice between her legs sparkled on her swollen cunt. He knew she was close to dripping on her lounge chair and considered just reaching over to that moist little furnace to sample her. Instead, he stayed inscrutable behind his sunglasses. To what lengths might he get her to go by playing hard to get?

The specter of Bill, ghostlike moments ago, now became a more tangible threat as he walked toward them from the water.

His slightly shrunken penis bobbed happily with every step, and his eyes sparkled nearly as much as Lillian's.

"I think there's something special in the water here," he grinned as he toweled off the sea from his body.

"I was just telling Jacques that today is my birthday," Lillian smiled.

"Indeed it is!" Bill agreed as he dropped into his lounge chair.

"And I was also telling him that you said I could have anything I wanted today."

"As you can year-round, my dear," he said, taking his wife's hand and giving it a squeeze.

"See? I told you." Lillian winked at Jacques.

"I never doubted you," Jacques chuckled. "I believe you also said you knew what you wanted." If she was going to flirt, he'd give her a challenge.

"Yes. I want Bill to oil me up, right here and now."

Sly woman.

"Well, that can be arranged," Bill said, getting up from his chair in search of the suntan oil. Meanwhile, Lillian lowered the back of her lounge and gracefully flipped over onto her front. Her beautiful ass curved deliciously upward, full and wantonly exposed for both men to view.

Bill stood over her now, looking mischievously from his wife to the Frenchman. He winked at Jacques conspiratorially. "You know you *really* want your front oiled, Lillian. I know you."

As she laughed, the muscles in her back contracted and relaxed with an ease Jacques found compelling. "Humor me. Start with my back and we'll work our way to the front."

Bill held the bottle several inches from the middle of her shoulder blades and carefully poured a thin stream of oil along her spine. The liquid snaked along her skin like an eager tongue, lingering in some spots, gliding over others, happy to be everywhere. She groaned when Bill's hands touched her skin.

"Oh, that's good," she moaned. She had turned her face away from Jacques so he couldn't see it.

What a fascinating connection she and Bill clearly had. As his hands massaged oil in and worked tension out, a brief silence descended that felt like theirs and theirs alone. Jacques dared not speak as Bill's palms communicated with Lillian's skin. The air around the three of them thickened with mystical overtones. Then he looked down and realized that the only real thickness was between his legs. He was hard now, harder than he'd been in weeks. So hard he could think of nothing pithy to say to break the awkward moment.

She turned her face toward Jacques but kept her eyes closed. "Bill, honey, my gluteus maximus is aching. Work a little magic on me, would you? You know what to do."

Bill positioned his hands where cheek melded with thigh and pushed upward with slow, sensual stealth. Her fleshy mounds yielded only slightly to his touch—they stayed firm but pliant enough for Jacques to wish passionately that he could trade places with Bill.

Lillian separated her legs slightly and opened her eyes. Looking directly at Jacques, she spoke to her husband. "Some oil has snuck in between my legs. I've always heard that oil and feminine juices don't mix well. You should probably lick it up," she advised, smiling.

Jacques stared as Bill bent to place his face between her ass cheeks. Dutifully, he licked.

Jacques looked around, to be sure that nobody objected to their little display. In France this would have been no problem, but he knew Americans were not known for their sexual tolerance. Fucking was great for them but sinful for others. At the moment, none of the other guests seemed to notice.

"I hope you don't mind," Lillian teased. She'd drawn up her arms so they framed her face, exposing the sides of her ample titties. "We've tried using towels, but nothing seems to clean like Bill's tongue," she giggled.

"I don't mind at all," Jacques commented. "I'm a little concerned for your neighbors, though. They may want to join in!"

"But I only have eyes for you," she winked.

Bill continued to lap away at her butt cleavage. Jacques waited to see what she'd do next.

"What do you think, Jacques? Am I done on this side?"

"Only you know your own body, *madame*."

"I know my body quite well, *monsieur*. I've gotten to know it intimately over the years, in fact. Bill knows my body pretty well, too, but that doesn't mean someone new couldn't teach me a few new things about it." She turned over on her back as Bill watched, grinning. The oil greased her movements.

"I'm harder to handle when I'm slippery," she added. The delight on her face at catching a glimpse of Jacques' erection was obvious. "And I see you're just harder when I'm slippery." Smiling at her husband, she directed her next comments to him. "Work my front, honey pie. Show the man how it's done."

Bill was at full tilt as well, Jacques noted as the man repositioned himself to fulfill his wife's latest request. The man's smooth balls gleamed from being so taut and covered with oil. Jacques had been so enthralled with watching Lillian, he hadn't noticed that Bill had indulged himself in a bit of the oil, too. He bent over his wife now, cock and balls hovering near her face as he leaned forward to focus attention on her breasts.

Jacques said nothing as he watched Lillian's beautifully tan and firm breasts being squeezed, kneaded, grabbed, and manhandled by Bill. Jacques made a conscious effort not to touch himself.

The oil gleamed seductively on her soft curves, beckoning to him. Bill had moved his ministrations to her shapely hips now. He stroked her lovingly from her thighs to her pretty bald beaver, and the couple seemed unaware of anyone but each other. Could Lillian so easily bounce between flirting with him and enjoying her husband? Of course she could–that's what made her so appealing.

As Bill massaged her toes and the mood lightened enough to allow conversation again, Bill announced he was going to Pedro's to pick up some ribs for lunch.

"All right, sweetheart. I think I'll just go back to the studio and shower off some of this sand. You'll keep me company, won't you, Jacques?" She sat up in her lounge now, glistening with oil, her feet on the beach sand, legs together. If he didn't know better, he'd say she looked downright demure. "I'll open a bottle of wine if you stay here."

Jacques looked to Bill cautiously to discern the correct course of action. One had to tread so delicately in these matters . . . But Bill nodded enthusiastically, eyebrows raised as if to add an exclamation point to his encouragement. Leaving his wife alone with the Frenchman seemed part of his plan.

And so Jacques followed behind the voluptuous beauty as she led the way to the studio. She swung her ample hips with the carefree, lascivious air of a woman who knows she's transferred a man's brain directly into his penis. Her firm ass cheeks had become so much a part of his fantasies now that he could almost taste them.

She sauntered up to the outside shower at the back of the studio, wordlessly beginning her shower. He removed his sunglasses and set them down on the small table. Running her hands along the slope of her waist, her eyes met his in sexual challenge. She did not invite him to join her with words, but her gaze lured him with unstoppable determination.

"May I join you?" He asked, mostly to be polite. His cock was doing the thinking for him now, so no matter what her response, he would have proceeded into the refreshing spray until he was close enough to touch her, just as he did now.

The cool water did nothing to squelch the sizzle between them. Her nipples, hard and pink under his wandering fingers, acted as barometers of her lust. When he kissed her mouth, her soft lips kissed him back. Suddenly, though, she stepped away from the shower, leaving him standing there alone.

"I just needed to rinse the sand off. I'll go get the wine now."

Her eyes sparkled and his erection bobbed with frustration. Rather than watch her distracting curves sashay into the studio, he shut his eyes and tried to get the water as cold as possible. There was no adjustment, though, so he remained under a steady cascade of tepid water. He would play her game, but he didn't like the idea that they had only as much time as it would take Bill to go to Pedro's. He wanted to enjoy Lillian now, rather than later, and wasn't sure whether Bill would take kindly to seeing his wife reamed by a visiting Frenchman. He did his best to summon up his Parisian laissez-faire attitude, vowing to leave things to fate, which had always served him well in the past.

The shower had no discernable effect on his raging hard-on, so he sat at the small round table near the shower and waited. Stroking himself as an interim measure occurred to him, but he dismissed it as amateur, unsophisticated behavior. When his cock got friction, it would be from that beautiful woman's wet pussy.

"Here we are," sang Lillian as she emerged from the studio. A bottle of wine and two glasses sat on the small tray she carried. "I've been saving this bottle for a special occasion."

"I'm flattered you feel this is it," he smiled.

"I think my birthday qualifies as a special occasion, don't you?" She stared at him, eyes ignited with mischief. "What shall we drink to?" She asked as she poured the wine. Normally, he would have intervened–a woman should never pour when a man is there to do it for her–but she seemed to have things well under control. Her control.

"Well, *madame*, we could toast to Mystic Beach, birthdays, French Telecom, or the beauty of the feminine form. I have fond feelings for all of them."

"I'd like to drink to handsome men with incredibly large cocks. How do you say that in French?"

"Like this," he said, leaning forward and making contact with her mouth before she could protest. She was warm, soft, fiery in spirit.

Her free hand wandered downward between his legs, seeking out the smooth heat of his shaft. She looped her index finger around his girth and brought her thumb around to close the gap. And then she stroked. Long, slow, perfectly timed sweeps upward then down, stopping short of his mushroom head on the way up and traveling all the way down to his dark brown pubes. His body trembled.

He couldn't reach her pussy amid the jumble of arms and wine glasses, so he put his glass down as he continued to gently tongue-wrestle with her. She emanated more heat when he tickled her shaved mons, and by the time he burrowed between her thighs to access her moist sweetness, their tongues were practically down each other's throats.

She broke free of the kiss first. Not abruptly, but firmly nonetheless. "You know, in this country, a woman with a birthday gets to make requests all day."

"Is that true?"

"Oh, yes," she whispered, smiling a crooked smile. "I ask you now to step inside so that you may ravish me."

He laughed in spite of himself. "Why do I get the distinct impression that I'm the one who will be ravished?"

"Scared?"

"Is this the erection of a frightened man?" He asked, directing both their attention to the rock-hard enormity in his lap.

She stood, took him by the hand, and led him into the studio through the sliding glass doors. The bed loomed, a wide expanse of white among small, simple wooden furniture. Though the room looked much like his own, its appeal was double–nay, triple–his.

Was it she who guided him on top of her, or had he placed himself into that dominant position? Regardless, he now looked down on her as she lay on her back, expectant and ready.

His cock had a purpose, a driving purpose in fact, but his mind wanted to explore Lillian more slowly. He wanted to play this woman as a musician plays an instrument, caressing her body for optimum performance, coaxing heights of excellence from it that only pure appreciation could evoke.

He put his lips to one large nipple and licked reverently while he listened to her gasp. Her sounds encouraged him to slip his other hand into her steamy folds, fondling and stroking until her cream coated his fingers.

"Luscious, luscious woman," he mumbled between laps at her breast. He squeezed her gently, enjoying the fullness in his hands.

Her fire was unrestrained now and her coquettish side had disappeared. Only her womanly essence was with him in the room at this moment, surrendering to her desires and stoking his. She spread her legs wide for him and he immediately slipped one, then two, then three fingers into her dripping wet hole. As he slid his digits in and out of her, he frigged her clit with his thumb. He was surprised by how large it became at his touch, and how sensitive it was. She writhed with happiness and rocked her hips in tandem with his thrusts to send him deeper inside her.

Her hands were not idle. They'd found his pulsing cock and pumped it in exactly the right rhythm. He could always tell when a woman simply went through the motions of playing with cock as opposed to thoroughly enjoying doing so. Lillian was of the latter variety, as obsessed with stroking him as he was with stroking her. Her enjoyment of his equipment turned him on even more. He could actually feel her swelling under his fingers and gushing into his hand.

"I have another request," she whispered.

"*Oui, madame. Quelque chose que vous voulez.*"

"What?"

"Whatever you want," he grinned. He was so lost in the moment, he'd retreated to his native language.

"I want you to fuck me. Slide that beautiful piece of meat inside me. I haven't been able to think about anything else since I saw you this morning."

"I'm afraid I cannot do that, *madame.*"

Her eyes opened wide in guileless wonder. "Why not?"

"Because my desire to eat you is greater than your desire to be fucked."

Her worried face relaxed into a knowing smile. "Well, then, by all means, eat my pussy."

He kissed his way down her body, from breastbone to navel, then slowed his pace as he approached her hairless mound. Her hands went to his head, where she grabbed handfuls of his hair. Her scent hardened him more and made him slightly dizzy. He couldn't recall ever wanting a woman so badly.

She tasted of salt air and fresh breezes but also of rich, spicy femininity. As his tongue played at her engorged clit, her juices dripped into his mouth, and he closed his eyes to keep from swooning. She spread herself wide for him, and as she did, her labia parted to expose every glistening pink part of her. Her clit grew larger as he licked it.

Her entire body stiffened and arched as she pulled more urgently at his hair. When she came, her shouts filled the room. She undulated and bucked as he continued to lick her, pushing her over the edge of whatever precipice she called pleasure.

"Now!" she cried. "Fuck me now!"

His only thought now was to please her. With his cock past the point of containment, he mounted her and gasped at the heat that suddenly surrounded his steely rod. Not only was Lillian the juiciest woman he'd ever experienced, she was also the steamiest. Any hotter and he might have felt pain.

He could not postpone his release as he could with other women. Looking at her now, with her pretty face in a kind of possessed state of transcendence, and feeling her tight cunt pull and squeeze his cock as if to milk the come right out of him, he surrendered to her, shouting nearly as loudly as she did as he filled her with thick, gooey fluid.

A slight movement in the corner of the room made him turn his head. The sight of Bill standing there, mouth agape, froze Jacques. Lillian, however, seemed undisturbed by his sudden and unannounced arrival.

"Hi, there." She smiled at her husband.

"Hi, yourself. You just couldn't wait, could you?"

Jacques did not, could not, breathe. In his elevated state of arousal, perhaps he had used bad judgment. Perhaps he should have waited to see what Bill preferred. He'd tried to read him, but maybe his lust clouded his judgment. He waited for Bill's next move, ready to apologize or flee, whichever seemed most expedient.

"No, baby, I couldn't wait. You saw the member on Jacques. Did you think I wouldn't want it as soon as I could get it?"

Bill smirked. "No, I knew you'd do this. It's what I hoped you'd do," he said, placing the bag of ribs on the coffee table. "Why would I get you a birthday present you wouldn't enjoy?"

Lillian looked from Bill to Jacques and back again. Jacques was relieved to have the plan exposed but wasn't sure how Lillian would react, now that she knew he'd been hired to please her.

"You mean you're a gigolo?"

"Well, not technically. A gigolo is more of a full-time job."

"Are you French, at least?"

"*Oui, madame. Je suis Français.*" He smiled. "But I am something else, as well."

"And what's that?"

"Very, very hot for you. You are an incredibly sexy woman. When Bill hired me, he said I should only do what felt right. Once I saw you, there was no question about what was going to feel right." He moved his hand to her still gushing pussy and stroked her swollen lips. She kissed his forehead.

Bill approached the bed, sturdy erection in hand. "I'd love to see Jacques fuck you from behind," he suggested.

"Mmmm, good idea," Lillian agreed. "And I can suck your cock while he rams me."

And so they assumed their positions. Lillian's cunt, a heady blend of scents from then and now, accepted Jacques' cock easily. The fact that he remained hard even after his orgasm of just minutes before was a testament to his rampant hunger for her. As he pumped her, he watched with fascination as her womanly ass cheeks jiggled provocatively. She even pushed up against him in time with his thrusts to force him deeper into her pussy. He found he could hold himself back somewhat more easily now that his first eruption had passed. So he watched her suck off her husband.

What a gift she had for knowing what a penis needed! As he followed the movements of her tongue around Bill's grateful cock, that cock became his own. He imagined his own meat stuffed far down her throat as her tongue swirled around it, tickling the underside of his knob and stroking the sensitive patch right near his come hole. The longer he watched, the harder he got.

Just as he was ready to let another load go inside her, the walls of her hot pussy clutched him. Bill's cock muffled her shouts, but she didn't let that impair her enjoyment. She ground her ass wildly up and back toward Jacques and made Bill's cock completely disappear down her throat.

Bill signaled Jacques to pull out. Confused but mindful of his role, Jacques obeyed. Bill held his tumescent, nearly purple member in one hand and Jacques did the same.

"Roll over, Lillian. We want to give you something," Bill

instructed.

Lillian turned over onto her back, and the moment she did, both men sprayed her face and torso with thick ropes of jizz. She looked like an X-rated Jackson Pollock painting.

"Mmmm," she said, rubbing the streams of come into her skin. "That was fantastic. I may never bathe again," she laughed. Jacques couldn't resist helping her massage the organic fluid into her supple skin.

"Good sex always gives me an appetite," Bill commented. "Ribs anyone?"

I intend to apply my whip to those luscious breasts of hers, gleaming and still unmarked in the light of the candles. Instead, I find myself kissing her, sharing the funky flavors that I just sampled from her butt hole. She opens to me, not only her mouth but her whole self, allowing me to feast upon her until I am sated. She keeps nothing back.

Candlelight and kisses. I may be a nasty old Dom, but I'm still an incurable romantic.

It's true that I've never known surrender as complete as what Ilsa offers. I find it a bit scary. She tells me that she will do anything for me, and I almost believe her. I'm sure that she has limits; everyone has limits, that's SM 101. But I haven't found them yet.

I've used paddles and floggers of every description, clamps and clothespins, electricity and chili oil. I've staked her out, naked and in full view of the world, on the balcony of my condo in January. This is in Minnesota, remember. After ten minutes, her ivory skin turned blue. She never complained, never used her safe word. I hastened to bring her inside, wrap her in blankets, and feed her hot tea and brandy. The clear light of adoration in her eyes never wavered. I was the one who felt chastened.

I've shared her at play parties, watching as my friends buggered and beat her. Afterward, she was more tender and attentive than ever. I'll never forget the night that I invited two rising stars in our community, Master Shark and Mistress Valentine, to come over and try her. They were far rougher on her than I could ever be. After an enema and a caning, being fisted by Shark and pissed on by Valentine, she was bruised and exhausted, but apparently in a state of bliss.

"You know you could always stop them, Ilsa," I told her later. "They know your safe word, and they would honor it."

"But Master," she murmured dreamily, on the edge of consciousness. "I wanted to please you."

She does please me, of course. Sometimes I can't believe my good fortune, to have won the devotion of this angel/slave when she could have chosen a younger, more handsome, more energetic Dom.

Often, though, I realize that there is something wrong in our relationship, something missing. Thinking about her brings on an unpleasant anxiety, vague but annoying.

I'm thinking about her now, as I sit sipping Starbucks cappuccino and trying to read Murakami. Could any person truly be so pliant and submissive? What kind of childhood did she have, to make her this way? When I asked, she told me that her upbringing had been "normal," unexceptional. Did I believe her? Why would she choose a master so much older than herself? Old enough to be her father? There must be some secret here, some story she won't, or perhaps can't, share, even with me.

All at once, my thoughts are rudely interrupted. Something slams into my chair from behind. My coffee leaps out of the cup and onto my lap. My cock is scalded, even through my trousers and undershorts. Anger rises in me as I turn to confront the culprit.

"What do you think you're doing? You should be more careful!" I don't need to shout. My voice naturally carries the authority of long years of dominance.

"Oh, I'm so sorry!" My first impressions are youth, plumpness, a certain disheveled quality that is not entirely unappealing. "Are you hurt?" The young woman notices the coffee stain spreading over my crotch. "Oh, dear! I am really such a klutz!"

an idea; I can literally see it light up her face. "Speaking of apartments, why don't you come over to mine for dinner some time soon?" She places her hand casually on my thigh. "I'm an excellent cook; all my friends say so."

She can see my hesitation. She turns up the pressure. "Please, Riordan, let me make up for my clumsiness by cooking you a nice dinner. How about tomorrow night?"

It's strange to have a woman call me by name instead of "Master." Once again I have a sense of disorientation. I know I should refuse, for my own sake as well as for Ilsa's. But somehow, I can't. Or at least, I don't.

"All right. What time?"

"How about seven?" She tears a sheet out of her notebook and scribbles something in a round, flowing script. "Here's my address and phone number."

"Uh, thanks." Where did my usual eloquence go?

Kate glances at her watch and stands up so suddenly that she nearly overturns her own coffee. "Oh, god, I've got to go! I'm really late. Is there anything you don't eat?"

I shake my head, speechless in the face of her energy.

"Great! Well, I'll see you tomorrow, then." She grabs my hand and squeezes it enthusiastically. "Thanks for being such a good sport, Riordan."

My hand and my cock are both throbbing in the wake of her whirlwind departure. I'm puzzled by my own reactions. My well-honed instincts tell me that Kate has no interest in kinky games. She's young, fresh, horny, and one hundred percent vanilla. Whereas I have had dominant fantasies since I was in grade school. I really can't understand why the prospect of ordinary, unadorned sex, without any paraphernalia or power exchange, suddenly seems so intoxicating.

Ilsa is waiting for me at the door when I return home. She is completely charming in her French maid costume: translucent black organdy top, frilly lace apron, and bare buttocks. And her collar, of course.

"Good evening, Master. Would you like a cocktail before dinner?"

"Scotch on the rocks. Please." I feel awkward with my sweet slave, in the aftermath of my encounter with Kate. "But I think we will go out for dinner tonight. Wear the green silk sheath. Without any underwear."

"Of course." Ilsa is trying to smother her smile and remain serious and respectful. She loves it when I take her out and show her off. She is already imagining the clinging softness of the silk against her bare skin.

The sting of my palm on her exposed behind brings her out of her reverie. "What about my drink, slave? Do I have to teach you how to provide such a simple service?"

"No, of course not, Master. Right away, sir."

She hurries off, swaying on her spike heels. I admire the reddening image of my hand on her white flesh as she disappears into the kitchen. Perfection indeed.

The next evening, I chain Ilsa to the foot of our bed. "I have to go out," I tell her, as I hand her the water bottle and the chamber pot. "I have some business. I may be quite late."

Why am I lying to her? We both know that I am the Master. I am free to do as I wish. She has chosen to accept that. If I want to see another woman, isn't that my prerogative?

I realize that if I were going to a play party tonight, or to help break in another Dom's slave, I'd be telling Ilsa the truth.

I have no illusions about tonight's dinner engagement. I can see very clearly what Kate wants, could see it long before she opens the door, wearing a tight red jersey dress that showcases her ample cleavage and plump, freckled thighs.

We don't even get past the second glass of wine. With dizzying speed, Kate propels me into her bedroom and sucks me into a hot, wet kiss. She tears off my clothes with such abandon that I worry, briefly, about damage. Then she sits me on the bed and does a slow, delicious striptease in front of me.

She slips one strap off her shoulder and I catch a glimpse of the black lace cradling her lush breasts. The other strap slides down and they're revealed in all their glory. No padding needed here. In fact, the lace is so delicate that her rigid nipples visibly distort it.

Next she gradually raises her hem to just below her pubis. "Want more?" she whispers. My swollen cock bobs in my lap. I suppress the urge to grab her, rip her dress open, and ravage her, and simply nod.

She pulls the dress over her head, displaying her black satin thong. Her breasts rise and tighten at the motion. My cock aches. I can't take much more of this.

Kate seems be losing patience, too. She slips the thong down her thighs and kicks it away, then unhooks the brassiere in front. Twin globes of ripe flesh spill out. I lick my lips, my mouth suddenly flooded with saliva. With a half-smile, Kate takes a step closer and feeds me her abundant tits, one at a time.

Before I can understand how it happens, I am on my back, with Kate astride me, riding me hard. She's wild, bucking and squirming, all her monumental energy focused on that spot where our bodies join. She rubs at her clit with one hand, pinches her nipple with the other. I grab her hips and arch up into her, trying to give her what she needs to push her over the edge.

I'm enjoying myself, of course, but I am somehow removed from the scene. I watch our bodies writhing with the same sense of detachment that I feel observing a couple fucking at a play party. I am simultaneously aroused and distant. I'm as hard as I have ever been, but it feels as though I am a long way from coming.

Her orgasm is a noisy cataclysm that, to my surprise, sweeps me away with it.

Afterward, Kate feeds me quiche and salad in bed, washed down with two bottles of white wine. Then she snuggles up to me, trapping me in her arms, feathering my cheeks with kisses. "Thank you, Riordan," she sighs, half-asleep already. "That was wonderful. You're a fabulous lover."

I don't respond. What can I say? *If you think that was good, you should try me when I've got a flogger and some nipple clamps?*

Kate sleeps. I don't. I'm turning the whole experience over in my head, wondering what I have done and why. I think about Ilsa, waiting for me in chains, and tears prick my eyes.

Near dawn, Kate rolls over, releasing me from her embrace. I tiptoe around the bedroom, gathering and donning my scattered clothes. I notice my shirt is missing two buttons, and that Kate snores.

I should kiss her good-bye, I know, but I'm afraid that I'll wake her. So I sneak out of her apartment like a thief, ashamed and guilty that I am abandoning her.

I haven't smoked in fifteen years, but now I buy a pack of cigarettes at a 7-Eleven and prowl the empty sidewalks of the city, lighting one after another, shivering in the October chill.

I've already forgotten Kate; it's Ilsa whom I'm worried about now. In some strange way, it seems, I've betrayed her trust. She asks nothing more from me than to be her Master, to train her and mold her, to guide her toward more complete submission. To perfect her.

And what do I do? I leave her alone while I chase some juicy but bland morsel who just wants me for my hard and willing cock.

I'm lazy, that's the plain truth of it. But that's not all. I'm afraid. I tell myself that I can't fathom Ilsa's limits, but have I really tried? Have I accepted the fact that I might need to give her more, push her harder, go deeper with her than I've ever gone with a slave?

Perhaps it's really my own limits that need to be expanded. There are things I could do, implements I could use, that I've never tried. To be honest, they make me uncomfortable. If this is what Ilsa requires, though, can I deny her? I understand, suddenly, that it is not only Ilsa who needs to be perfected.

She's asleep, curled up on the carpet, when I tiptoe into the bedroom. A stray beam of early morning sunlight filters through the drapes and gilds her coppery curls. She looks like an angel, but what angel ever displayed the fading pink marks of a caning on her unblemished skin?

A pang of guilt and regret lances through me, as excruciating as physical pain. I don't deserve her. I should set her free.

I am about to turn away and slink out of the room when she stirs.

"Master," she says, not trying to hide her smile. "You're home." She raises herself onto her knees, thighs spread, wrists clasped at the small of her back, as I taught her. She dares to look up at me. "I missed you."

I need to be stern with her, I remind myself. I need to offer her extremes of pleasure and pain that far surpass anything we've yet experienced together. I must be willing to bring her to the point where she trusts me enough to utter her safe word, without fearing my displeasure. No matter what it takes.

I must be fierce and implacable, cruel and merciless, immune to any doubt or fear, in order to be the Dom that she needs.

Incurable romantic that I am, I can only kneel beside her and take her in my arms.

Common Place

MARILYN JAYE LEWIS

LOOKING BACK NOW, I see my mistake. Naturally, in hindsight it's as plain as day. I was consumed with self-doubt. I was trapped between right and wrong, doing battle with my conscience and wanting to come out on top. I wanted it to be okay, doing the wrong thing.

Why is it the moments that could accomplish something productive wind up being charged with something too volatile? Wind up being too full of ignorance to accomplish anything kind? Making us blind–all that ignorance, all that "living in the moment" stuff. Why can't we live in hindsight instead, where everything is crystal clear–all our ulterior motives? And let's be fair; you were different then, too. It wasn't all just my immature insanity. You were feeling your way blind just as much as I was; I just expressed myself more loudly. That was the only difference, really. I expressed myself, and you were as quiet as a mouse. A passive-aggressive little mouse. You bitch.

There, I've said it. She was a manipulative little bitch. Too bad I had to fall in love with her. Too bad she couldn't have been honest about what she wanted and saved me so much constant grief . . . Jesus, I've got to put a stop to this tape-loop already. I'm making myself insane. What time is it? Two-fifteen. She's late. As usual. She was always running just a few minutes late. And me? I was always maniacally punctual. Showing up everywhere, right on the dot. And since being on time is the good thing, I was always good and she was always bad. It was fundamental to our relationship. But maybe she's not late this time. Maybe she's just not coming?

And why should she come? I was the one who was the real bitch. Merciless. I couldn't give her any slack. I couldn't let her veer one iota from what was commonly accepted as "right," even though there I was, secretly trying to convince myself that it was okay to want the wrong thing.

"I'm flattered," she'd said. "But I'm married." And she said this as if she were ashamed of it, being married. Then she added in her defense, "Besides, I'm not . . . well, I'm not into women. I'm not gay."

"You don't have to be gay," I said, finding it amusing. "I just wanted to have sex with you."

Could I really have been that amoral? I couldn't see that she was married, for chrissakes, and that a commitment like that meant something to her?

Now what time is it? Two-sixteen. Sixteen minutes, that can still be considered "running late." When is it no longer running late? When is it clear that she's just not coming?

"The truth? You want to know the truth?" This was some time last month. I was having lunch in the city with Jeff. We were talking about her because he'd just recently run into her again. "The truth is," I finally confessed, my voice dropping to a painful whisper in that noisy bistro, "the truth is that she was one of the great loves of my life. She was. And I fucked it up. But she drank too much, you know? That was real." My voice went even lower. "She wanted to fuck only when she was drunk. It made me insane. What was I supposed to do? It's not right to allow yourself to fuck only when you're drunk. It means you're conflicted about it, you know? That you can't be *honest* with yourself."

Jeff seemed skeptical about the way I tried to justify my long-ago behavior. "She was *married*, you know. Or don't you remember that part? She left her husband for you. I think she was trying. She was trying to be honest with herself–and you."

His frankness had stung. Still, it was like the slap I really needed, at long last. *Get real*, he was trying to tell me. *So she wasn't perfect? She tried and you blew it.*

I blew it. I really did. I see that now. I was to blame. I couldn't accept myself for who I really was, so I focused all my rage on her, on trying to get *her* to accept *herself*. Fixing her problems, that became all I could see. Never mind that jumping into bed with me in those days required a person to go to the depths of utter insanity right along with me. How many people are really prepared to do that? I guess she *was* trying. Maybe the reason she was always drinking when we had sex was because my insanity was insufferable otherwise.

I want I need I crave . . . who the hell knows what I needed back then? An orgasm sure wasn't enough. That much was obvious. And yet what is more than an orgasm? An orgasm is the greatest gift, really. It's the thing we all strive for on some level, that peak sensation so that everything can subside, can feel calm again, satiated.

My face between her legs. That was all I wanted at first. Something as simple as that, and she denied me that pleasure for the longest time. "I'm married," she would say. "I can't even be talking about this." But as time went on, she said it with less conviction. That first night we went out alone together and she got so drunk, I took advantage of the situation. I knew she was scared. I knew the booze was her comfort zone, the buffer she was trying to wedge between her fear of herself and my lust. I wasn't exactly sober, but I wasn't as drunk as she was. My lust had the upper hand.

We were out on the street again. I purposely aimed her down that alley so that I could get her really alone. "Come on," I said, backing her up against the cold stone side of a building. "Don't tell me you don't at least think about it. Having oral sex with a girl for a change." I was standing so close to her then, closer than I'd ever been, forcing my point to penetrate her comfort zone. "Tell me you don't at least think about it. Convince me."

I made sure she had nowhere to run. I made sure that she couldn't even escape the judgment of my gaze. "Come on," I challenged her. "Tell me you don't have fantasies. That you don't at least try my tongue on for size in your head."

Only a faint smile, but it gave her secret away in spades.

From that moment, I had her. I slipped my hand inside her leather jacket, feeling for one of her tits. I searched her eyes for even a hint that she was going to deny me that quick feel. It was warm inside her jacket. I imagine my hand must have felt ice cold, even through her shirt, her bra. But she didn't refuse me. She let me feel her tit without saying a word, just staring at me. And when I reached down between her legs, running my hand up the seam of her jeans, she let me do that, too.

"What do you want?" she finally said, her voice sounding helpless.

"To have sex with you, that's all. I want to have sex with you."

"But why? I don't like women."

"How do you know? Have you ever tried it?"

She was back to being wordless, just staring at me.

"What if I like it too much?" she finally said.

"Wouldn't that be a good thing?"

"But I'm married," she said, as if she needed to remind me.

"I know."

Another tortured, interminable pause. Another eternity to stand too close to her in that dark, quiet alley and force her to show her hand.

"But I wouldn't know . . ." Her voice trailed off.

"What?" I asked. "You wouldn't know what?"

"What to do, you know? In bed. I don't know how to have sex with a girl. I wouldn't know how to please you."

She wouldn't know how to please me. It was too quaint. What an image that brought to my mind, full-blown and salacious as hell.

"Don't think too much," I said. "I wouldn't worry about it."

"No?"

"No."

"Why?"

"Why? Because you don't have to *do* anything to please me. I want to do the pleasing. I want to please you."

She gave this some consideration. "I don't think I understand," she said.

"It's not complicated. Just touching you would please me. And I like to think that me touching you would please you."

To my sublime delight, she popped open the button of her

jeans and pulled her own zipper down. She urged my hand to go inside and touch her.

You'd think it was the first time I'd ever felt slick lips before, as if I didn't know that girls' bodies did that. And yet for some reason it surprised me, that she was that wet.

When my fingers slipped through the tangle of hairs, went between the slick lips and found her clit, it was as if the tension in her body fled–the burden of her indecision, perhaps her guilt. It was gone when she collapsed her weight against the building. She tugged on her jeans a little, trying to inch them down discreetly, to make more room for my fingers between her legs.

The ecstasy was immediate. For me, as well. It wasn't easy getting a good feel of her with her pants still up like that, but it still felt incredible. My fingertips slipped all over her clit and it made me feel excited. Like I'd never felt up a girl before.

"Come home with me," I said. "Just for an hour."

"No," she said. "I can't. I shouldn't even let you do this."

"Can I at least kiss you?"

"No," she said.

I applied more pressure to her clitoris. I watched her eyes roll up, her lids flutter, her face give over to her pleasure.

"Okay," I said. "Just this, then. Until you're ready."

But I lied. I crouched down then, right there in the alley. I didn't expose her too much–I pulled down her jeans just enough to reveal her hairs, the top of her mound, where I knew her clitoris was primed.

"Don't," she said very clearly. "Don't do it, not here. Don't."

But I did it anyway. I put my mouth on her, letting my tongue find her clitoris, trapping her against the wall. I pushed her until she betrayed herself. Until she shoved her jeans down even more and let me seriously lick her. She came quickly. And when she came, she also started to cry.

"I have to go now. I need to go home."

I let her go, because I knew it was finally the beginning. Her denial of me was as good as over.

"IS THIS SEAT taken?"

"Holy shit, where did you come from?" She's as pretty as ever. Older, but still very pretty.

"You looked like you were a million miles away."

"I was," I admit.

She isn't smiling, but she's here and she's sitting down.

"Sorry I'm late," she says. She slides an envelope across the table to me. "I wrote this. I wasn't sure I'd have the guts to say the things I really wanted to say to you, so I wrote them down. You can read them now or later. Either way, I just wanted to make sure I had my say. I didn't want to come, you know. I almost didn't, in fact."

I look at my watch. She's over half an hour late. Funny, after being glued to the clock all day, I'd somehow lost track of the time.

"You look good," she says.

"I do?"

"Yes, you do. You always do—or did, I should say."

"Are you drinking anything today? Can I order you something?"

"Tea."

"Tea?"

"Well, what are you drinking?"

"Wine."

She hesitates. "That's not the best idea, considering . . . but I'll have a glass of wine, too."

We order the wine. We don't say anything. Now I'm the one who feels like crying.

"Thanks for coming," I say. "For agreeing to meet me after, well, after all these years."

She doesn't reply. I consider the envelope on the table in front of me, but I don't think I have the guts to read its contents in front of her, to face her wrath, her rage, her contempt or perhaps her disgust, and then have to look into her face as well.

"So how are you?" she finally says.

"Pretty good."

"Are you happy?"

I give it some thought. "Yeah, I'm happy."

"Good, you deserve to be happy."

I'm not sure what that's supposed to mean. She looks now as if she could cry, as if she's battling that urge.

"Christ," I finally say. "Shelley, I'm so sorry. I know it's too little too late, but I just wanted to say that. When Jeff said that he'd run into you, that you were back in town, I wanted to at least try, to at least say I finally figured out what a bitch I was. How mean I was, how inexcusable some of that stuff was that I put you through. You were my very best friend. I don't know–I was just crazy."

"Yeah, you were. But it was part of why I loved you. I think I was a masochist, too. In that particular way, anyhow." It's finally out, that word, *masochist.* It's hanging in the air, over the table, crowding in between us. "It's not the same as what you were doing," she goes on awkwardly, "but in my own way, I was a masochist, too. Just by putting up with you for as long as I did."

Ouch, that hurt. But I'm not going to say what I'm thinking now in reply. It's too defensive. It's not my mission to point out her faults from twenty years ago and try to change her.

"It sounds funny, doesn't it?" she asks.

"What?"

"Me, using the word *masochist* as if I know what I'm talking about. I was always so ridiculously naïve, wasn't I? A real fool."

"I wouldn't say that."

"I would. In fact, I just did. Can I ask you something? Something personal, I mean, that I should have asked you a long time ago?"

"I suppose now is as good a time as any."

"Why were you like that? What did it do for you that being in bed with me couldn't do?"

I look around uneasily, feeling like we're onstage, as if everyone in the place were listening to us, poised on the edge of their seats, waiting for my reply: why was I a sexual masochist? But no one is paying us any mind. It's just my own insecurity, my fear of being exposed. It's fucking with my head.

"Is it too personal to explain it me? Is it none of my business?"

"No, it's not that."

"Because I have to tell you. Over the years, I gave it a lot of thought, and I feel like I should have tried to understand you better. I should have. Maybe it would have kept you from straying, kept you in our own bed. But honestly? You scared the hell out of me when it came to sex. I was always in over my head around you."

I want to say, *I know that.* I want to say, *I used it to my advantage.* I want to confess once and for all that I was just as manipulative as she was. She used the booze to drown her feelings of guilt over leaving her husband and to hide her fear of not knowing how to have sex with a woman, for wanting the sex and not wanting it at the same time. And I hated her drinking, but I used her drunkenness to get her to spread her legs for me. Then afterward, I used her drunkenness to punish her for feeling inadequate. Because I believed in punishment back then. To me, it was an essential component of good sex–to be the punisher sometimes and to be punished all the other times. But she was too confused by her own conflicting desires to ever be a suitable punisher for me. She was always caught up in her own head, trying to reason everything out, to come to some grand conclusion about us, about lust, about what people might be thinking about her and me together. So I had to go elsewhere to get my punishment. The lure of it was irresistible.

"Did I offend you?" she asks. "I'm sorry, I can be so damn blunt sometimes."

"No, you didn't offend me."

"You got so quiet."

"I was just thinking. Trying to answer your question. And then it got me thinking about other things. Memories that I'm not very proud of, things I was doing back then."

"Listen," she says, extending her hand and touching my arm. "You don't have to explain yourself after all these years. You really don't. I came here today just to see an old friend after a really long time. And to say some things I should have said, but I'm still too much of a coward–I had to put it down on paper. Because there are some things I still can't stand to hear coming out of my own mouth."

Now I want to read what's in that envelope. I want to tear it open with my teeth and read her letter feverishly, find out what the hell she's talking about. But that seems like a clumsy thing to do at this moment.

afraid to see you in person, you know. Afraid of revisiting who I used to be. I was . . ." her voice drifts off. She looks nervous.

I want to kiss her, standing this close to her, with her looking so vulnerable. When am I going to get over that?

"I've come to terms with a lot of things over the years. I really have . . ." She attempts to continue but falters again.

"If you keep this up, Shelley . . ."

"What?" she asks quietly.

I look at her. I suddenly remember her very well. "I'll do something we'll regret," I try to explain.

"Like what?"

"I'll kiss you."

"Let *me* be the one to kiss *you* this time."

I'm almost afraid to believe my ears.

"Will it offend you?" she asks. "I mean, with me being married again and all that? After everything we went through the first time?"

"I'm not sure how to answer that. It wouldn't offend me, exactly." I can't help but notice that she's trembling. I wonder why it's so hard for her to be brave. But then it used to be hard for me, too. It took a lot of rope and a succession of dominant women violating me in unspeakable ways before I figured out how to be brave in this world.

Finally she leans close and kisses me on the mouth. A real kiss: she's giving me her tongue. I can't help but hold her when she's kissing me this way. She presses her whole body up close to mine. This is kissing, all right, and yet it's so much more.

I try to extricate myself, but I'm only partially successful. "Shelley, don't. This is trouble. This is playing with fire."

"I know. I know, you're right. Damn it. Why is it that when I had you in my life, I was too afraid to move? And now? Now that it's over, done, history, there's so much I want to do with you? I have to be honest. I still think about you a lot. In all those sexual ways. Part of me still wants that. I keep wondering, am I really gay? Have I just been in denial my whole fucking life?"

I can't help but smile. She's doing it again–thinking herself into a tailspin, trying to reason everything out. "You think too much, Shelley. I wouldn't worry about it if I were you."

"Can I see you?" she asks.

"You're seeing me now."

"No, I mean . . ."

"What?"

"See you, as in 'see you.'"

"Have sex?"

"Yes. That."

"But you're married."

"Since when did that matter to you?"

I feel like smacking her, but she's right. "True," I say. "That's true."

"Can we?"

No, I tell her in my head. *No, we can't. I'm not that woman anymore. I learned from my mistakes, from my selfishness, my cruelty. I can't go backward.* And yet I'm kissing her again. I'm nearly devouring her mouth, mauling her tits through her blouse. I can't wait to have my mouth on her once more, down there between her legs, to have my tongue jammed up her hole. Make her squirm and writhe and then listen to her whimper, as I make her come all over my fingers.

Odd Habit

B. D. FAW AND MIKE RESNICK

AS THE DAMAGED coach pulled to a stop beside her, Melissa peered inside, cautiously separating the rich, royal velvet curtains that shaded it. A handsome young nobleman was alone, slumped back in his seat, eyes closed, shoulders wedged into the corner, as still as death. The severe damage sustained by the coach and the wounded coachman bore silent witness to the ferocity of the attack they had survived. The footman was missing, probably dead. The unknown lord inside was very likely dead as well. Melissa reached her hand up to the door handle and slowly twisted it. She took a deep breath and then jerked the door open in a smooth, decisive motion. It was, she decided, as if Fate had put her in this particular spot at this particular time, and who was she to argue with Fate?

She reached up into the coach and laid her hand on the man's leg to see if he was still alive. He groaned, and she moved her hand up his leg, probing for different signs of life. His response was immediate, involuntary, and impressive. The swelling under her dainty fingers took Melissa by surprise, and she involuntarily clenched those fingers, causing the swelling to increase.

Suddenly the prim, virginal Melissa that she displayed to the world was gone, replaced by the true, secret, passionate vixen. Melissa yielded without an argument to her wanton alter ego.

Suddenly, an arm snaked out from the coach and pulled her inside–at least, that is how she would remember it. In a desperate attempt for balance, she clenched her hand tighter–and the now fully engorged member she gripped throbbed wildly in response. The door swung shut behind her, and the interior of the coach was plunged into near-darkness by the rich velvet curtains barring its windows. She felt, rather than saw, the silk ruffle on the sleeve of a man's wrist, as a hand swung up and rapped thrice upon the roof of the coach. The coach lurched forward in response to the coachman's whip, and Melissa was pitched sideways into the man's lap. His pulsating manhood still clutched in her viselike grip.

The throbbing in her palm shot bolts of excitement up her arm and into her heart. *I should feel guilty and degraded,* she thought, *but somehow all I feel is excited.* She was overcome with a desire so strong, so immediate, that it made her most lascivious fantasies seem like innocent dreams and pushed all sense of propriety from her mind.

A deep, guttural moan rose from the man, and her quivering buttocks felt the sharp upward thrust of his hip. A faint light filtered through the soft velvet curtains, barely enough to see by. She trembled as the moan began anew: lower, deeper, and rising in mixed passion. How can anything that feels this good be sinful?

Another moan: no specter's wail, but rather emanating from her own dainty lips, suddenly cut short by another pair of lips pressed against her own. His hungry lips were both firm and soft at the same time, searching her own for some secret entrance. Her lips parted slightly, and sensing the breach, like a cavalry commander in full charge, his hot tongue flickered through, quickly exploring the barricades of her perfect teeth and then thrusting beyond. Her tongue rose up to do battle with his, and a lustful war that both sides would win raged inside her mouth.

She gripped tighter with one hand and reached out with the other, thrusting her fingers through his dark wavy curls. Her body stiffened, almost a mirror of his manhood.

A deep throbbing pulsation accompanied the spreading wetness between her legs, while the pulsating organ in her hand beat a strong counterpoint. Her body began pulsing in slow, rising contractions, sending tendrils of bliss throughout her, until the throbbing manhood within her grasp exploded with its own convulsions. As their personal rhythms converged, as their bodies locked into the savage, synchronized death-grip of irreversible lust, the intensity of her own release overwhelmed her and she completely surrendered to the wanton wench within.

That which he could no longer do with his diminishing manhood she urged him to do with his hands and then his mouth. She sailed on gossamer wings among clouds of delight, over the verdant valley of her secret garden. Water cascaded down the mountain of her mind, tumbling over sun-warmed rocks and exploding into the tepid pond below–into her lap, where the dampness continued to grow as her body twisted and writhed, released at last in maddening lust. Wave after wave of pure delight rolled over her arched body, until she finally fell limp and helpless into the arms of the handsome stranger.

She slowly relaxed her grip upon his shrinking member, but not before she gave it one last affectionate squeeze. Then she retrieved her errant hand, extricated herself from his embrace with all of the self-assurance and nonchalance she could muster, and slowly twisted her body around until she was seated directly across from him. She arranged her skirts neatly around her hips and stared directly into his appraising eyes.

"That's a lovely blue gown you're wearing," said the man.

"Thank you," said Melissa. And then, because she knew she would never see him again: "I think you're beautiful."

He seemed taken aback by her comment but soon regained his composure. "I don't believe we've been introduced." He smiled, his calm manner belying their so recently shared passion. The sincere warmth of his smile and the intelligent fire in his eyes allayed any regrets she might have had. He seemed to radiate a vibrant zest for life. "Permit me to do the honors, my dear," he continued in a deep, sonorous baritone. "I am the Count Francisco Alonzo de Cabernet. And you?"

"I cannot tell you my name," replied Melissa.

"Why?"

"Because if you knew my name, you might seek me out again, and what we did tonight must last us a lifetime."

He stared at her, curious. "Have you some explanation?"

"It would be too dangerous," she replied. "I would not want my husband to come after you."

"Your husband?" he repeated, startled. "You are married?"

"Oh, yes."

"And you do this often?"

"That is none of your business, Francisco Alonzo de Cabernet."

"You make your husband sound murderous," he said.

"No, my husband is very understanding."

“He does not participate in duels?”

“I have never known him to pick up a sword.”

“Then perhaps I shall challenge him to a duel for you.”

“You would lose,” she assured him.

“I very much doubt that,” he said confidently. “I have won many duels, my dear.”

“Nevertheless.” She uttered the word with such confidence that he dropped the subject.

In the silence that ensued, Melissa twisted the handle beneath her hand and slipped quickly from the coach, vanishing into the night.

THE SOFT RUSTLE of the dark velvet curtains barely disturbed the absolute silence of the confessional. The attractive young woman, now clad totally in black, slipped through almost unnoticed and seated herself on the hard wooden bench within. The silence was broken only by the sound of a small wooden door sliding softly back on its well-worn grooves, just beyond the filigreed grille separating the woman from the priest.

“Forgive me, Father, for I have sinned. It has been three days since my last confession.”

“And what do you have to confess, my child?”

“I have lain with a man.”

Father Benedicto sighed wearily. “Again?”

“I know it was wrong, but I could not help myself.”

“A different one?” Why do I bother asking? It’s always a different one.

“Yes, Father.”

“You must understand,” he said slowly, “that I cannot keep absolving you if you persist in committing the same sin again and again.”

"Does not the Bible tell us that the flesh is weak?" she said.

"It also tells us that we are supposed to avoid sins of the flesh, not seek them out. This is becoming tedious."

"But my husband forgives me," she protested.

"Everyone knows that your husband's compassion is boundless," said Father Benedicto. "But sooner or later even your husband will decide that you must be cast out and punished."

"You know that will not happen," she said. "He loves me completely and unselfishly." She made no attempt to hide her impatience. "Give me my penance and let me be on my way."

"It is not like paying a fine," said Father Benedicto. "You must truly repent of your sin and vow never to commit it again–and you must mean it."

"I do repent, and I will never lay with a man again." *Until the next time. Already I can feel myself yearning for it.*

"You said that last week."

"I am only flesh and blood," she replied. "I will try harder."

Sure you will–until the next time. "All right, my child," said Father Benedicto with a defeated sigh. He briefly outlined her penance.

"Thank you, Father," she said. "I know Satan will tempt me again, but I shall try to never commit this particular sin in the future."

But as Father Benedicto watched Sister Melissa walk away toward her sparsely furnished quarters in the convent, he knew she would be back.

Sins of Omission

STACY REED

HE HAS ALWAYS sought absolution in his writing and has yet to write a story that is purely imagined. He does write erotica, sexual fantasies–but never his own. He would rather admit to the sins that he is actually guilty of than confess those he dares not commit.

This makes him wonder whether writing about his fantasies is more honest than writing about what has actually happened to him, if his loyalty to the facts is not a smoke screen masking the deeper truths his erotic visions would reveal. Long dedicated to grounding his every word in reality, he now suspects his dreams are no less true–maybe even more so. Perhaps he is even more obliged to confess them. If they are truer, the desires he doesn't act on tell far more than those he pursues.

TREVOR'S AN ESTABLISHED writer who's been teaching erotica-writing classes for years. I enrolled in his first class, and I've been his student ever since. He says he's taught me all I can learn from him, but the idea of leaving his class worries me; even though he says the key is keeping the audience in mind, the secret to my writing is that he is the only reader I am speaking to. This makes me nervous; I fear outside his class I might not produce, might never publish.

Tonight, the last night of class, Trevor has promised us a story he has written especially for the occasion. As I watch him walk to the podium, I feel unfounded pride, as if I could have anything to do with his creativity or success. He takes a drink of water and says, "You are all promising writers. And as I promised, I wrote a story for you tonight, since you've written so many for me." We fall silent, and Trevor begins to read.

Sins of Omission

He has always sought absolution in his writing, and has yet to write a story that is purely imagined. He does write erotica, sexual fantasies–but never his own. He would rather admit to the sins that he is actually guilty of than confess those he dares not commit.

This makes him wonder whether writing about his fantasies is more honest than writing about what has actually happened to him, if his loyalty to the facts is not a smoke screen masking the deeper truths his erotic visions would reveal. Long dedicated to grounding his every word in reality, he now suspects his dreams are no less true–maybe even more so. Perhaps he is even more obliged to confess them. If they are truer, the desires he doesn't act on tell far more than those he pursues.

Trevor's voice trails off; he takes another sip from his glass of water, cautiously, as though he's testing coffee to see if it's cool enough to drink. He runs his fingers through his unkempt hair, hair the color of mushrooms and so fine at times, in certain light, it seems liquid. He adjusts his glasses and continues–

EVEN SO, TREVOR hesitates to share his fantasies with his students, and he feels guilty for this; he takes great pleasure in reading theirs. Sometimes he receives a manuscript that is clearly accurate reporting, but most of the stories his students submit are obviously imagined. Sometimes–apparently–they are fantasies about him or fantasies starring the author, but they are fantasies nonetheless. Still, the lines sometimes blur; occasionally, a female student confuses him with a character she's created. Or gets herself confused with a woman in one of his stories. But never has he had an affair with a student. That is one line he cannot cross.

Writing his fantasy–that is another.

He'd like to believe his fantasy started when he discovered hers. Slipped in quietly with the other manuscripts was one he saw himself in. And once Trevor saw what might be, the temptation overcame him.

So he began to write.

> Every morning before dawn she comes to him. At first he can only smell her, flowery, but underneath the dance of rose and lilac, woman. He's afraid if he opens his eyes she will vanish, so he lets her insinuate herself into his vision, into his mind. Her beauty is bracing, ethereal, but so true, right now, for him. Her hair falls over his face, and

her face is the only thing he can see. Those eyes that take in everything and reveal so little, cheeks that admit it all with every blush, and her lips the color of ripened plum skin.

She feels him grow excited and settles against him. She relaxes, grants him the forgiving softness of her perfumed body but offers no more. It's nearly impossible for him to resist moving beneath her, but he fears that any movement of his body would chase this precious fantasy from his bed, from his mind. This is when he notices he is inside her, safe, where he somehow understands he is supposed to be.

Still wary, Trevor remains completely passive. He surrenders to her. She slides up and down the length of him, repetitively, patiently, slowly. Maddeningly. He senses she is daring him to crack, to push into her, to grab her hips. But he also senses that if he were to show the slightest shred of the desperation he feels—for the urge to spill himself into her is overwhelming—that she would melt into the air.

Like yesterday morning and the one before, the longer he commands himself to stay still, the more stimulated his lover becomes, and her very excitement has antagonized him to nearly painful arousal. He wants to tell her to slow down, but worries that doing so would break the spell. Before his lips can form any words, they catch in his throat. As if in answer to his escalating arousal, she begins to rub herself against him more vigorously, more urgently, and shoves her pelvis against his with increasing abandon. Her breasts sway in front of his face as she works herself against him. Her nipples are so close to his lips that if he were to dart his tongue between his clenched teeth he could taste them, the delicate aureole. His lips part, but he realizes she is not so close anymore; he could now grasp her nipples with only his fingers, the chance to take them in his mouth is gone. He imagines reaching for a round breast, feeling its weight in his palm, tracing the perfect nipple with his fingers—but he dares not.

A moment of eagerness, and he knows she will be gone. He must exercise restraint, must tolerate this naked beauty writhing against his body as though he were mere water through which she were swimming. He tries to ignore the screaming between his thighs. She is moving so fast, her body is so alive with frenzy, it comes in fragments: her collarbone, delicate and vulnerable; the veins straining against the gauzy skin of her neck; her almond eyes wet, set deep; the swoop of her hips; the heft of her thighs; the soft slap of her long, wavy hair against his contorted face as she brings herself pleasure. It is at this moment that he falters and entertains the idea of the ecstasy coursing through her. As soon as he imagines her coming, it is too late: He shudders helplessly as his lust overcomes him, and when he opens his eyes, she is no longer.

TREVOR STOPS READING abruptly; the story seems cut short, unfinished. We are slow to applaud, but I soon clap enthusiastically along with the rest of the students. My face feels hot. I hope no one—especially Trevor—notices, so I stare at my shoes. Caught off my guard, I feel stunned and vaguely panicked. I am anxious this might mean something, anxious what it might mean. I am particularly worried that it might mean nothing at all.

Once the applause dies, Trevor skips over several pages and concludes, "Thank you for inspiring me to write what I have never written, what has never happened." He shuffles his papers, though they are already stacked neatly between his fingers. "I've told you to reap your imagination, but I confess I never had. 'Write what you know.' I believed that, but I didn't understand that I could know fantasy as well as reality, that both are true."

Some of the students look awestruck, as if a profound and essential secret has been revealed. Others smile nervously, as if their teacher has said too much. Amid their agitated whispers and uneasy glances, he leaves the podium while his favorite students–or at least the most eager–hover nearby. Others leave or cluster around the snack table.

Once Trevor begins to mingle, I take my place in his inner circle and say, "I deeply admire your writing; it is important to me." But what I want to say is *you are deeply important to me.*

I don't say this; I wrote it. He knows. *He'd like to believe his fantasy started when he discovered hers. Slipped in quietly with the other manuscripts was one he saw himself in. And once Trevor saw what might be, the temptation overcame him.* I invited him. And he has made his admission in return. *So he began to write.* This is all I have tempted him to.

It's not enough. I bide my time, and when only a few clumps of people remain, I steer my teacher away from his admirers, mumble excuses about a manuscript I want to mail to him. I tell myself this is not exactly a lie; though I submitted only that one story about him, there are more–enough for a manuscript.

When we are safely segregated, I say, "That story–"

"You gave me the idea."

The pride I found so illogical an hour ago resurfaces with conviction, but I try to hide any bravado in my voice. "That was me you wrote about."

This is where our writing should come to life, joined and shared in the moment between us, but nothing happens. I set this all into motion, he has admitted his feelings for me, but Trevor says only, "You are a fine writer. Your work moves me."

The praise is not enough. "Do I?"

"Yes, I told you that." Suddenly exasperated, he speaks in controlled, carefully measured words. "I told everybody."

It still is not enough. I can't help testing; I kiss his cheek quickly, then wait.

It takes him forever to say, "Kate. You are my student. I told you that, too."

He did. *But never has he had an affair with a student. That is one line he cannot cross.* But writing his fantasy—that is another line he said he cannot cross—yet he did cross it. That temptation overcame him—why not another?

In case Trevor might stand by this principle, I boldly erase the line by saying, "I don't have to be a student." The idea of giving him up as my teacher terrifies me—could I write without him?—but I have to see if I can. Only then could we exist in three dimensions.

"You can't be *my* student. Not after what you wrote. Not after what I read tonight."

"You're right," I say. As soon as I speak the words, I realize how right he is; I can't go on writing for him, about him. "I'm not your student anymore."

"No," Trevor says. "You've taught me too much."

"That's quite a compliment," I say as I look around for my purse. "I'm sorry; I have to go."

As I head toward the door, he catches up with me and asks, "Hey—aren't you going to get my address?" The next question he asks with light irony—"For the manuscript?"

I realize that he has not only taken my offhand excuse seriously, but he also believes the book is about him. He thinks I intend to send him more stories like the one I submitted. He expects another literary come-on, but the extended remix this time. But what for? He has reciprocated my one story-bound flirtation with a confession of his own, nothing more. It isn't enough. "No," I say. "It's okay, really."

He scrawls on a napkin and presses it into my palm. "Just keep this anyway."

"Sure. Good night." I hurry out the door and drive home. That night I fall asleep reading all the stories I have written about Trevor, all but one he has never read.

MONTHS LATER, AND his address hangs tacked to my bulletin board. I never sent him anything; there was never anything to send. Well, there were the stories I had written about him, the ones I had written to him even though I never wanted him to actually read them. I could never publish them though; they weren't meant for the public. Besides, I could not chance Trevor discovering them.

There is a manuscript now, however, a real one. A whole collection of stories, even though I have never taken another class from Trevor. He's no longer my teacher or my audience or my sympathetic character—and to my surprise a publisher wants this book that Trevor has shaped in no way.

I pull up in front of the post office and am surprised to see Trevor walking toward my car, carrying a package of his own. My impulse is to sit in the car, wait until he walks away—but that's ridiculous. I'll say hi, we'll chat—it'll be over in no time. What harm could come of saying hello?

He spots me immediately. "Kate! It's been so long! Kate—how are you?"

I'm shocked by his enthusiastic greeting, inexplicably

embarrassed, as though I've been caught lying. But of course I say, "Fine."

He sees the package I'm carrying and says, "I always thought you should publish those."

I know the stories he's speaking of, the ones he intuits I have written about him, the ones he assumes I have never shown him. The "manuscript" we discussed the last night of class, the last time I saw him. But those fantasies are all saved to disk, filed away. "These stories are all new; I wrote them since I last saw you. These aren't the ones I asked you about sending."

"No? Whatever happened with those? Why did you never send me anything?"

"Back when I asked you if I could send you my manuscript . . ." The words taste like a lie on my tongue. "I mean, the stories I had back then don't work," I say honestly. My next words ring even more true—"The characters are too flat. They don't come to life off the page."

I scrutinize his face to see if he takes my meaning, but he only grows more composed. "Really?"

"Yeah. They need to fill out; I want them to be real."

"Give them a chance," he says, but I can't tell if he is speaking of the characters or us. If he is referring to us, he won't let on. "Anyway, where are you taking classes now?"

"I'm not."

"I guess you were right: You don't have to be a student."

I can't help correcting him: "I can't be *your* student." The words call back the reason why—*not after what you wrote . . . not after what I read*—and his dream returns to me now in variations and slivers: *underneath the dance of rose and lilac, woman . . . bracing, ethereal, but so true . . . her face is the only thing he can see . . . eyes that take in everything and reveal so little, cheeks that admit it all with every blush . . . lips the color of ripened plum skin . . . he is inside her, where he is supposed to be . . . she is daring him to crack, . . . threatening to melt into the air . . .he is water through which she swims . . . in fragments: her collarbone, delicate and vulnerable; the veins straining against the gauzy skin of her neck; her almond eyes wet, set deep; the swoop of her hips; the heft of her thighs . . . he opens his eyes, and she is no longer.*

What's it been? Nearly a year? And still the words affect me like he just spoke them. I hope Trevor doesn't notice how flustered I've suddenly become or guess why. I'm about to walk past him and mail my manuscript, say good-bye politely without acknowledging anything more, when he says, "Wait–you *aren't* my student anymore. Why not . . ."

"What? Exchange more erotica about each other?"

Surprising me, he says, "I haven't written any."

I feel slighted, then annoyed with myself for feeling anything at all. Before I think about what I am asking, I hear my voice–"Why?"

He echoes the words that kept propelling me the last night I saw him. "It's not enough. Imagining you is no good now that I don't see you anymore. Kate," he says, gesturing toward my neatly taped manuscript box, "that is good. But this," he says and at last kisses my cheek in return, "this is much better."

I don't want to spoil this real-life kiss that I've imagined for so long, but the truth is too insistent. "These stories are all new," I repeat. "They are not about you. I haven't written about you since that night." The words sound mean-spirited, rude coming out of my mouth. But I need him to know that I can write without his mentoring, his influence, the way his body for so long insinuated itself into my imagination. *I* need to know that. At the same time, I feel a contradiction rising: I want him to be proud of me for this. I repeat myself as though I'm reporting an accomplishment, "They aren't about us."

"One was."

"That was only a fantasy," I say. "It wasn't real."

"It was true. Make it true again, but this time make it real, too."

Surely I could never live up to Trevor's virtual Kate. Could he compete with the character I based on him? "Do you want that?" I ask.

"Do you?"

"I don't know," I say. Back when I was still his student, I was convinced that I did. But I knew only Trevor the teacher and the embellished Trevor of my imagination–not the real man. "I don't know you," I admit to myself as much as to him.

"I'm someone who wants you more than the dream of you."

"Do you? You don't know me, either."

"I know it's not enough," he repeats. "The dream is not enough."

I can feel him pushing me the same way I tested him. I feel flattered and intimidated at the same time. He presses on, "That story you wrote about me–was that enough?"

Of course not. Why would there be dozens more? The thought that I have dedicated so many words to this one man weakens my defenses. "No," I say. "It's not." It's not enough, and I want more even though I don't know what "enough" might be. The thought excites me, but I am drained by this conversation. I don't have the energy to discuss what might be enough, so I try changing the subject. "Hey, I have some stories I'd like you to read."

"I'm pleased you still value my opinion."

"I just want you to read them. Promise that you won't be my teacher." Of course I am the only one with a promise to keep—that my writing be neither for him nor about him. Really, I have no problem now with Trevor as my teacher—I just don't know if I can be his, too.

But he dismisses my doubts by saying, "People learn from each other, Kate. Look, you've taught me, too. If it weren't for you, I'd be at home imagining this, writing about it—not doing it."

"And you really think doing is better?"

Trevor's candor surprises me. "Not always. But now, yes: I think doing is better. Let's get together—I'll read those stories."

Is this man who I have worked so hard not to need as my inspiration or my audience, this man I have banished from my writing, the one I want now to bring into my waking life? Now that I don't need him as my teacher or my main character, could I want him? Is he right—could he really learn from me, too? Since I have no idea what the answers are, I say, "Sure."

Trevor seems genuinely pleased. "Tomorrow at Jitters? Seven?" Though I can't remember whether I have any plans, I nod, and he says, "See you then!" He bounds up the steps to the post office, turns, and asks, "Hey—want me to mail that for you?"

I hand the package to him, eager to escape to a place where I can stop to consider what has been set into motion. "Thanks. Save the receipt."

"It's nothing. See you tomorrow!"

I GO TO the coffee shop at 6:30—I want time to order, find a seat, and check my makeup and my papers, though not necessarily in that order. I want to prepare myself.

Ten minutes later Trevor walks in and waves at me

sheepishly. I imagine he realizes I've caught him at a trick I know well–he wanted to get here first, to brace himself for my arrival. I relax a little; he's as scared as I am. He's apprehensive, but he's here anyway. Thinking of this simple bravery–the mere fact that both of us have shown up–I feel less anxious.

After a redhead wearing a Yale sweatshirt finishes making his cappuccino, Trevor joins me. "I'm so glad you made it."

"I got here early–thought I'd get some reading done." I realize I have no book with me and switch topics: "I brought some stories for you to read." This, at least, is true, so I push a stack of folders across the table. "If you want."

I wait for him to open the first folder, flip back the title page. He reads quickly, like a practiced writing teacher would, and I pretend to read a newspaper some patron left behind. Though the story is short, it seems like an hour passes before he looks up and says, "This is not about us."

I'm taken aback. I'd expected criticism or maybe praise, but not this blunt observation. Have I shocked him simply by not writing about him? "No. It's not. It's not about anyone."

"I know. It's just that I thought–"

"Look, I said I had some stories I'd like you to read," I say in a tight, brittle voice. I'm both intrigued and put off by his presumption, but I realize how I might have sparked the confusion. I lower my voice and try to speak lightly. "I never said they were about you."

"None of these are?" He speaks too loudly, too quickly. "But you wrote one–you must have written others."

"These are not those."

"You did write others about me!" The excitement in his voice is flattering. Is it also condemning? Am I guilty of writing about him? Is he guilty of caring whether I did?

Then it hits me: He *knows*. He knows I wrote not just the one

I submitted to him in class, the one he responded to with a story of his own—he knows I wrote more, other stories about him. He knows he was not just a one-night stand of my imagination, but a recurring figure—maybe once he was the star. But he knows.

Does he also realize that every story of mine he has read was to him, that it was his ear alone I was whispering in?

I said it. *These are not those.* I had planned to lie; I had not intended for him to know I had written more than that one story about him. But I guess I wanted to tell him. Yes, I feel glad I've told him, relieved. So relieved that I know my admission is not for his benefit; I told him for me, out of the selfish desire to be free of the secret. All this hiding, so many lies and evasions, exhausts me. I am tired, worn thin enough to read through. Admitting the truth is invigorating; more than I am worried about the reverberations of revealing this secret I am exhilarated by the possibility of reverberations.

He drinks his cappuccino quickly. "I've been writing about you, too. I have nothing like this," he says and gestures to my stories. "Unless I write about you, I no longer write."

"You told me that you haven't written any erotica about me."

"I lied. That package you saw me mail—"

"You can't be serious!"

"—stories about you."

"About *me*?"

"No, not exactly. About the you I imagine. Are you angry?"

"Why are you telling me this?" I ask, needing to hear his reason more than any one answer. "If I am angry, it hardly matters now."

"I just want to be honest with you."

He no doubt counts on me to accept his compliance with such a virtue, so I challenge him: "And which one of us will sleep easier? Maybe I'm concerned about how you depicted me, what you've imagined."

Trevor shifts in the booth uncomfortably. "I guess I just wanted to get it off my chest."

"You want me to absolve you. Right?"

"Yeah."

In the face of his honesty I assure him, "You have done nothing wrong."

He knits his brow. "I haven't?"

"No." If he had tried to convince me he was spilling his guts for my sake, that would be wrong—but not writing a book about some Kate who lives in a parallel universe that only Trevor can access. Nothing wrong at all—in fact, I feel put at ease that he has written about me, less embarrassed for him to know I have written about him. Even so, it also disturbs me that he writes about me only—even now. He can never know the real me until he says good-bye to the one he imagines. If he can't let go, then I might be mad.

"Then you aren't angry?

This time I speak frankly. "It depends on whether the fantasy really is not enough."

"I told you it isn't."

"You also said you had written nothing more about me." But he has—an entire manuscript. As much as this admission makes me want to trust him, the fact that he had something to confess makes me suspicious. But I have been less than forthcoming, too. And he has come clean now.

In the spirit of reciprocity I say, "You can read those stories, the ones I wrote about you. I wrote them a while ago, and I haven't looked at them in months." This is not a lie; I want to make clear that I no longer write about him. I want him to know that I have long given up the dream of him, that there is now room in my life for the reality of him. I didn't make that space thinking he might fill it, but I want him to know it is there.

In response he offers me a space to step into. "No. I'd rather experience us than read your fantasies about us."

This is what I want to hear, but I fear one secret will stand in the way of having that experience. "I wrote them for you," I admit. I don't say this to prod him into reading the stories; I just need him to know. "Everything you read I wrote specifically for you."

"Not just that last story?"

I shake my head. "That is why I had to leave. Everything was for you, and then everything was about you."

"Why did you not want to tell me?"

I feel buttressed by his admission, by knowing that his latest book is about me—or some metaphor for me. Besides, now he knows anyway—that I wrote other stories about him, that at one time everything I wrote was for his eyes. I speak more candidly. "Why did I not want to tell you that you were my only audience? That you were my leading man? You'd have thought I was in love."

"Is that what you think of me?"

"Because of the manuscript I saw you mail? No. Maybe you're in love with your idea of me, but not with me." It's true; Trevor has no idea who I am beyond the classroom or outside his imagination. He is as mysterious to me. "We barely know each other."

"I know enough to want to know you." He picks up the folders on the Formica table. "Can I read these?"

"That won't help; you've already read scores of my stories."

"But you did not write these for me, did you?"

I shake my head. "I never imagined you'd read them."

"Then it's a start."

Maybe, but it isn't the right one. "No. You just read a story of mine. Now it's your turn to let me read something." I am eager to see his writing, eager to see if any insight of mine can shape it the way Trevor's advice has shaped mine.

"But *everything* is about you," he protests.

"Then you will have to write something new."

"I know I have to let go of the fantasy," he says. "Like you did."

"Is that what you want? Wouldn't you prefer the ideal to the real?"

He dodges my question with one of his own, but a good one: "Wouldn't you?"

"That depends on how the real compares."

"It's up to you to find out. I want to find out. I want this," Trevor says earnestly, evading my question no longer. "I want us to build it together; what I have written about you, what you've written about me–none of it counts anymore."

"Then why did you have to tell me about that manuscript? Why did you have to know why I quit taking your classes?"

He finishes his cappuccino and says, "Kate, I just want to know if you have thought about me. I need you to know I've thought about you." He takes my hand and says, "But now it is *this*, this reality, that counts."

Coming from his lips it sounds so simple, but I need for him to prove it. "Then start working on something new. A story about Not Kate. This week. We can meet next Thursday and talk about it." I have to find out if he can stop writing about me if I am ever going to know whether he can have what he says he wants: me–me in 3-D, me in a rotten mood, me smelling of sweat. Could Trevor abandon the sparkling Kate of his breathless writing? Does he really want the curve of my belly against his back at night? Is he truly meaning to invite me, a real woman with insecurities and faults, into his life? I wonder if I would not disappoint him, fall short of the two-dimensional Kate he has created. I wonder if he would not disappoint me.

I realize Trevor must wonder no less.

TONIGHT TREVOR ARRIVES a little late. "I hope I haven't kept you waiting."

Of course he has, but I say, "No, of course not." A couple of small amendments to my original response–is that really so big a lie?

"I brought you a new story," he says as he slides into the booth. "As you requested."

I take a sip of my latte and ask, "Should I read it now?"

"I think so."

He hands me a thin manuscript. I turn to the title page: "Candace." I try to concentrate on the plot, the witty dialogue, but I can't help searching for myself in every word. When I finish the last sentence I say, "It's brilliant, Trevor." I didn't know if he could resist the temptation to write about me again. It was one he had given in to for so long. But this story is not about me–he has given up the fantasy; maybe he wants me. I hand him back the manuscript. "I made a few notes–I think you've got a comma splice on the last page–but I like it." It would be polite and deferential for me to shut up now, but I cannot accept any more of his instruction unless I am certain he can learn from me. "Except the ending," I say. "It's a little awkward."

"How would you change it?" he asks.

As I tell him, he jots notes on the manuscript. I smile; he takes my advice seriously. Maybe we can teach each other. Maybe we can be peers–no longer student and teacher. When he finishes writing, he looks up and says, "But you did like it?"

I am surprised he needs my reassurance. "It's very good."

"I was worried you wouldn't."

"Why?"

"It's not about you."

"I didn't want it to be. I wanted–"

"It is about someone else."

"Is it?" I ask, trying to keep my voice even. All that really happened? Candace exists?

"I told you: I write what has happened."

He did tell me. *He would rather admit to the sins that he is actually guilty of than confess to those he dares not commit.* I insisted that he stop writing fantasies about me, but he knows almost nothing of the real me; I've made it impossible for him to write about me at all. But I didn't entertain the obvious possibility that a writer who hesitates to bare his imagination would give me a true story about another woman. What had I expected? Trevor's not inclined to write his fantasies but to report his adventures.

"Really, it's very well written, Trevor," I say in what I hope is a brisk voice. I pause. Someone else? "Are you trying to tell me something? I mean, you can stop penning your confessions–if you are seeing someone, just say so."

"That's not what I meant! What I am saying is if we get involved, you would become my muse. You would replace all past loves, Candace included. I would write about *you*, the *real* you; you would no longer be a fantasy. What I have written about you so far will reveal nothing; it is my conception of you, and not the real Kate, that people will read about. But if we actually get involved . . ." He closes his eyes and says a bit vehemently, "You should know: *I will put on display every intimate detail of our lives.*"

"And if I do the same—write about the real us?"

"I hope you do. But I certainly will—I need to know now if you can live with that; Candace could not."

"The woman in the story." The past love. The story is no admission to some lover he expects me to tolerate. It is no provocation to jealousy. This story is an example of what has driven away other women. He could have claimed writer's block, a busy schedule, absentmindedness. Any number of lies could have excused him from showing me what he fears might repel me.

That he would rather be forthcoming than seductive pleases me. Or maybe he is seducing me, for I feel sudden empathy and ask, "Did others leave?"

"Some women would rather be immortalized on canvas, in oil."

I don't need the details; he has let me know what matters now, for us. Having me read that story is coincidental to what is really on his mind: Could I accept an erotica writer publishing accounts of our sex life? I could—I think.

"If you ever want to immortalize me, use any medium you choose." I am not exactly sure what I have just granted him permission to do, but the fact that he has confessed his intentions makes me trust them. That he would make this admission now, before the "transgression" could possibly happen, tempts me to trust him.

"Are you sure you can handle that?" he asks.

Now it is my turn to tell the truth. "No, I'm not." I think I can handle the uncertainty, though; the next words I say are also true, even more so: "But I promise to try."

Mia Culpa

ELIZABETH COLDWELL

I MEANT TO tell him, I really did. I mean, I know we all keep secrets, even from the people we love the most, but on the other hand, I felt it was something Josh should know, however much my revelation might damage our relationship. It was just that I could never find the right time. After all, when exactly do you break the news to the man you've been living with for the last year that when you were just nineteen years old his father introduced you to kinky sex?

Of course, in those days I had no idea Josh was related to Mitchell, could never have dreamed that the gap-toothed nine-year-old in the silver photo frame on the desk in Mitchell's study would grow up to be the strapping, six-foot hunk I shared my bed with. But then I dreamed about very little beyond getting a decent mark for my term paper on *Great Expectations* and managing to make any of the guys in my residence hall take enough interest in me that I wouldn't, as I was convinced I was destined to, die a virgin.

So it came as something of a shock to me when I realized that out of all the people who could possibly be interested in initiating me, the one who was most keen was my English tutor, Mitchell Summers. Looking back, it's embarrassing to remember how naïve I actually was and how long it took before I realized that all the attention he was paying me had some motive other than ensuring I understood the reasons why Estella was playing mind games with Pip. By the end of our studies together, he'd taught me a few mind games of my own, but perhaps that's more than you need to know at this point.

What complicated things further was that my best friend at the time, Lucy, had a massive crush on Dr. Summers. She didn't care that he was married, a fact she had picked up on the first time he started idly fiddling with his wedding ring in a tutorial. If Lucy wanted someone, she got him, so it seemed only a matter of time before she took the teacher-pupil relationship to a more intimate–and probably highly inappropriate–level. And I wouldn't have been at all surprised if Mitchell had responded to her obvious flirting. Lucy had all the tricks: the coy glance she would break as soon as he returned eye contact; the extra button unfastened on her top, so that as he walked behind us, his gaze could not help but be drawn to the generous cleavage nestling in her lacy bra; the skirt so short that when she crossed her legs, it showed anyone who cared to look the tight white triangle of cotton where her thighs met. She was top-heavy and had long, glossy hair the color of flame; I was dishwater blonde, with almost nothing in the way of tits and neither the guile to consider padding my bra nor the experience to know that the man who looks beyond the superficial is the man worth having.

So you can understand why I was confused by the fact that I would sometimes look up when one of the other students was reading from their latest essay and catch Mitchell looking at me with an expression so hungry it made me blush. I mentioned it to Lucy once, but she just told me I was imagining things. As far as she was concerned, the man had eyes for no one but her.

All of which meant I was completely unprepared for the afternoon he asked me to stay behind after a tutorial session. I honestly thought he wanted nothing more than to discuss the content of the last essay I'd submitted–which he did, but only as a starting point for something I had never imagined might ever happen to me. We had been asked to place various literary characters in modern contexts, to examine how they would react today if faced with the trials that confronted them within the novel and, from there, to discover how much of their behavior was shaped by the conventions and expectations of their time. I can't remember exactly which book I had been asked to comment on, though in truth every last aspect of what led up to that unbelievable afternoon should be burned into my memory, but I do know that I had made the statement within my essay that the woman in question "deserved a damned good spanking." I noticed immediately that Dr. Summers had vigorously circled that point in red ink, and I felt my heart sink. He was not averse to ridiculing a student whom he thought had made a particularly naïve or crass comment, and I was sure I was in for a thorough tongue-lashing.

"So she deserves a spanking, eh, Mia?" Dr. Summers said, the hint of a grin causing his lips to curve upward. "And what makes you say that?"

"Well, she's petulant, she's spoiled–she's just a brat. I don't think she's ever had anyone say no to her, and I think she just needs something to happen that will make her realize there are people other than her in the world." It was a longer speech than any I'd ever made in a tutorial, but I couldn't stop the words tumbling out of my mouth.

"It's an interesting theory, Mia, but has it ever occurred to you that there are some women for whom a spanking might not have that effect–indeed, that by their bratty behavior, as you put it, they are actively seeking to have their backside tanned because it gives them pleasure?"

His words completely baffled me. There I was, a girl who had never gone any further than a few sloppy kisses during a slow dance at the end of a party, being asked to contemplate a world of sexual behavior that was completely alien to me. Surely it would hurt, wouldn't it? Surely no woman could get any kind of pleasure from the humiliation of being hauled over a man's knee and spanked 'til she squealed?

But that was nothing compared to what came next. "Have you ever actually been spanked, Mia?"

I shook my head. I couldn't even remember receiving the sort of sharp smack many parents dish out when a small child runs into a busy road or tries to pull a pan of boiling water off the stove. So why I had such a strong conviction that a spanking would solve the problems caused by a willful woman, I had no idea. It just seemed to make sense.

"Perhaps it's time you had that experience, Mia. There's an obvious gap in your education that needs to be filled." His voice was low and strangely seductive. That was the point at which I should have left his study and gone to report him for sexual harassment. With a few well-chosen words I could have ended his career at the university, perhaps even in the teaching profession as a whole. But as I said, I was young and I trusted him–

until then, I had no reason not to. And since a confession demands utter honesty, I have to admit that if I had my time over again, knowing as I do now how he was calculatedly exploiting my innocence, I would not change a thing about what I did that afternoon.

"What do I do?" I asked.

"I want you to bend over the desk, and leave the rest to me," was his reply.

So I did as he requested. I bent over the edge of his big wooden desk. If I had been at all alert, I would have noticed how a space had been deliberately cleared away from the piles of books and papers that usually littered it, but I was sleepwalking into the situation that had been prepared for me.

It seemed suddenly very quiet in the small room. The English department was based on the seventh floor of the arts building, insulated from the world outside by thick double glazing. All I could hear was the clock ticking on the bookshelf by the desk, and the pounding of my own heart.

Dr. Summers came to stand beside me. He didn't say a word, just quietly went about the business of getting me ready for my spanking.

He lifted up the hem of my skirt–in those days, everyone dressed in the grungy style that was fashionable, and my wardrobe consisted mostly of cotton sundresses worn over T-shirts, and tights that were more like an elaborate pattern of holes–and then he did something that caused me to suck in my breath. Slowly, deliberately, he pulled down my tights and my skimpy white panties, until they were lodged in the groove just underneath the cheeks of my bottom.

I had not expected this, and I tried not to think of the vision I was presenting to Dr. Summers as he stood silently observing me.

"Beautiful," he murmured, and I felt his hands run over my buttocks, gently stroking. When that stroking movement finally altered, it took a little while to register that he had actually slapped me. This wasn't the punishment I had been expecting, designed to shock and smart. This was something altogether more subtle. Yes, it hurt a little, but it was a good hurt–an exciting hurt. As he continued to spank me, I began to feel breathless and slightly exhilarated. He was building up a rhythm, alternating from cheek to cheek and steadily increasing the force of each slap, but alongside the tingling in my flesh, I was starting to feel a deeper, darker sensation. I was getting turned on.

"So tell me, Mia," Dr. Summers said, as his hand snaked down between my legs to touch me where no man's hand ever had, "do you still think a spanking like that would teach a woman how to behave? Would she feel it was a punishment, or would she find it pleasurable?"

As he spoke, his fingers were dabbling in the wetness that had started to well up at the entrance to my pussy. I was confused; I couldn't deny that it was pleasurable, but I didn't want to admit it to Dr. Summers, since that would turn everything I had believed when I walked into his study on its head.

"I– I–" My words were coming out as little more than shallow pants. Dr. Summers had unerringly found the little bud of flesh that held the key to my arousal and was stroking it with the lightest of touches. I couldn't stop myself from thrusting my pelvis backward, not knowing whether I was encouraging him to spank me or play with me. I was rewarded with a few harder slaps as he switched quickly between each cheek, and then, just as I was starting to think that this was punishment after all, his finger slipped back onto my clit and began to rub with precise circular movements. This was too much for me: My knees buckled and I clutched the edge of the desk. As Dr. Summers continued to frigfinger me, the tension that had been building in me since he first told me to bend over and take my punishment finally broke. I gave a small cry and surrendered to my orgasm.

When I finally regained something approaching my composure, Dr. Summers told me to pull up my underwear and handed me my essay. My one-on-one session was over.

That set the pattern for our private tutorials. They always followed the same routine: Mitchell would find some pretext to keep me behind after the other students had left, and then he would raise my skirt, pull down my panties, spank me, then bring me to orgasm. In all that time, he was never less than fully dressed. Indeed, he never so much as unzipped his fly. Though I remember the feel of his solid cock pressing against me through the thick fabric of his trousers, I never saw it, never even touched it. He never asked me to play with it, or to suck it, even though he was happy to lick me from clit to asshole till I came my brains out. He put his fingers inside me, even masturbated me with the wooden handle of a hairbrush that he had just used to redden my ass cheeks, but nothing more. At the time, I never questioned this, never wondered why he did not go further. I realize now that he obviously thought as long as he never fucked me, he wasn't actually being unfaithful to his wife. Never mind that we were carrying on in a kinky enough fashion to send most women screaming to the divorce courts if they'd found out about it. No, in Mitchell's mind he was not committing adultery if he didn't penetrate me, and that enabled him to rationalize his behavior.

And so it went on, for the next five months or so until the

start of the summer, when I went back to my hometown to spend my vacation working behind the counter in a sandwich bar, and Mitchell took up the offer of a teaching post in some obscure little college in the southern United States. He left me with "A" grades for my final exams, and with memories of his hand working its slow, seductive way over my bared backside and his tongue playing wicked tricks with my clit–memories that would surface when I lay in bed alone at night, playing with my pussy. Though I tried my hardest, I never quite found anyone else like him. Until Josh Carpenter came along.

I wouldn't even have considered Josh as a lover–he was ten years younger than me and worked as a waiter in the pizza parlor across the road from my office to help him pay his way through college–but I was trying to break my pattern of sleeping with–and seeking punishment from–older men. My relationship with Mitchell had had such a profound effect on me that I had fallen into the classic trap of trying to re-create that first experience with every other man I dated. It was a mistake, of course: Half of them treated me as though I was a complete freak the first time I asked them to spank me; the others made one or two halfhearted attempts, but I could always tell they weren't really into it, and if there's one thing guaranteed to kill a scene, it's feeling like the other person is just humoring you. So when Josh scribbled his phone number on the bottom of the bill and asked me to call him after he'd served me and some of my friends one lunchtime, I decided to take him up on his offer. He was cute, he was intelligent–and he definitely wasn't Mitchell. Or so I thought.

All I learned about his family background on the first couple of dates was that his parents had split up when he was a kid, and that his mother had later remarried. So the first time he took me back to his place, I was doing the usual nosy thing of examining the photographs on his bookshelves, and stopped abruptly as I picked up one of the frames. I knew exactly where I'd seen that gap-toothed little boy before–and I couldn't fail to recognize the man who was with him.

"So how do you know Mitchell Summers?" I asked casually.

Josh's answer threw me completely. "He's my father. My real father. That was taken the summer before he went to work in the States." He took the photo from me and looked at it, brow creased in thought. "That was what split my parents up. I was nine, and my mom thought I was too young for all the upheaval of moving. So my dad went over there on his own, with the idea that we would follow him in time, and six months later he told my mom he was leaving her for one of his students."

So some things never changed. I wondered if that girl was someone else he'd introduced to the joys of a reddened ass. "He used to teach me, you know," was all I said. "Small world, isn't it?" And then I went up behind Josh, put my arms around him, and started nibbling his ear till he put down the frame and pulled me onto the sofa with him, thoughts of his long-absent father forgotten.

Within a couple of weeks, Josh had left his apartment and moved in with me. Things moved faster between us than was usual in my relationships, but it hadn't taken me long to reach the conclusion that despite the difference in our ages, Josh was the one. Not only could I hardly keep my hands off his body, but I also genuinely loved spending time with him. He made me laugh, and we struck sparks off each other intellectually. The only area where things could have improved was in bed.

Once the initial excitement of experimenting and getting to know each other's body had settled down to steadier, less intense sex, I began to realize that Josh was inherently vanilla in his tastes. He was happy to go down on me for hours, and he adored having his cock sucked, but apart from that he was as straight and unadventurous as I had been before Mitchell had introduced me to his unique brand of adult education. I loved feeling his long, thick cock slide into me as his fit, young body rose and fell above mine, but I still counted it as a moral victory the night I got up on my hands and knees and persuaded him that I would feel him even more deeply–and he would get the benefit of my increased pleasure–if he entered me from behind.

Of course, the one thing I really wanted was to have my gorgeous stud dominate me and order me to do whatever would please him most, but he didn't appear to have a shred of desire to instigate kinky games, and I didn't want to frighten him away as I had done so many other men who were afraid to discover what really made me tick.

So I would lie there as Josh fucked me with my hands above my head, crossed at the wrists, and imagine he had tied me in place and I couldn't get free until he decided. And I would have gone on like this forever, having sex that wasn't quite what I wanted but getting everything else I needed from Josh, until the night I was fantasizing that I was having my bottom spanked with one of my own bedroom slippers and realized that the face of the man who was wielding it in my mind's eye belonged to Mitchell Summers.

That was when I decided I had to tell Josh about my true sexual nature, and the part his father had played in shaping it. I put it off for as long as I could, but one night, when we were lying in bed, horny and slightly giggly after a night out, during which we had sunk a bottle of champagne to celebrate Josh passing his final exams, I took a deep breath and dived in.

I confessed everything to him just as I've confessed it here, reliving every deliciously naughty moment of those illicit encounters. Josh listened in silence, and I could only imagine how he was reacting to the tale of how his father had used me—and no doubt many girls before and after me—and how, instead of being demeaned by his treatment of me, I had grown and blossomed under his expert guidance. I wasn't ashamed of what I had done, I told Josh, although I knew he would probably expect me to be, because I didn't believe that what we had done had precipitated the breakdown of his parents' marriage. However, I did think Mitchell had used our sessions to find something that was lacking in his sex life at home, and I knew that a kinky nature could never be fully suppressed. I hadn't loved his father the way I loved Josh—if anything, I had simply been in thrall to the man's dominant personality—and I really, truly wanted our relationship to work. Indeed, I wanted to spend the rest of my life with him, but he had to appreciate that from time to time, if I was to be a contented and fulfilled woman, I needed to have my backside warmed.

When I finally came to the end of my story, I looked at Josh, not knowing whether he had understood what I had been trying to tell him, and fully expecting him to say that it was over between us. Instead, he caught hold of my hand and placed it on his cock, which seemed bigger and harder than I had ever known it.

"Look what you've done to me, you bad girl," he said, with an authority in his voice I had never dreamed he could possess. "There's only one thing I can do to someone who's behaved the way you have." He hauled me over his lap as he sat up in the bed. "Mia, I'm going to have to punish you . . ."

Regrets

M. CHRISTIAN

SITTING ON A chair, arms on the desk, fingers on the keyboard, words on the screen . . .

Sandy,

I never wanted this to happen. Please believe me. Every day since I met you ten years ago has been delightful. More than delightful, it's been incredible. You are truly the most wonderful and extraordinary woman I have ever known, and I'm a weak and sniveling idiot for what I've done.

Seeing you the first time, when you were working the counter at the Kwiki Mart, I knew you were something special. Not only were you fantastically beautiful, but I could tell that silly, pointless job was just a step on the ladder for you, that you deserved not just to be the night clerk but also manager, or maybe district manager.

Even though I was with that slut Marsha, the moment I saw you I knew that there was a unique and powerful connection between us. When you gave me my change after getting us our hot dogs and two MegaGulps, I felt an electric-like spark between us when our hands touched. I knew right then that we were meant to be together.

I know it was rude of me to wait two weeks before coming back to the Kwiki Mart, darling, but to be honest with you I had spent all that time trembling with fear at seeing you again. I was terrified, you see, that perhaps you didn't feel the same way about me, or that you'd see me for the quivering little boy that I am deep down inside.

But I had to see you again, so I risked it. So I got Earl and Frank–and you are so right, beloved, that Frank is a no-good fool who never has and never will amount to anything–to go with me, in case I should be too taken with fear and insecurity at being around you, and we went down to the Kwiki Mart. I know we all acted like idiots, Sandy, but it was all an act. I really didn't mean to spill all that beer, or make fun of that stupid paper hat they made you wear. I really didn't mean it when I said that you must have been a loser to be working in a place like that. It was all nerves, you see, because I knew, deep down in my heart, that you were the one woman I wanted to spend the rest of my life with.

It was all a foolish game. All of it. The way I teased you, the insults, when Earl, Frank, and I grabbed the Coins for Cripples jar and pretended to steal it. It was all my way of trying to get to know the most beautiful woman I had ever seen.

I'm sorry if I made you cry after we left. I was a rude and

self-centered jerk. But I was scared, Sandy. I was terrified that you wouldn't like or love me the way I loved you. It's because I felt this way about you that I had to come back after dropping off Earl and that no-account Frank and see you again.

I can see it all like it just happened. I was in the parking lot, nervous and frantic with anxiety, putting on an act of calm by leaning against my car and smoking a cigarette. I must have been there for hours, though to you I'm sure it must have been only a few minutes. Finally, it was the end of your shift and you came out. There you were, my angel, a vision despite that stupid paper hat and ugly striped uniform. I have to tell you, darling, that even though you were hauling a big bag of stinking garbage over to the dumpster, I have never seen a more beautiful and sexy woman in my life.

It was all I could do to stand there and smoke my cigarette. I wanted to take you in my arms and sweep you away, carry you off, and make sweet love to you. I wanted to drop down to my knees and proclaim my eternal affection for you. I wanted all that and more, Sandy, but as I have said, I am a total fool and a complete idiot.

But I did manage to speak with you as you walked over to your car. I know I may have been gruff and rude to you, and for that I am very sorry, but in my heart what I said instead of "Hey, you look kinda hot" was "You are the most beautiful woman I have ever seen." And instead of "Wanna do it sometime?" what I meant was "I want to marry you and take you away from all this, treat you like the lovely woman you are, and shower you with diamonds."

That first time, in the alley behind the Kwiki Mart, was magical. I know it should have been in a fancy hotel with champagne and roses on the bed, and you should have been in one of those Victoria's Secret fancy lace panties and bra, but I was with you and that's all that matters. I remember how beautiful you looked, even with garbage on your tennis shoes and that stupid paper hat on your head. Your eyes were dancing in the moonlight, looking like two gold beads and not like "cheap orange drink in a paper cup" like Marsha says.

It was one of my best times, much better than with any other woman in my entire life—which actually isn't that many, even though I may have said different to Frank and Earl. I really am a simple and caring soul under my T-shirt and smelly old jeans. That's what made our first time behind the Kwiki Mart so special, Sandy. I know I may have acted gruff and crude and all, using four-letter words when I suggested that you kneel down on the asphalt to perform oral sex on me, but that was just nerves again.

So many things I'm sorry for, Sandy. So many bad things I wish I'd had the courage and strength to do right with you. Like that first time. I wish I hadn't been so gruff and rough with you, making you do things with your mouth, then pulling your jeans down, tearing a perfectly good pair of panties, and then putting my penis into you from behind. Even though I'm pretty sure you were having a pretty good time, it wasn't the first time I wish it could have been. I'm also very, very sorry that I ejaculated inside of you even though you had said that I shouldn't.

I'm very sorry, too, that it was a month before I saw you again. I was very busy going to job interviews, cleaning up my mom's house, reading books to blind children, and definitely not—never ever, seeing that slut Marsha or doing stupid guy things with Earl and that idiot Frank. But I did come by to see you; stopping in for a couple of Twix bars and a MegaGulp was just a lame excuse. I know that my pretending not to recognize you was a very cruel and mean thing to do, but I really thought I was being funny in a stupid, loser kind of way.

I know I was very bad about freaking out like I did when you told me you were late, very politely and sweetly I have to add, just like a lady would, and not like a slut who "did" you in an alley like that slut Marsha said. I like the way you said it directly and to the point, with only a little screaming and crying. It was just hard for me to accept that the dream I've had since I was a little boy of having a beautiful wife and a wonderful little house with a white picket fence was finally going to come true. It just took a call from your daddy and a visit from your three brothers for me to realize that it really was happening and that it wasn't just some kind of fantastic dream I was having.

I know that our wedding wasn't as good as you wanted. I really wanted to take you to a nice hotel with real silverware and tablecloths and flowers on the table, a really good dance band, and a real big cake with white sugar frosting, and that we could have taken a real trip somewhere for a honeymoon. But even though I really did want to find a real good job where I might even have to wear a suit, I wasn't making enough money at Bob's Auto Body to afford the wedding you deserved. I seriously thought that it was better to save my money for my wonderful family—and not spend it on stupid things for my stupid car, or, tragically, our wedding–even though I know you wanted and deserved something so much better, my wonderful, beautiful wife.

I just wish I could go back in time and give you that fantastic wedding, one that would have showed how much I care for you and how happy I was that we were becoming man and wife. I hated that we had to get married in city hall, and I'm sorry that I kept calling it "getting hitched" and introducing you to everyone as "the new ball and chain." It was nerves, beloved. Just nerves. I really didn't like that we had the reception at Smelly O'Douls and the dance in a suite at the Budget 8 down by the railroad tracks, and I'm very embarrassed that I went around asking people for money to help pay for "beer and shit." I'm really glad your dad took me behind the restaurant and talked to me about that and how I was acting, because I really had no idea of how much of a jerk and an idiot I was being, and no matter what Frank and that stupid Earl said, your dad never touched me in any way, and I really did slip and fall and hit my eye on a doorknob.

I really wanted a good band to play for us, not Frank's cousin who was just out of jail and needed a job. But he was good enough, I guess, and I really liked it when he played "Freebird" and we danced. But I agree with you, darling, that someone had to have stolen your sweet uncle Ray's wallet and broken into the cars parked behind the Budget 8 and, yes, absolutely he was the only person who could have done it. You're right, you're absolutely right.

More than anything, though, I wish we could have had a proper and romantic honeymoon. Your uncle Ray was very nice to give us the money to go to Mexico; I just wish I hadn't had to use it to take care of my mother, who was suddenly very sick and needed that operation on her "guts." But even though we spent our three-day honeymoon in Chicago with my friend Skylark, who you're absolutely right in calling a "smelly hippy," and one of those three days was spent with him driving around some very scary parts of the city while he did some "business," I still had a great time, because I was with the woman I love.

The best time, of course, was that afternoon when Skylark had to go see his probation officer and we had his awful little place all to ourselves. It wasn't a nice hotel with mint chocolates on the pillows, but it was wonderful because I had you all to myself. I still think back on that time, about how beautiful you looked, how happy I was that we were man and wife, and that we had our whole lives before us to raise a family and have good times together. That day was also the best, because we woke up late with the sun streaming through the dirty windows and I looked over at you, staring into your golden eyes, and said, "So, you wanna do it?"

Sex with you, Sandy, is an incredible experience—more than that, it makes my heart sing with pleasure and my body tense with excitement. Seeing you in bed that day, your bosoms surging with sensuality, was more than I could stand. My manhood became engorged, my ardor became profound—it was all more than I could stand. I particularly remember how much pleasure you gave me with your lips and mouth, more than anything because I knew how such an act made you feel, how people had told you it was dirty, a bad thing to do. But for me, for us, it was a good and pleasurable thing. But that was only because we were now man and wife.

After your mouth, I remember how excited you became, how moist your sex had become. I realized that you were ready to be taken in a womanly way, and I was more than happy to oblige, and slid myself into your wet woman-space. I just wish it hadn't been as good for me as it was, for maybe I would have been able to hold off on my orgasm longer and not been as tired as I had become and so would have been able to give you your own share of bodily pleasure.

The next few months with you were a delight, even though I was idiotic not to say how much pleasure you gave me with your body and in making us a home we could share together. I know my salary wasn't enough to buy a house, but even though we had to make do with my little apartment over my mother's garage, I was happy there with you. I particularly liked the little "homey" touches you gave to the place, the lace curtains, new TV trays, and plastic flowers you put in bottles and jars in the kitchen. Even though I cruelly teased you about them, in my heart I knew you were just trying to give us a pretty home.

I just wish my frequent late nights at Bob's Auto Body didn't keep me away from you and our house, but I was really trying to earn enough so that we could have the best of lives. I know that coming home at one or even two o'clock in the morning was a rude and thoughtless thing to do, even worse being how I snapped at you for being upset. But, darling, I was very tired from trying hard to earn us enough to make a happy home, and was feeling very guilty and ashamed for not doing enough for you and our lives together. I appreciate your also not mentioning how my breath often smelled of beer, even though I knew you knew I'd been drinking. You are a wonderful woman in so many ways, and your not humiliating me by pointing out my problem with alcohol is just one of them.

I understand that you have needs, and I especially understand that because I was not in our wonderful and beautifully decorated home enough, you felt unloved and unappreciated. I also understand that you'd been craving my love as well as the return of the fantastic sex life we'd shared together. I only have myself to blame for your reaching out to someone else for love and comfort. I agree with you that of all the people you could have reached out to to get what I had been so foolish to deny you, Frank was the worst. I do not fault you for being intimate with him, darling, though I now share your hatred of him, because he told me about your affair in such a coarse and ungentlemanly fashion. That he bragged to me while we were out drinking with Earl, telling me that he "banged her silly," was unspeakably rude and insulting to you. I consider that to be more insulting than the fact that he touched you. You are, and always will be, a lady. Even though you may still work at the Kwiki Mart, not be as thin or beautiful as those models in my insultingly sexist *Playboys* (which I know you hate me for having around and am so sorry make you feel uncomfortable), you are beautiful and sexy, and I was always happy with our relationship.

Even when you told me that you weren't actually pregnant, I may have acted very badly and said all sorts of rude and insulting things, it was only because of my disappointment that we would not be having a new life to raise children together in our pretty and well-maintained little home. My being gone for a few days was just my way of dealing with the sadness I felt that we would not be a family, even though I knew that we could always try again and that it would be as lovely and sensual as all of our other sexual interludes.

Perhaps it's because of the pure depths of my love, Sandy, that I can find no fault in anything about you. You are a pure red rose, a woman beyond compare, as lovely as a woman from one of those romance novels you read—which I apologize for calling "girl trash." They are lovely stories, with very good writers, as I would know if I would ever pick one up and read one.

Every moment with you, no matter how fleeting, has been magical. I would never want to hurt you in any way, and the thought of it sickens me to my very depths. That is why I'm writing to confess to you my deep and shameful sin.

As I've said, Sandy, sex with you has always been a remarkable and magical experience, not at all like the cheap and tawdry images in my stupid magazines. I could never have sex with another woman and have it ever be as good as it was with you. But I am a fool like most men and did not realize how much you meant to me until I'd committed the ultimate idiotic act.

Not that I am completely innocent. I know how you felt about Marsha, but when I saw her I did not respect your wishes to stay away from her. What did you call her? "A villainous vixen." I remember saying that you were wrong–in a very coarse and rude way–about that, but now I realize that you were absolutely right about her. Instead of listening to you, I allowed myself to be deluded by one of her cheap, slutty outfits and her bargain basement perfume. I thought she just wanted to talk, honestly, and thought that a beer or two wouldn't hurt.

But it did hurt–and it hurt the one most precious to me. I allowed myself to be led astray and seduced. I was weak, thinking of my own physical pleasure with a slut who everyone knows has slept with everyone in town, and in so doing, hurt you tremendously. I have to say, though, that the experience was horrible and shallow–despite what that jerk Frank may have told you about it being "better than anything I've ever had." Although she put her mouth on my manhood, it was bad, the worst I've ever had, and when we performed intercourse, it was so disappointing that afterward I swore that I would never, ever have sex with another woman–except for you, my darling.

But I know now that I can never have the infinite pleasure and happiness I've shared with you. I've betrayed the magical connection we'd shared together through one stupid act of carnal pleasure. I've lost through my own foolishness the one who's meant the most to me, my reason for living. I've lost you.

That's why I can't go on, Sandy. That's why I can't live any longer. That I've hurt you and ruined our lives together has made living unbearable. That's why I've decided to take my own life with my father's shotgun, which I shot myself with from across the room. I'm sorry for the mess it might cause, but more than anything, I'm sorry for the pain I've caused you, the most beautiful woman I've ever known, much prettier and sexier than anyone, especially that slut Marsha.

Regrets,

Tom

Sitting on a chair, arms on the desk, fingers on the keyboard, words on the screen ... Tom, a hole in his chest. Sandy smiled at the note that was long overdue to her, if she did say so herself.

Before she picked up the phone, touched fingers to buttons, dialed the police, Sandy had one quick, certain thought: *I'm sorry I didn't do this sooner.*

Appetites

SAGE VIVANT

IN BETWEEN HER first and second Overeaters Anonymous meetings, Julia had an epiphany. She realized that the slim, pretty woman everybody flocked around during the break at her first meeting was the woman whose husband she had fucked for nearly a decade.

How could Julia be faulted for failing to recognize Paulette? For the many years that Matthew had been her lover, Julia had faced the rosy, round cheeks and strangely tired smile of his wife every time she visited his cubicle. Although it was often obscured by piles of error reports, the photo of Paulette always served as a prickly reminder of who had staked claim to Matthew first and who shared his bed each night. Julia's only comfort then came from noting Paulette's obvious girth. Whenever she thought of Paulette in the days of the affair, she envisioned the lumbering, overweight matron who couldn't hope to compete with Julia's younger, svelter charms. Paulette's size was her principal flaw, the ingredient in the cocktail for lust that soured the matrimonial drink.

Something had happened to Paulette since those days, though. The same bizarre twist of fate that had removed Paulette's excess weight had reapportioned it to Julia. Although it had been years since Julia had even spoken to Matthew, seeing Paulette in her new sexy, confident persona upset the sexual status quo that Julia had previously accepted as incontrovertible.

So she skipped the next weekly OA meeting, which would have been her second, in order to think about what Paulette's transformation meant to her.

"SHE'S A GOOD PERSON," Matthew would say to Julia when the subject of leaving Paulette came up, as it inevitably did each time they were together. "And I have Sarah to think about."

"Sarah is in high school now," Julia would remind him. "How old does she need to be to understand that her parents are miserable and need to split up?"

And then he would look at her with brown eyes full of pain and desire and conflict, and nothing mattered except the smooth heat of his neck against her lips.

She recalled a certain regrettable phone call she'd once made.

"May I speak to Matthew, please?"

"He's out right now. May I ask who's calling?" came the unbearably courteous inquiry.

"This is Christine in IT," Julia lied. "He's not answering his pager, and there's an emergency here at work he needs to deal with. Can you have him call this number as soon as he gets in?"

"Oh, of course. What is it?"

Julia gave the unsuspecting, trusting wife her home phone

number, which Matthew promptly called when he returned from his bike ride some thirty minutes later.

"I've got some drives that are really overheating," Julia purred into the telephone. "How soon can you get here?"

She heard his silent confusion, imagined him turning away from a questioning Paulette. She ignored the sickness in her gut.

"I'll be right there," he said after a long pause.

The urgency of her request precluded the shower he might have otherwise taken after such an extended bicycle excursion, and that was fine by Julia—she adored the scent of his sweat. The only time he showered whenever they were together was after sex. It was a precaution he felt was necessary to keep at least the olfactory evidence of the affair hidden from Paulette.

Julia recalled that particular visit well. Her hunger for him, always at barely manageable levels, had been so intense that day that she'd broken their rule about no calls to his home. When he arrived, his face a paradox of reprimand and excitement, they fell to the stairs leading to her apartment the moment she closed the door to let him in. Their bodies tumbled in a blur of kisses, gropes, and erratic breaths. With his rigid cock in her hand and her swollen nipples at his tongue, they somehow inched their way upstairs to her freshly made bed (white linen, to mirror the one he shared with Paulette).

The strange thing about depravity and deception is how beautifully it feeds an already corrupt and selfish obsession. Never before had he thrust into her with such ferocious need. Never before had she wanted to feel him so deep inside her, pushing and pounding against her, filling her so full that grateful tears stung her eyes. But the door to one moral misstep always miraculously leads to another, and with Julia's disregard of one rule came the reckless and heady freedom to violate new ones. They soiled more than the pristine white linen that afternoon, but the all-consuming joy they felt in each other's presence helped them justify the rightness of it all.

Julia had always been one of those students who read ahead to future lessons. So naturally she acquainted herself with not just the first step in OA but with the entire dozen.

Step Four: Made a searching and fearless moral inventory of ourselves.

The reading materials explained that this step required an honest examination of one's past. Because wrongs weren't faced honestly, it said, feeling shame was common.

Okay. Her affair with Matthew was wrong. She knew that. She could even face it, but could she face it with Paulette in the same room? Was an outright confession absolutely necessary?

Step Five: Admitted to God, to ourselves, and to another human being the exact nature of our wrongs.

Shit. Letting Paulette in on the results of her searching and fearless moral inventory might actually be what was supposed to happen.

Underneath all the grousing she'd done about Paulette during the affair, she'd always wanted to apologize. No, that wasn't entirely true. She wanted absolution, then and now. That need had never abated—Julia carried it around like a marble stuck in her spine. She was accustomed to the discomfort but always aware that it needed attention. Steps Four and Five might very well be the opportunity she'd been craving all these years. But was she ready for this opportunity?

Maybe the OA people would allow her weeks or months to get to Step Five. Or even Step Four, for that matter.

Maybe she should have signed up for Weight Watchers instead.

There was no question that Paulette had probably lost more than a hundred pounds. This fact continued to bewilder Julia, who had most assuredly gained that amount since her breakup with Matthew.

Paulette moved about the church basement in a friendly, almost motherly way, looking positively waifish in her soft, black jersey pencil skirt, flat sandals, and simple knit top. She had nice but modest breasts, Julia realized, surprised that she had never thought of Paulette with breasts of any kind. Along with her excess weight, Paulette had also ridden herself of her signature loosely tied bun that controlled her graying but long hair. Now she sported a sassy layered cut with ends that skimmed her jawline–and the gray had been replaced with a subtle blonde color. As she spoke to the people milling about before the meeting, her smile was warm and wide, not at all like the pained pretense of happiness in the photo that once graced Matthew's desk.

The women had met before. Julia had once come to Matthew's home under the pretext of his researching some bicycle options for her, but Paulette obviously had no recollection of the meeting. She had been so kind to Julia, even offering her lunch, which Julia politely declined because the thought of sharing a meal with this woman disturbed her more than the thought of sharing her husband. Julia couldn't remember now whether Matthew or she herself had thought the meeting was a good idea, but she would never forget the urgent desire to run screaming from that house into the street.

As she watched Paulette now, the woman felt her gaze and turned to her, still smiling. "Hello. Nice to see you again."

Julia's heart felt like it was creeping past her esophagus. She searched Paulette's face for signs of what might be coming next. Did she finally recognize her? Would she now launch into some wildly shrewish tirade about the place in hell reserved for women who break up marriages? Would she really do that in public?

"You remember me?" Julia stammered, trying to return the smile and irritated to find that her mouth was twitching.

"Of course! I remember everybody who attends our meetings," she said, placing a delicate hand on Julia's arm. "It's how friendships begin."

To Julia's relief, the meeting was then called to order. Despite Paulette's genuine greeting, there was some kind of vapid quality in her eyes, something that reminded Julia of a Stepford wife.

As they sat in a circle and listened to someone read about one of the program's twelve traditions, Julia's attention was continually diverted to Paulette, sitting there in an aura of such disconcerting serenity. She was sorry for her—sorry that she didn't know her husband had been screwing around on her, sorry that she didn't recognize the woman seated directly across from her who'd been the catalyst in their ultimate divorce. *It must be heavenly to be that delusional, Julia thought.*

ONE NIGHT, MATTHEW had eyed the collection of scarves that hung inside Julia's closet door and decided to tie up her tits while he fucked her from behind. The two of them watched themselves in her bedroom dresser's mirror, mesmerized by the image of his pulling on the scarves like reins as her tits reared upward in response. One orgasm wasn't enough to satiate them, and because her lips were still slick with need, she mounted him, still wearing the scarves. Her breasts bounced and jiggled with her enthusiasm, and he came again, this time before she did. She continued to grind her cunt into him, spreading her juice over his balls and thighs until he sought out her clit and moved against it until she shouted her climax.

How she loved it when his balls contained an endless supply of what she needed, when she needed to work him to exhaustion to stem his series of comes. The payoff was only partially the sex. When he'd given her everything he had and laid there quietly snoring, she could pretend that he was spending the night, sleeping in her bed. She could pretend that he was her husband and that the bed was conjugal. She could pretend that Paulette did not exist.

"So WHERE DOES she think you are tonight?" Julia had asked him one Friday evening as she rode his lap. In her mind, Friday nights were reserved for them, despite his tendency to fill his time after work drinking with the guys before finally heading over to her place.

"Why do you ask?" His expression always darkened whenever she brought up Paulette. He was still hard, but a definite pall had fallen over the proceedings.

"I'm just curious. Does she think you're out with the boys every Friday night?" Julia raised and lowered her hips in slow, dramatic movements, enjoying the sound of her wetness as it consumed Matthew's cock and released it again.

"Well, she's not stupid. I'm sure she wonders why I stay out so late, or why I come home so much cleaner than I should after a day of work and a night of drinking."

But Julia disagreed. She thought Paulette must be supremely dense not to realize that her husband was in love with somebody else. If Matthew were *her* husband, she'd know within hours of any dalliance. She would just know. It was a further testament to their malfunctioning marriage that Paulette had no idea that Matthew spent so much time with another woman. Julia said nothing, though. She had learned that Matthew would come to Paulette's defense whenever Julia criticized her.

She had tried to imagine what life was like for the rotund Paulette, filling her mouth and her life with food and driving her husband away in the process. Julia gradually decided that Paulette's determination to stay overweight was her way of keeping Matthew at a safe distance. Julia had heard about wives like Paulette, wives who craved the security of marriage but didn't want to feel the intimacy of it. The fear of losing oneself, of becoming a boring hausfrau, or simply being too bored to care any longer were all possibilities, although Julia never really knew which situation best described Paulette's. All she knew was that a woman who wanted to keep her husband was unwise to puff herself up with candy and cookies.

And if Paulette chose not to see that Matthew was having an affair, she either had to be oblivious or, in some twisted way, complicit to the grand act of deception in which they all played a role.

SHE LINGERED AT the literature table, staring at the pamphlets and booklets she'd already read many times at home. She didn't want to watch Paulette make her way through the small group, smiling encouragement and touching support to all she encountered. If Julia proceeded with her plan, would she be destroying this woman's happiness for a second time? No, she decided. She would be completing Step Five.

When the meeting officially began, Julia did not wait for some other needy soul to share what was on his or her mind. She launched into her own without delay.

Newcomers were not expected to speak at their first or even their second meetings–unless they had a burning desire to do so. Julia waited until her third meeting to tell her story.

"Hi, my name is Julia."

"Hi, Julia."

"I really want to thank all of you for making me feel comfortable enough to speak about what led me here." She smiled at the kind, nodding faces, the kindest of which was Paulette's.

Julia took a deep breath and began the speech she'd rehearsed in the shower, in the car, in the elevator, and lying in bed at night for the past week.

"I've been coming for a few weeks now and have been so touched by the love that's here. I feel honored to be able to work my program with people who really seem to care about my welfare." Her words caught in her throat–she hadn't realized how true the words were until she said them. But she had a mission, and tears would not help her accomplish it.

"I'm working Step Five now." Knowing nods dotted the circle of concerned faces. "I know why I became powerless over food, and I'm not going to keep it bottled up inside me any longer, because I'm tired of the shame." Her throat tightened. She took a deep breath and continued. "I'm powerless over food because I am powerless over sex."

The silence in the room suddenly felt oppressive. Everybody stared at her with that insipid loving kindness when she would have preferred a snide remark or shocked expression. Anything to distract her from her confession. But none came, and as she played with the hem of her plus-size jeans, she knew that the only real elephant in the room was her disclosure, sitting big and heavy and smelly until somebody could figure out how to remove it.

"I fell wildly in love about twelve years ago," she began. "The man was married, so I fought the desire to sleep with him for as long as I could, which ended up being a lousy two months. He quickly became the reason I got up each morning. I dressed for him, listened to music that he liked, shifted my political beliefs closer to his.

"I still don't know whether our sexual connection made me that compliant, or whether I was compliant because of the sexual connection. Whatever it was, I craved him constantly and took every foolish risk I could have taken. I gave him blow-jobs in the office, made love to him in the backseat of my car, and told friends and family that my travels to meet him in far-away places were business trips.

"I honestly thought he would leave his wife. Couldn't imagine any other outcome, in fact. She was heavy and I wasn't at the time, so I thought I'd naturally be more desirable. She was older than I was, too, and I thought the combination would make his decision to leave her even easier. But as the years went on, it became clearer to me that he was afraid to upset the life he'd made for himself and his family. He told me he couldn't abandon his little girl. He bought a house with his wife. But none of it mattered to me, because when we were naked together, the world stopped and every fantasy I had was realized."

Julia glanced at Paulette, whose big blue eyes were locked on her with worried attention. What was she thinking? Was she fitting the pieces together in her mind, figuring out timetables and slowly recognizing Julia as the woman who once came to that new house and refused her offer of lunch?

"He fed me. Not with food but with sex. I was satiated only when our skin met. He could make any promise to me–or I could imagine that he made any promise–and I would have no reason to eat.

"Yet, I always wondered about his wife. Did she know? Did she hate me? Did she wonder why her husband pulled away from her, or why he woke up in the middle of the night with the sweats? I tried to put myself in her position, and each time I did, I felt a little more disgusted with myself. As time went on, my sex with her husband got raunchier. We delved to levels that I'd never gone with any other man."

As Julia spoke, she remembered how he had bent her over her raised bed and pushed his cock into her ass while she wailed her acceptance. How even the pain had been surreal and heady, and how even now, the memory of it made her body melt. She would have undressed for him right at that moment had he walked into the room.

Was this how Step Five was supposed to feel?

"After nine years, the frustration of waiting and hoping got the best of me, and for my sanity, I stopped seeing him. I learned later that he and his wife did divorce. Ironic, isn't it?"

Paulette's eyes were bloodshot, and it seemed that the corners of her mouth trembled. Yet, when Paulette met her gaze, she smiled at her as if to urge her to continue.

"I've been eating ever since," Julia confided. "I'm still grappling with whether I eat to recall the fullness he provided, or whether I have an appetite for something greater than either food or sex.

"But that's for me to figure out. For now, all I can do is tell you good people about my mistakes. I've justified my sexual hunger, and now my food consumption, with all kinds of excuses, none of them terribly enlightened. I've always been hard on myself, rough even, but my capacity for denial is immense. Kind of like my size right now."

She waited for the laughter, but of course the room remained silent. Nobody guffawed at fat jokes at an OA meeting.

"I justified my behavior with the weakest excuses: She was fat and unlovable, she couldn't have cared about him, I deserved happiness, blah blah blah. With every morsel of food I've eaten since I broke up with him, there's some little piece of my subconscious that says 'take that!' for hurting a woman I didn't even know. I hurt his wife then, and I'm hurting myself now. I'm truly sorry. I can't hide behind lame justifications anymore."

She looked down at her lap, which was spotted with tears. Her hands, so carefully placed there, bore the wet streaks of emotion. And when she looked back up at her fellow compulsive overeaters and realized she'd been crying throughout, she choked and wept aloud until the person next to her had to reach over and hold her hand.

"It's okay. You're safe here. Go ahead and cry," the woman whispered, obviously trying to fight back the urge to hold and comfort Julia.

Because no cross-talk was allowed at the meeting, somebody else filled the awkward silence that followed Julia's confession with a description of his day and how he fought back his cravings. Julia struggled to regain composure as he spoke, and within ten minutes or so, she had stopped weeping and was breathing normally.

She didn't know what she expected after the meeting, but what happened was not among the possibilities in her imagination. Paulette did not make a point of going up to her, didn't go out of her way to reassure her that her disclosure was a positive step. Instead, she talked with other attendees and laughed with a kind of gaiety Julia found offensive in light of her admission. She showed no indication of recognizing Julia as the woman who drove the wedge between herself and her husband of fifteen years. Julia stayed attuned to her every movement, right up to the point where Paulette got in her car and drove away.

Hot nausea percolated in Julia's stomach as she realized that for a second time, important information had presented itself to Paulette and been completely, almost blithely, ignored.

JULIA HAD NEVER made a confession to which no response had been forthcoming. What was the point of baring one's soul if not to cope with the reaction of the listener?

"I love you," she had said softly into Matthew's ear one night after the third or fourth time they'd made love. It was the ultimate confession.

And it had been met with silence.

"Did you hear me?" she asked, half-expecting that he was teasing her by not responding.

"Yes, I heard you. I don't know what to say. I love you, too. As much as I can."

She'd been fondling his balls as she snuggled against him, but stopped to look at him. "As much as you can?"

"I can't give you everything you need while I'm still married. You know that. I love you as much as the situation will allow me to."

Confessions, it would appear, were rarely the catharsis they were touted to be, thanks to the unreliable nature of those who were hearing the confessions.

There was so much she wanted to say to Paulette. What she'd

divulged at the meeting was only the beginning. She wanted to right every wrong, sex act by sex act, yet knew such enthusiasm ran counter to the tenets of Overeaters Anonymous.

She longed to pour her disappointments into a bowl, mix them with ice cream and chocolate sauce, and reintroduce them to her body, where she'd nurtured them for such a long and unrewarding time. Instead, she devoted herself to repeated reading of the remaining steps she needed to complete.

She learned that her disclosure at the meeting might have covered not only Step Five but also *Step Nine: Made direct amends to such people wherever possible, except when to do so would injure them or others.* Could the completion of one step coincide with the completion of another, she wondered? Or worse, could one step contradict another? Had her confession injured Paulette? Had it been just as self-serving as the affair itself?

It was times like this she knew that having a sponsor might be helpful. But the only person at the meeting who emanated the kind of peace Julia hoped to have someday was Paulette, and the likelihood of turning to Matthew's ex-wife for guidance felt disingenuous as well as counterproductive.

PAULETTE DID NOT attend the next week's meeting, which infuriated Julia, who had endured the previous week only to arrive at this evening. What could the woman be doing that would take precedence over an OA meeting where her ex-husband's former lover awaited some reaction from her?

But Paulette did show up at the following meeting, smiling and warm but uncharacteristically subdued. Because it was only a few days before Christmas, attendance was low, creating an especially intimate atmosphere in the room.

"Hi, everyone. I'm Paulette. And I'm a compulsive overeater." As if everyone didn't already know her.

"Hi, Paulette."

"I was very affected by Julia's share a couple of weeks ago, and it made me start to think about some of my own issues. How maybe I haven't taken as thorough an inventory as I need. How maybe I haven't admitted all the wrongs in my past that led me to this point in my life."

Julia's pulse fluttered and twitched. Her ears rang, and her palms sweated right through the fabric of her jeans.

"I was in a friendly but loveless marriage for a long time. There was warmth and devotion but not much passion. I turned to food to sustain me during that time, because it was there when I needed it and I never had to wonder if it split its affection between me and somebody else.

"It took me a long time, probably years, to face the fact that my husband was involved with another woman. When I finally faced it, I would imagine myself as his lover when we had sex. I thought that if I could convince both of us on some subconscious level that he wanted me as much as he wanted her, I would be able to keep him. I wanted to be her, and I wanted him to believe he was with her whenever he was with me. But it never worked, and the more he distanced himself and lied to me, the more I turned to food for solace.

"I remember how much I hoped that one day that woman he loved would be as rejected by him as I was, and that she, too, would get as big as a house. I wanted her to be alone and fat and miserable, because that's what she'd done to me. I ate *at* her in direct proportion to how much of him she got. I despised her as much as I despised myself."

I do not come often with my clients. It is my *job* to have sex. Not my desire. Just like an actress does not fall in love with every leading man she plays opposite.

But sometimes she does. And tonight in the theater, this fantasy is too sweet. And Peter Pan's fingers are too expert.

He strokes harder, then softer; he kisses me in rhythm to the tension he is building. I almost slip, almost forget. But I can't. This is not my game.

I reach out. Oh, so slowly, scared, unknowing. I touch his knee, I hear him sigh. Encouragement. His fingers stop moving. Desperately I want to get them moving again. But this isn't my game. I move my fingers up his thigh and find the bulge in his pants.

Still sixteen, I stop, react, then try again. My fingertips run up and down the length of his erection. Testing it. Learning it.

"Is this what you want?" I whisper.

"More, Jenny, more." He is using her name, he has paid for the right to do that. I don't mind. I am enjoying Jenny, who is the teenager he was in love with thirty years before.

I get braver and unzip his fly and fumble in his pants to release him. I stroke him with my hand, and he moves in his seat, thrusting out. And rather than this being the end, his fingers begin to circulate deep within me again. He mimics my movements so that we are doing the same thing to each other now. My hand slides down and up, his fingers probe. We are in tandem.

Faster. He pushes forward. So do I. Faster yet. He pushes his lips at me, presses hard. I can feel his teeth and his fingers in me and my fingers on him and the sounds of a guitar in the background and the feel of mohair velvet on the back of thighs and my breasts loose under my shirt.

The first wave hits me with a shock. It is very rare that this happens. But I don't fight it. I give him the benefit of the feeling, I let him hear the pleasure, and it is what he needs to take him over the edge, and the forty-seven-year-old man who has never quite stopped wanting Jenny, whoever she was, throws his head back and lets me milk him to orgasm.

Not bad for a three-thousand-dollar night's work.

I'm sorry.

I know you don't want to believe it. I know it hurts. You want to be his Jenny. You are his wife, and his friend, and the mother of his children. But it just can't be her. At least not in real life. That's for the movies and the make-believe. And that is what I'm in the business of doing. Making make-believe real—for a few hours at least.

collections *Six-Inch Spikes* and *Death Drives a Semi*; and the nonfiction how-to books *Writing Horror* and *Writing Erotica*. He is also a frequent contributor to several men's magazines such as *Hustler Fantasies*, *Score*, and *Gent* under the pseudonym Evan Hollander. Visit his Web site at www.vanbelkom.com.

SAGE VIVANT operates Custom Erotica Source (www.customerotica-source.com), where she and a small staff of writers create tailor-made erotic fiction for individual clients. Her stories have been widely published in anthologies such as *Best Women's Erotica*, *The Mammoth Book of Best New Erotica*, *Stirring Up a Storm*, *Wicked Words: Sex in the Office*, and *Naughty Detective Stories from A to Z*. She is the editor of *Swing!* and, with coeditor M. Christian, has edited *The Best of Both Worlds: Bisexual Erotica*. Upcoming anthologies with M. Christian include *Amazons* and *The Garden of Perverse*. She is the author of *29 Ways to Write Great Erotica*, available at Custom Erotica Source.